OECD Sovereign Borrowing Outlook 2017

OECD
BETTER POLICIES FOR BETTER LIVES

This work is published under the responsibility of the Secretary-General of the OECD. The opinions expressed and arguments employed herein do not necessarily reflect the official views of OECD member countries.

This document and any map included herein are without prejudice to the status of or sovereignty over any territory, to the delimitation of international frontiers and boundaries and to the name of any territory, city or area.

Please cite this publication as:
OECD (2017), *OECD Sovereign Borrowing Outlook 2017*, OECD Publishing, Paris.
http://dx.doi.org/10.1787/sov_b_outlk-2017-en

ISBN 978-92-64-27125-8 (print)
ISBN 978-92-64-27127-2 (PDF)

Series: OECD Sovereign Borrowing Outlook
ISSN 2306-0468 (print)
ISSN 2306-0476 (online)

The statistical data for Israel are supplied by and under the responsibility of the relevant Israeli authorities. The use of such data by the OECD is without prejudice to the status of the Golan Heights, East Jerusalem and Israeli settlements in the West Bank under the terms of international law.

Photo credits: Cover © Inmagine/Designpics.

Corrigenda to OECD publications may be found on line at: *www.oecd.org/about/publishing/corrigenda.htm*.

Foreword

The 2017 edition of the OECD Sovereign Borrowing Outlook *provides data, information and background on sovereign borrowing needs and discusses funding strategies and debt management policies for the OECD area and country groupings, including:*

- *Gross borrowing requirements*
- *Net borrowing requirements*
- *Central government marketable debt*
- *Interactions between fiscal policy, public debt management and monetary policy*
- *Funding strategies, procedures and instruments*
- *Implications of a low interest rate environment for government debt markets*
- *Liquidity in secondary markets*
- *Overview of and outlook for inflation-linked sovereign bonds*

Each year, the OECD's Bond Market and Public Debt Management Unit circulates a survey on the borrowing needs of member governments. The responses are incorporated into the OECD Sovereign Borrowing Outlook *to provide regular updates of trends and developments associated with sovereign borrowing requirements, funding strategies, market infrastructure and debt levels from the perspective of public debt managers. The* Outlook *makes a policy distinction between funding strategy and borrowing requirements. The central government marketable gross borrowing needs, or requirements, are calculated on the basis of budget deficits and redemptions. The funding strategy entails decisions on how borrowing needs are going to be financed using different instruments (e.g. long-term, short-term, nominal, indexed, etc.) and which distribution channels (auctions, tap, syndication, etc.) are being used.*

Comments and questions should be addressed to the Bond Markets and Public Debt Management Unit within the Financial Affairs Division of the OECD Directorate for Financial and Enterprise Affairs (e-mail: Publicdebt@oecd.org*). Find out more about the Bond Markets and Public Debt Management Unit online at* www.oecd.org/finance/public-debt/.

Table of contents

Tables

Figures

Follow OECD Publications on:

http://twitter.com/OECD_Pubs

http://www.facebook.com/OECDPublications

http://www.linkedin.com/groups/OECD-Publications-4645871

http://www.youtube.com/oecdilibrary

http://www.oecd.org/oecddirect/

This book has...

StatLinks

A service that delivers Excel® files from the printed page!

Look for the *StatLinks* at the bottom of the tables or graphs in this book. To download the matching Excel® spreadsheet, just type the link into your Internet browser, starting with the *http://dx.doi.org* prefix, or click on the link from the e-book edition.

Acronyms and abbreviations

AFT	Agence France Trésor
AKK	Hungarian Debt Management Agency
AOFM	Australian Office of Financial Management
ATM	Average Term-to-Maturity
BIS	Bank for International Settlements
BOE	Bank of England
BOJ	Bank of Japan
BTP	Buono del Tesoro Poliennale
CACs	Collective Action Clauses
CEP	Council on Economic Policies
CEPR	Centre for Economic Policy Research
CGFS	Committee on the Global Financial System
CPI	Consumer Price index
DDA	Dutch Direct Auction
DMO	Debt Management Office
ECB	European Central Bank
EM	Emerging Market
EMGILB	Emerging Markets Government Inflation-Linked Bond index
EMILSI	Emerging Markets Inflation-Linked Securities Index
EMTIL	Emerging Markets Tradable Government Inflation-Linked Bond index
EU	European Union
FED	Federal Reserve
FILP	Fiscal Investment and Loan Program
FRBSF	Federal Reserve Bank of San Francisco
FRN	Floating Rate Note
GBR	Gross Borrowing Requirement
GDP	Gross Domestic Product
HICP	Harmonised Index of Consumer Prices

IGCP	Portuguese Treasury and Debt Management Agency
IMF	International Monetary Fund
ISIN	International Securities Identification Number
JGB	Japanese Government Bond
LSAP	Large-Scale Asset Purchase
MEP	Maturity Extension Programme
MiFID	Markets in Financial Instruments Directive
NBER	National Bureau of Economic Research
NBR	Net Borrowing Requirement
NTMA	National Treasury Management Agency
OECD	Organisation for Economic Co-operation and Development
PD	Primary Dealership
PGB	Portuguese Government Bonds
PSPP	Public Sector Purchase Programme
QE	Quantitative Easing
RPI	Retail Price index
STRIP	Separate Trading of Registered Interest and Principal of Securities
TIPS	Treasury Inflation-Protected Securities
UK	United Kingdom
UNCTAD	United Nations Conference on Trade and Development
US	United States
WPDM	Working Party on Public Debt Management

Editorial

A continued decline in government borrowing needs has limited the pace of debt accumulation in recent years, although fiscal policies are expected to become more expansionary

The *OECD Sovereign Borrowing Outlook 2017* (the *Outlook*) indicates that the pace of government debt accumulation in OECD countries has stabilised in recent years as a result of fiscal consolidation efforts. The aggregate central government marketable debt across the OECD area, which increased by 40% between 2008 and 2010, has grown by a modest 10% in the last three years. Government debt-to-GDP ratios in OECD countries started to decline in 2016. Among country groups, the decline in the debt ratio is more significant for the G7.

With the outlook for economic activity set to remain weak in spite of very accommodative monetary policies, several OECD countries are expected to use fiscal policy more actively to stimulate growth, if they have not done so already. Policy recommendations of the *OECD Economic Outlook of November 2016* on using fiscal space emerged in light of a favourable interest rate-growth differential environment, which reduces cost of debt-servicing and relieves debt sustainability concerns. As the fiscal policy stances of several governments are slowly becoming expansionary, gross and net borrowing requirements are projected to remain flat in 2017 in the OECD area. The government debt-to-GDP ratio is projected to decline further to 73%, from 74% in 2016, reflecting expectations for higher economic growth.

Sovereign issuers have lengthened debt redemption profiles and limited rollover risks amid a low interest rate environment

Prolonged low interest rates have reduced the cost of borrowing in OECD countries considerably and helped to improve debt dynamics. In fact, sovereign debt management offices, which set policies in light of constraints and opportunities provided by market conditions, have been increasingly issuing long-term local currency financing instruments to mitigate exposures to refinancing risk and currency volatility. Correspondingly, average-term-to-maturity of outstanding marketable debt has increased considerably in recent years and reached historic highs in 2016 for several countries including Belgium, Mexico, the United Kingdom and the United States. One reason for this is the growing issuance of ultra-long bonds which has doubled since 2008. This edition of the *Outlook* examines the issuance of debt with maturity of 30 or more years and discusses the potential implications for investors and issuers.

The increasing popularity of ultra-long debt issuance is partly driven by attempts to benefit from low long-term interest rates, however debt managers are also careful about potential market risks related to efforts to lock in current long-term interest rates which may fall further in the future. From an investor perspective, the strategy of investing in long-term and ultra-long-term has been profitable, with central banks purchasing long maturity government debt and lowering the long end of the yield curve in many markets over the past few years. This strategy obviously also carries duration risk, especially if central banks decide to raise rates faster than market participants expect.

A new phenomenon: Issuing debt with negative yield-to-maturities

The previous edition of the *Outlook* highlighted the potential implications of low interest rates for government bond markets. This edition of the *Outlook* takes an in-depth look at this with a special focus on negative yielding government bond issuance, a new phenomenon in public finance. While volumes of sovereign debt trading at negative yields surged to record levels in 2016, some sovereign debt management offices, including France, Germany and Japan where respective central banks hold a significant portion of the outstanding government debt, have issued negative-yielding debt and received premiums from these issues in recent years. Calculations reveal that, between 2014 and 2016, the volume of negative-yielding, fixed-rate bond issues in 14 OECD countries stands at USD 1.25 trillion, total premiums received reached a substantial level, and the maturity of negative-yielding issues has gone out to 10 years in Japan, Germany and Switzerland. From an investor perspective, the demand for negative yielding bonds is mainly driven by expectation of further decline in yields which would push the prices up.

Why and how sovereign debt management offices are taking measures to support market liquidity

Government securities markets are usually the largest and most important markets in each country. Therefore, their orderly operation is crucial for financial market players and for the pricing of other instruments, such as repos and futures contracts. This also has important implications from a public finance perspective. Reduced liquidity impairs the price discovery process and even small changes in rates can result in significant costs or savings to taxpayers. Against this backdrop, an OECD survey of liquidity in secondary government bond markets highlights that sovereign debt managers have continued to observe deterioration in liquidity conditions in their local currency debt market. The survey also shows a change in the appetite and behaviour of investors in response to the low –sometimes negative– interest rate environment. In response to market liquidity concerns, debt managers in several countries have introduced policy measures such as tap sales, buy-backs and switch operations, and smaller auctions to improve liquidity conditions.

Globally, sovereign debt managers face policy uncertainties. Whether, when, how much and how fast major central banks will unwind quantitative easing policies remains unknown. The same applies to governments' use of fiscal policy tools to support economic activity. Looking forward, these are the two main factors that will determine the agendas of sovereign issuers. These factors will require further strong co-ordination with monetary and fiscal authorities to ensure the smooth functioning of financial markets.

Pierre Poret

Pierre Poret
Director, OECD Directorate for Financial and Enterprise Affairs

Executive summary

Shaped primarily by fiscal policies, sovereign borrowing levels in the OECD area have stabilised in recent years, although sovereign debt burdens remain high by historical standards and redemption profiles still pose serious challenges.

The pace of debt accumulation has stabilised compared to the first years of the global financial and economic crisis. Sovereign borrowing requirements (both in gross and net terms), which had risen rapidly as a result of the policy response to the crisis, have since declined due to fiscal consolidation efforts made mostly from 2011 to 2015. Net borrowing requirements have also declined but remain positive and are projected to stay level in 2017 in the OECD area, reflecting that underlying fiscal balances are slowly becoming more expansionary. As a result, outstanding debt has continued to increase, albeit at a slower pace. Survey results indicate that aggregate central government marketable debt across the OECD area will gradually increase from USD 41.3 trillion in 2016 to USD 42.2 trillion in 2017, while sovereign net borrowing requirements are expected to remain at USD 1.7 trillion in 2017, approximately the same level as 2016.

Against this backdrop, sovereign debt burdens remain high by historical standards. After surging from 49.8% to 74.6% between 2007 and 2015 in the OECD area, central government marketable debt-to-GDP ratio has started to decline and is estimated to be 73% in 2017. This decline is more significant for the G7 group than other country groups, despite sluggish economic growth in these economies. The November 2016 edition of the *OECD Economic Outlook* indicated that fiscal space was created by lower interest payments on rolled-over debt in several advanced economies. The recommended policy response is to use fiscal space to support growth in public investment which would require additional borrowing.

Since 2008, the high level of debt servicing, combined with large net borrowing requirements, has generated challenging rollover ratios and aggravated refinancing risk for sovereign debt management in the OECD area. In response to the drastic increase in government debt levels, most OECD countries have deployed a funding strategy geared towards issuance of long-dated instruments. The total debt service of OECD governments has decreased from 45% in 2015 to around 40% of the outstanding marketable debt in 2016. While this service burden has eased, it still poses a serious challenge to sovereign debt managers.

The persistent ultra-low interest rate environment has had a significant impact on both primary and secondary markets for government securities.

Short- and long-term interest rates have continued to fall, reaching very low and – in many cases – negative levels in recent years. More than USD 10 trillion of outstanding high-credit-quality sovereign debt is currently trading at negative yields. This *Outlook* examines the implications of the ultra-low interest rate environment for debt dynamics, sovereign funding strategies, investor base, and government market liquidity. Lower interest rate yields – entering into negative territory in several countries – have improved debt dynamics and eased government debt funding. Since interest rates have declined by more than GDP growth which more than offsets the increase in the debt-to-GDP ratio, debt-servicing has been facilitated and debt sustainability concerns have been alleviated in a number of OECD countries. Also, historical evolution of the average term-to-maturity of outstanding central government debt, representing refinancing risk exposure, indicates a 1.5-year increase compared to the pre-crisis period.

With volumes of sovereign debt trading at negative yields attaining record levels in 2016, some countries, including France, Germany, Japan, and the Netherlands, have received payments for issuing domestic government bonds. Specifically, an examination of sovereign bond auctions in 14 OECD countries indicates that the volume of negative-yielding fixed-rate bond issues reached USD 1.2 trillion between 2014 and 2016.

Survey results indicate that debt managers witness structural changes in the investor base for government securities. Large central banks and public funds have become dominant holders of sovereign debt in major OECD countries. While the share of buy-and-hold type investors increased in the sovereign debt investor base, secondary market liquidity remains an important source of concern for debt managers.

Inflation-linked sovereign bonds have become a standard type of sovereign debt and their supply has grown significantly in recent years.

This edition of the *Outlook* also reviews inflation-linked sovereign debt in OECD countries which has grown significantly in recent years, currently standing at around USD 3 trillion. A substantial portion of inflation-linked bonds are issued by countries characterised by both low inflation rates and price stability. While G7 countries are the dominant players in this asset category, regional aggregates also indicate increased popularity of linkers in emerging market economies where near-term inflationary pressures are arguably more of a concern.

In light of prolonged low interest rates and low inflation in several jurisdictions, current policy discussions focus on the potential impact on supply and demand for these securities. Indeed, break-even inflation rates, simply defined as the difference between nominal yield on a nominal fixed-rate bond and real yield on an inflation-linked bond of similar maturity and credit quality, have been decreasing in several countries. This development, which can be attributed to market expectation for future inflation and poorer liquidity conditions of linkers relative to nominal bonds, has raised concerns over the potential impact on the linker market. In terms of demand, inflation-linked bonds stand as a unique asset class offering a perfect hedge against inflation for investors, particularly for pension funds and insurance companies. Looking ahead, underlying demand for linkers is likely to remain robust as the future level of prices is uncertain and liability-driven investments increase. In response to continuing strong demand, sovereign issuers remain committed to inflation-linked programmes and to maintaining a well-functioning market for inflation linkers.

Chapter 1

Sovereign borrowing outlook for OECD countries

This chapter provides an overview of, and outlook for, sovereign borrowing, deficits and debt in the OECD area for the period 2007-2017. It examines net and gross borrowing needs of OECD governments in the context of fiscal policy challenges and developments. Fiscal policies are shaped by two imperatives: the need to reinvigorate economic growth, including through debt-financed public investment over the short to medium term; and continued pursuit of measured fiscal consolidation over the medium- to long-term. Debt management offices react to these challenges by making redemption profiles somewhat lighter over the short-term.

The statistical data for Israel are supplied by and under the responsibility of the relevant Israeli authorities. The use of such data by the OECD is without prejudice to the status of the Golan Heights, East Jerusalem and Israeli settlements in the West Bank under the terms of international law.

1.1 Introduction

This chapter[*] examines net and gross sovereign borrowing in OECD countries from 2007 to 2017. It first looks at net and gross borrowing needs of OECD governments in the context of fiscal developments. It then considers recent trends in central government marketable debt in the OECD area and central government debt ratios for groups of selected OECD countries. Finally, the chapter examines funding strategies and growing issuance of debt with 30 or more years of maturities.

Key findings

- Sovereign gross borrowing needs in the OECD area have continued to decline from the peaks attained in 2012. They are expected to be USD 9.5 trillion in 2017, approximately the same level as 2016.
- Net borrowing needs have also declined but continue to be positive and are projected to remain flat in 2017 for the OECD area, reflecting the fact that underlying fiscal balances are becoming more expansionary. Until 2016, net borrowing requirements in the OECD area declined steadily from the peaks attained in 2009.
- Sovereign debt levels have continued to increase and debt levels are high by historical standards, although exchange rate developments are complicating the interpretation of such aggregates.
- After surging from 49.8% to 74.6% between 2007 and 2015, the central government marketable debt-to-GDP ratio has started to decline and is estimated to be 73% in 2017. Among country groups the decline in the debt-to-GDP ratio is more significant for G7 countries.
- Interest rates remain low and are even negative for approximately USD 10 trillion of outstanding high-credit-quality sovereign debt. This situation facilitates the servicing of debt. It also makes debt-funded public investments to kick-start real activity growth relatively less costly and more attractive, without obscuring the medium- to long-term need for continued measured fiscal consolidation.
- Debt managers are reacting to fiscal challenges by lengthening redemption profiles, thus limiting rollover risks. This strategy tends to involve higher debt-servicing costs over the short term but, at the current juncture, such costs are very limited.
- Ultra-long government bond issuance has increased significantly, partly driven by attempts to lock in low long-term interest rates. Annual volumes of ultra-long bonds almost tripled between 2006 and 2016, with the number of issues doubling over the same period.

[*] This chapter was prepared by Fatos Koc and Sebastian Schich, Senior Policy Analyst and Principal Administrator respectively, OECD Financial Affairs Division, with research and statistical support from Gary Mills, Statistician, OECD Financial Affairs Division.

1.2 Gross and net borrowing needs of OECD governments have declined

The gross and net borrowing needs of OECD governments have continued to decline, while net borrowing needs are expected to remain flat in 2017, reflecting the fact that fiscal consolidation has slowed. The fiscal stance is expected to move from broadly neutral to moderately supportive and net borrowing requirements for the OECD area are not expected to contradict this (Figure 1.1).[1]

Looking back, the financial crisis, and the policy response to it, implied drastically increased additional borrowing requirements in 2008 and 2009. From a peak of USD 3.3 trillion attained in 2009, net central government marketable borrowing requirements have fallen considerably since then. Requirements are estimated to amount to USD 833 billion in 2017, a slight increase on 2016.[2] As net borrowing in the OECD area continues to be positive, this observation is reflected in the continued growth of central government marketable debt.

Figure 1.1. **Fiscal and borrowing outlook in OECD countries, 2007-2017**

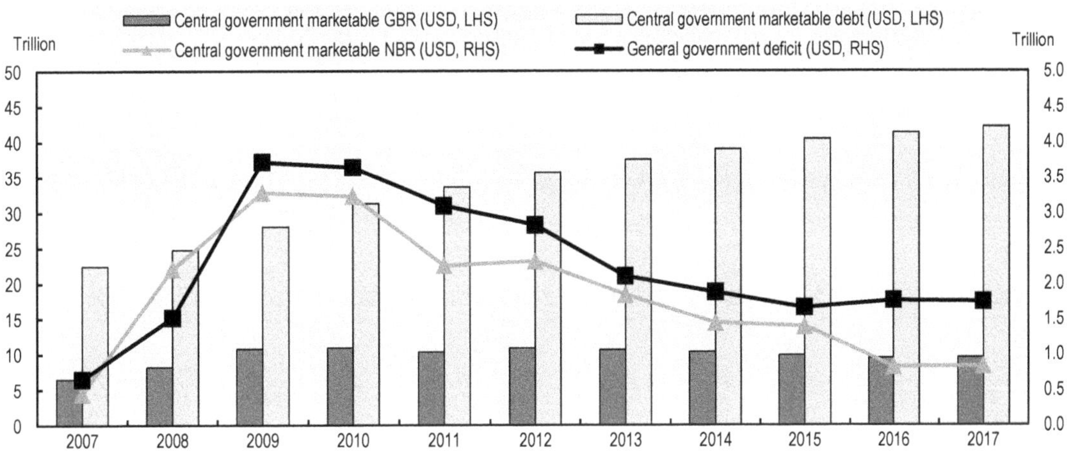

Notes: GBR = gross borrowing requirement, NBR = net borrowing requirement. General government deficit is derived from the general government net lending as published in the OECD Economic Outlook No. 100 for all OECD countries except for Chile, Mexico and Turkey for which the source is the IMF World Economic Outlook (October 2016). Figures are calculated based on data in national currencies using exchange rates as of 1 December 2009.

Source: 2016 Survey on central government marketable debt and borrowing, carried out by the OECD Working Party on Debt Management; OECD Economic Outlook No. 100; IMF World Economic Outlook (October 2016); Thomson Reuters, national authorities' websites and author calculations.

StatLink http://dx.doi.org/10.1787/888933474598

Outstanding central government debt is expected to increase by 2% from USD 41.3 trillion in 2016, to around USD 42.2 trillion in 2017 (Table 1.1). Compared to the financial crisis period, the pace of debt accumulation has stabilised significantly in recent years. Specifically, central government marketable debt in the OECD area grew, on average, by 3% annually between 2014 and 2015, compared to 6% between 2011 and 2013, and 12% between 2008 and 2010.

Table 1.1. **Central government marketable gross and net borrowing and marketable debt in the OECD area 2007-2017**

USD trillion

	2007	2008	2009	2010	2011	2012	2013	2014	2015	2016	2017
Central government marketable GBR	6.5	8.2	10.7	10.9	10.3	10.9	10.6	10.3	9.9	9.4	9.5
Central government marketable debt	22.5	24.7	28.0	31.3	33.6	35.7	37.6	39.0	40.4	41.3	42.2
Central government marketable NBR	0.4	2.2	3.3	3.2	2.3	2.3	1.8	1.4	1.4	0.8	0.8
General government deficit	0.6	1.5	3.7	3.6	3.1	2.8	2.1	1.9	1.7	1.8	1.7

Notes: GBR = gross borrowing requirement, NBR = net borrowing requirement. General government deficit is derived from the general government net lending as published in the OECD Economic Outlook No. 100 for all OECD countries except for Chile, Mexico and Turkey for which the source is the IMF World Economic Outlook (October 2016). Figures are calculated based on data in national currencies using the exchange rates as of 1st December 2009.

Source: 2016 Survey on central government marketable debt and borrowing carried out by the OECD Working Party on Debt Management; OECD Economic Outlook No. 100; IMF World Economic Outlook (October 2016); Thomson Reuters, national authorities' websites and OECD calculations.

Figure 1.2. **Central government marketable gross borrowing in OECD countries, 2007-2017**

As a percentage of GDP

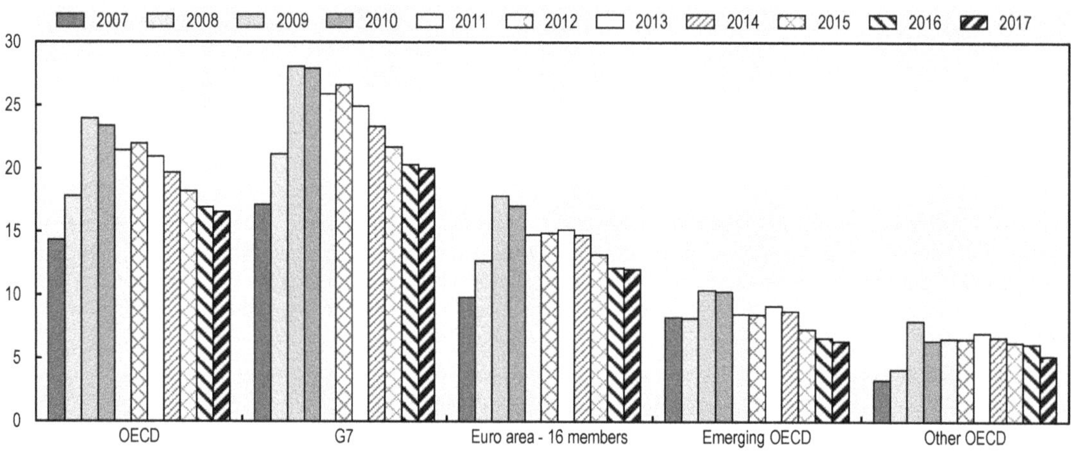

Notes: Central government marketable GBR without cash. Values of marketable GBR and GDP have been aggregated by using fixed exchange rates, as of 1st December 2009, for all years. "Euro area - 16 members" includes the following OECD countries: Austria, Belgium, Estonia, Finland, France, Germany, Greece, Ireland, Italy, Latvia, Luxembourg, Netherlands, Portugal, Slovak Republic, Slovenia and Spain. "Emerging OECD" includes Chile, Czech Republic, Estonia, Hungary, Latvia, Mexico, Poland, Slovak Republic, Slovenia and Turkey. "Other OECD" includes Australia, Denmark, Iceland, Israel, Korea, New Zealand, Norway, Sweden and Switzerland.

Source: 2016 Survey on central government marketable debt and borrowing carried out by the OECD Working Party on Debt Management; OECD Economic Outlook No. 100; IMF World Economic Outlook (October 2016); Thomson Reuters, national authorities' websites and author calculations.

StatLink http://dx.doi.org/10.1787/888933474604

Amongst selected OECD country groupings, aggregate borrowing expressed as a percentage of GDP is relatively high for the group of G7 countries, although it is expected to decline for its fifth consecutive year in 2017 (Figure 1.2). The figure is based on data collected through a survey on central government marketable debt and borrowing for the period from 2007 to 2017 carried out by the OECD Working Party on Debt Management, and includes author projections where applicable.

1.3 Enhancing real activity growth through debt-financed public investment

The global economy appears to be caught in a low-growth trap of weak investment and productivity, reflected in low potential per capita output growth (Figure 1.3). As the role of monetary policy to address these issues is limited and monetary policy support for real activity growth is already exceptionally strong, policy advice is reassessing the role of fiscal policies. In addition to structural reforms, a need to reassess fiscal policies has been diagnosed, with the suggested focus of such policies to be placed more sharply on the consequences for growth as opposed to budget balances and debt reduction. According to the recent OECD Economic Outlook No. 100, fiscal space (broadly defined as additional room available for sovereign debt levels to grow before access to new borrowing would be compromised) has increased in many advanced economies, mainly as a result of declining interest rates.

Figure 1.3. **Potential output growth in the OECD area has slowed markedly, 1998-2018**

Contribution to potential per capita growth

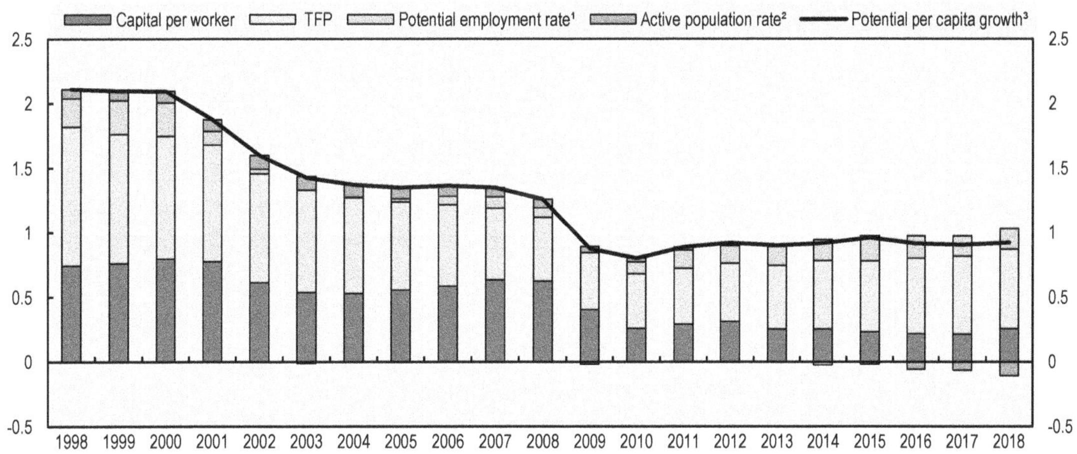

Note: Assuming potential output (Y*) can be represented by a Cobb-Douglas production function in terms of potential employment (N*), the capital stock (K) and total factor productivity (E*) then y* = a * (n*+e*) + (1 - a) * k, where lower case letters denote logs and a is the wage share. If P is the total population and PWA the population of working age (here taken to be aged 15-74), then the growth rate of potential GDP per capita (where growth rates are denoted by the first difference, d( ), of logged variables) can be decomposed into the four components depicted in the figure: d(y* - p)=a* d(e*) + (1-a) * d(k - n*) + d(n* - pwa) + d(pwa - p).

1. Potential employment rate refers to potential employment as a share of the working-age population (aged 15-74).
2. Active population rate refers to the share of the population of working age in the total population.
3. Percentage changes. Growth in Ireland in 2015 computed using gross value added at constant prices excluding foreign-owned multinational enterprise dominated sectors.

Source: OECD Economic Outlook No. 100.

StatLink http://dx.doi.org/10.1787/888933474615

As a result of this favourable interest rate-growth differential[3] environment, even though debt-to-GDP levels remain at historically high levels, debt-servicing is facilitated and relatively larger burdens of debt can be sustained at current levels of interest rates. A case has been made for fiscal measures to supplement structural reforms in attempts to raise the productive capacity of the economy. For example, according to the OECD Economic Outlook No. 100 published in November 2016, OECD governments could finance a 0.5 percentage point of GDP productivity-enhancing fiscal initiative in OECD countries for three to four years on average, without raising the debt-to-GDP ratio in the medium term, provided the selected activities and projects are sound. An easing of the fiscal stance through well-targeted growth-friendly measures is not expected to aggravate the debt-to-GDP ratio in the short term, whilst well-targeted fiscal measures are expected to raise potential output (not only raising soft and hard infrastructure or education spending, but also cutting harmful taxes) so that a temporary debt-financed fiscal expansion need not increase debt ratios in the longer term.

Some countries, including Canada, Japan and the United States, have recently announced expansionary fiscal measures, including raising spending on investment. Elsewhere, fiscal policies in most of Europe were only marginally easier in 2016 than in the previous year, though the United Kingdom has signalled an easing of its fiscal stance. In this context, a communication from the European Commission on fiscal policy in the euro area calls for a "positive fiscal stance", defined as both expansionary (a fiscal expansion of 0.5% of GDP in 2017) and of high-quality composition (with regard to the cross-country distribution of efforts and, within a country, with regard to the tax and expenditure mix). It recognises that countries which have not reached their medium-term objective or are under an excessive deficit procedure would find it difficult to achieve a fiscal expansion of 0.5% of GDP in 2017.

Interest rates continue to be low by historical standards in OECD countries (Figure 1.5). Ultra-low or negative interest rates provide opportunities for governments, given that they tend to have much larger interest-bearing liabilities than interest-earning assets. Interest rates have declined by more than GDP growth and the decline in interest rates more than offsets the increase in the debt-to-GDP ratio. As a result, even though debt-to-GDP levels are still at historically high levels, debt-servicing is facilitated and relatively larger burdens of debt can be sustained at current levels of interest rates. Obviously, these currently favourable metrics should not obfuscate the need to enact necessary structural and fiscal measures that ensure long-run fiscal sustainability.

The OECD Economic Outlook No.100 argues that a continuation of low growth observed during recent years could undermine fiscal sustainability and, eventually, the capacity to address future fiscal challenges. Given the low growth rate environment, there is a case for structural and temporary deficit-creating, well-targeted fiscal measures are required to raise the productive capacity of the economy. Simulations shown in Figure 1.4 suggest that, compared to general government debt[4] interest rate payments during 2014, cumulative interest payment "gains" on an unchanged stock of debt during the subsequent three years from 2015 to 2017, would be considerable if a large proportion of long-term debt (carrying much higher coupons than most recent issues) would be rolled over into debt at currently lower interest rates. The considerable magnitude of effects obtained through these simulations reflects the lower interest rate during the period from 2015 up to mid-2016 compared to 2014, as well as the assumed large proportion of refinancing. The expected effects are particularly high for countries with higher levels of debt and the greater the assumed debt rollover rate, the higher the increased effect. As regards to central marketable government debt in the OECD area, the present Sovereign Borrowing

Outlook estimates that, on average, about 20% will be due in year one and about 40% over the next three years (see also Figure 1.8).

Figure 1.4. **Fiscal stance in OECD countries, 2000-2018**

Underlying primary balance changes, including projections

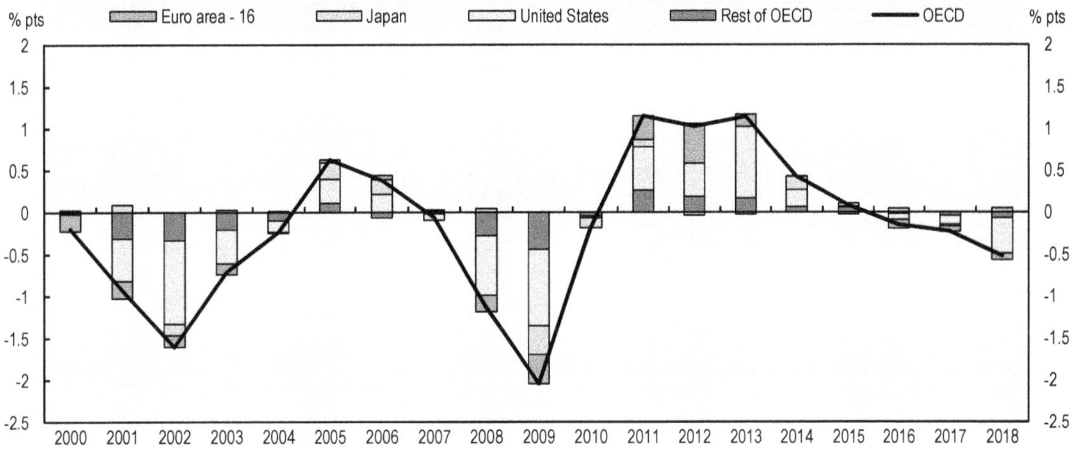

Notes: "Euro area - 16" includes the following OECD countries: Austria, Belgium, Estonia, Finland, France, Germany, Greece, Ireland, Italy, Latvia, Luxembourg, Netherlands, Portugal, Slovak Republic, Slovenia and Spain. "Rest of OECD" are all other OECD countries excluding the Euro area - 16, Japan and the United States.

Source: OECD Economic Outlook No. 100.

StatLink http://dx.doi.org/10.1787/888933474623

1.4 Interest rates and developments in relative debt burden measures

In recent years, the Bank of Japan and several smaller European authorities, following the European Central Bank (ECB), embarked on the uncharted territory of negative interest rates and expanded their monetary policy measures by purchasing government bonds. These developments contributed to unusually low interest rates in financial markets, which also influenced government bond yields. Already low, sovereign bond yields have turned negative in some countries. As a result, instead of paying interest, a number of OECD governments, including Germany, Japan, France and Switzerland, are now being paid for safe bonds up to 10-year maturity (Figure 1.5). As of December 2016, the amount of government bonds yielding negative interest rates is about USD 10 trillion, with Japan, France and Germany accounting for well over two-thirds of that amount. This is an unprecedented phenomenon in financial market history. A more detailed assessment of the implications of low interest rate environment on government debt markets is provided in Chapter 2 of this *Outlook*.

Figure 1.5. **Government benchmark interest rates in OECD countries**

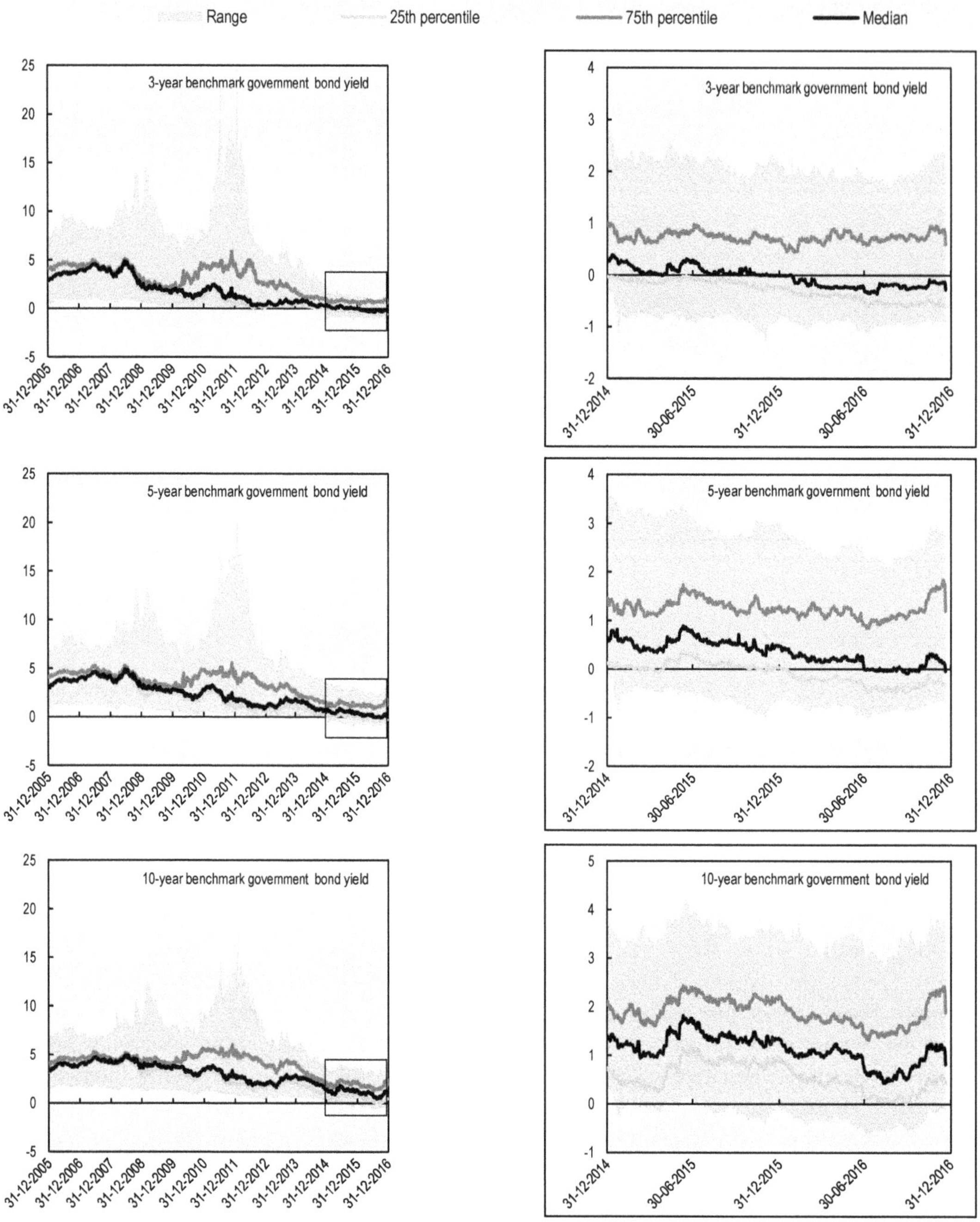

Notes: Interest rates in percentages. The charts show the evolution of several metrics (minimum, maximum, 25th percentile, 75th percentile, median) of 3-year, 5-year and 10-year benchmark government bond yields, calculated on the following group of countries: Australia, Austria, Belgium, Canada, Denmark, Finland, France, Germany, Hungary, Ireland, Italy, Japan, Netherlands, New Zealand, Norway (5-year and 10-year yields only), Poland, Portugal, Spain, Sweden, Switzerland, United Kingdom and the United States. The grey area shows the range of minimum and maximum values among all the included countries.

Source: Thomson Reuters and author calculations.

StatLink http://dx.doi.org/10.1787/888933474636

The ultra-low interest rate environment has changed the trade-off between costs and risks[5] and made it cheaper to insure against rollover risk. Weighted average term-to-maturity (ATM) of borrowing has increased significantly in several OECD countries and a higher ATM figure implies a slower pass-through impact of changes in interest rates to government's interest costs in the future. As the ATM of outstanding marketable debt is reaching eight years and gross borrowing needs are decreasing recently in the OECD area, the impact of falling interest rates on government interest expenses will be somewhat limited.

Figure 1.6. **Central government marketable gross borrowing, interest payments and long-term interest rates, 2007-2017**

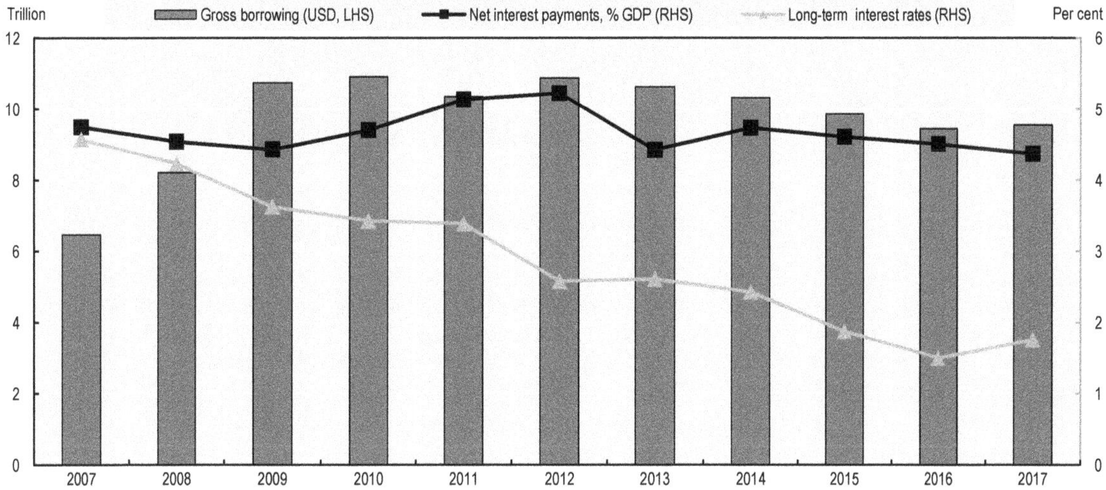

Notes: OECD area estimates. Long-term interest rates derived from long-term interest rate on government bonds calculated as a GDP weighted average.

Source: OECD Economic Outlook No. 100 and author calculations.

StatLink http://dx.doi.org/10.1787/888933474649

After surging from 49.8% to 74.6% from 2007 to 2015, the central government marketable debt-to-GDP ratio decreased slightly to 74.1% in 2016 (Figure 1.7). In terms of country groups, the group of G7 countries has the highest debt ratio at 86.7%, followed by the Eurozone country group. As discussed in the OECD *Sovereign Borrowing Outlook 2016*, current levels of debt burden are high by historical standards, particularly in G7 countries and some Eurozone countries. Looking ahead, central government marketable debt-to GDP ratio is expected to fall gradually to 73% in 2017, mainly driven by the decrease within the G7 country group.

Weak economic activity in Eurozone countries has continued to put pressure on debt-to-GDP ratios. Indeed, the central government marketable debt-to-GDP ratio is expected to remain at the 2016 level in 2017. Financing concerns are currently mitigated by low sovereign funding costs for almost all sovereign rating categories and robust demand for government bonds against the backdrop of the ECB's ongoing asset purchase programme. Despite the fact that debt servicing is currently much easier, risks to debt sustainability are still on the downside in several Eurozone countries.

Figure 1.7. **Central government marketable debt in OECD countries, 2007-2017**

As a percentage of GDP

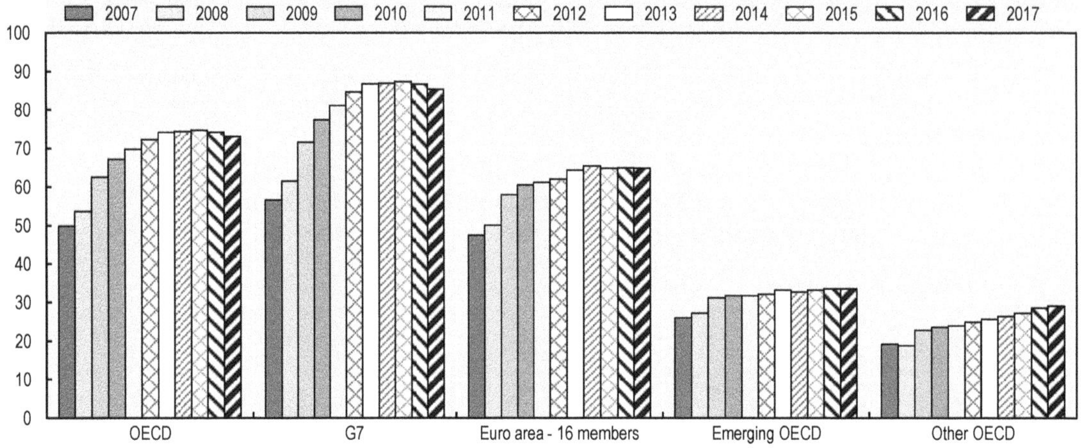

Notes: Central government marketable debt without cash. As of 1 December 2009, values of marketable debt and GDP have been aggregated by using fixed exchange rates for all years. “Euro area - 16 members” includes the following OECD countries: Austria, Belgium, Estonia, Finland, France, Germany, Greece, Ireland, Italy, Latvia, Luxembourg, Netherlands, Portugal, Slovak Republic, Slovenia and Spain. "Emerging OECD" includes Chile, Czech Republic, Estonia, Hungary, Latvia, Mexico, Poland, Slovak Republic, Slovenia and Turkey. “Other OECD” includes Australia, Denmark, Iceland, Israel, Korea, New Zealand, Norway, Sweden and Switzerland.

Source: 2016 Survey on central government marketable debt and borrowing carried out by the OECD Working Party on Debt Management; OECD Economic Outlook No. 100; IMF World Economic Outlook (October 2016); Thomson Reuters, national authorities’ websites and author calculations.

StatLink http://dx.doi.org/10.1787/888933474654

1.5 Risk-based government borrowing strategies are in place to manage refinancing risk

Government debt managers routinely measure and monitor refinancing risk exposure of the government debt portfolio by using various metrics. The three most commonly used indicators are: *i*) the ratio of debt maturing in a specific period to the total debt portfolio; *ii*) maturity structure of debt stock; *iii*) the Average Time to Maturity (ATM). As elaborated in the 2016 OECD Sovereign Borrowing Outlook, debt portfolio indicators that measure rollover risk: (*i*) play a diagnostic role for identifying vulnerabilities in the government debt structure; (*ii*) also serve as an important portfolio benchmarking role for reducing portfolio risk. Against this backdrop, an overview of these risk metrics is provided in this chapter.

Figure 1.8 presents the debt service of outstanding medium- and long-term central government marketable debt for the next 12, 24 and 36 months. Total debt service of OECD governments for the following 3 years is around 40% of the outstanding marketable debt, one fifth of which is due in the next 12 months.

Figure 1.8. **Cumulative percentage of debt maturing in the next 12, 24 and 36 months**

(As a percentage of total marketable debt as of 2016)

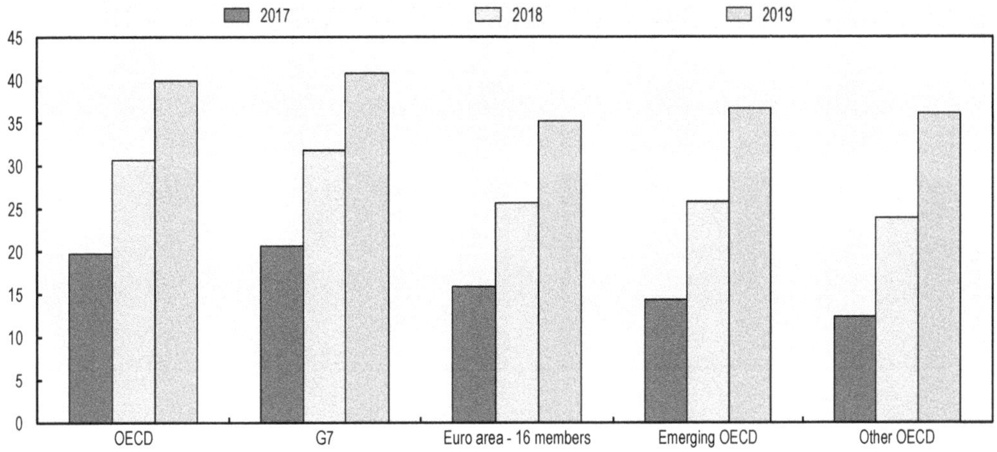

*Notes:*Cumulative percentage of debt maturing in the next 12, 24 and 36 months (i.e. in 2017, 2018 and 2019),) as a percentage of total marketable debt stock (without cash) in 2016. Values of principal payments and marketable debt have been aggregated into a single currency by using fixed exchange rates, as of 1st December 2009, for all years. "Euro area - 16 members" includes the following OECD countries: Austria, Belgium, Estonia, Finland, France, Germany, Greece, Ireland, Italy, Latvia, Luxembourg, Netherlands, Portugal, Slovak Republic, Slovenia and Spain. "Emerging OECD" include Chile, Czech Republic, Estonia, Hungary, Latvia, Mexico, Poland, Slovak Republic, Slovenia and Turkey. "Other OECD" includes Australia, Denmark, Iceland, Israel, Korea, New Zealand, Norway, Sweden and Switzerland.

Source: 2016 Survey on central government marketable debt and borrowing carried out by the OECD Working Party on Debt Management; OECD Economic Outlook No. 100; Thomson Reuters, national authorities' websites and author calculations.

StatLink http://dx.doi.org/10.1787/888933474661

Since the onset of the global crisis, the high level of debt servicing, combined with large net borrowing requirements, has generated challenging rollover ratios, and aggravated refinancing risks, for sovereign debt management in the OECD area. In response to the drastic increase in government debt levels, sovereign debt managers in most OECD countries have strategically increased the issuance of long-term as opposed to short-term instruments (Figure 1.11). The share of long-term debt in gross issuance operations in the OECD area has increased by more than five percentage points in 2016 compared to 2007 (Figure 1.9). Also the recent rising maturity of long-term issues, driven partly by growing ultra-long bond issuance (defined here as maturities of 30 years or more), has further mitigated the refinancing risk, as well as maturity mismatches, on the balance sheet.[6]

Although the long-term trend implies a surge in the share of long-term debt in gross issuance operations, Figure 1.9 indicates a slight rise in short-term issues in recent years. The maturity structure of gross issuance operations in the OECD area indicates around a six percentage point increase in the share of Treasury bills from 2015 to 2017. The main driver of this development was the United States Treasury's strategic policy decision to raise its liquidity buffer by increasing the supply of Treasury bills in May 2015[7] which it did to meet growing demand and raise liquidity buffer to an amount equal to 5 days of liquidity subject to USD 150 billion minimum amount in case of market disruption (US Department of the Treasury, 2015). As a result of this policy change, the share of US Treasury bills in gross short-term issuance in the OECD area, which has already increased by 4 percentage points from 2005 to 2016, is expected to exceed 43% by 2017.

Figure 1.9. **Maturity structure of gross issuance operations in the OECD area, 2007-2017**

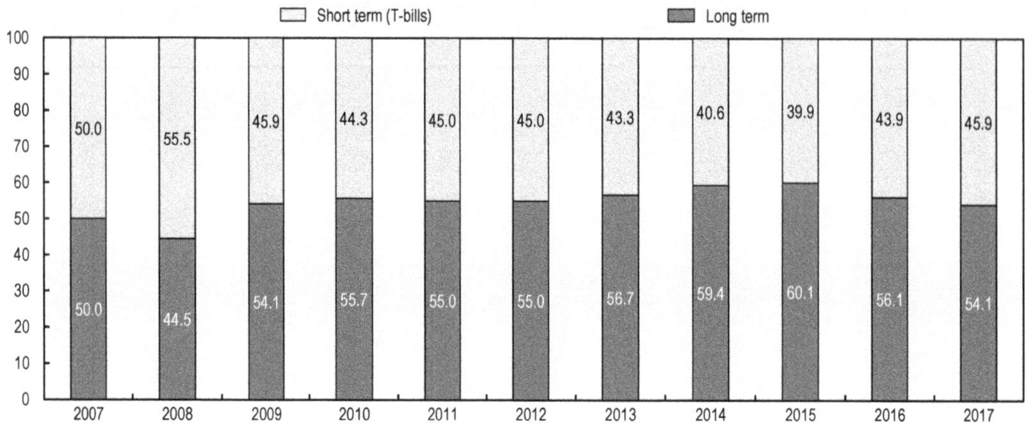

Source: 2016 Survey on central government marketable debt and borrowing carried out by the OECD Working Party on Debt Management; Thomson Reuters, national authorities' websites and author calculations.

StatLink http://dx.doi.org/10.1787/888933474671

As has been noted, the prolonged low interest rate environment and flattened yield curves in several OECD countries has enabled debt managers to lengthen average maturity of issues by easing the trade-off between expected costs and risks[5] along the efficient frontier in favour of costs. Current estimates for debt maturing in the next 36 months are slightly lower than the figures of previous editions of the OECD *Sovereign Borrowing Outlook.* The estimates cited in the 2013, 2014 and 2016 editions of the Outlook suggested an average of 44% of debt maturing in the following 3 years. Clearly, continued efforts of sovereign debt managers to extend the average maturity of debt stocks are starting to bear fruit.

Reduction in rollover risk exposure also manifests itself in maturity composition of outstanding debt. In parallel to increased borrowing maturities, the share of long-term debt in total central government marketable debt in the OECD area has risen since 2008. This figure has been stable at around 90% in recent years (Figure 1.10).

High rollover risk implies that debt can be refinanced at an unusually high cost or, in extreme cases, cannot be refinanced at all; in turn this weakens investors' confidence and can exacerbate or even trigger a debt crisis. This vicious cycle turns into a virtuous cycle when rollover risk is considered low. In recent years, an ultra-low interest rate environment and lengthening average maturities have generated a virtuous cycle in which rollover risk has been further mitigated at relatively cheaper costs.

Figure 1.10. **Maturity structure of central government marketable debt for the OECD area**

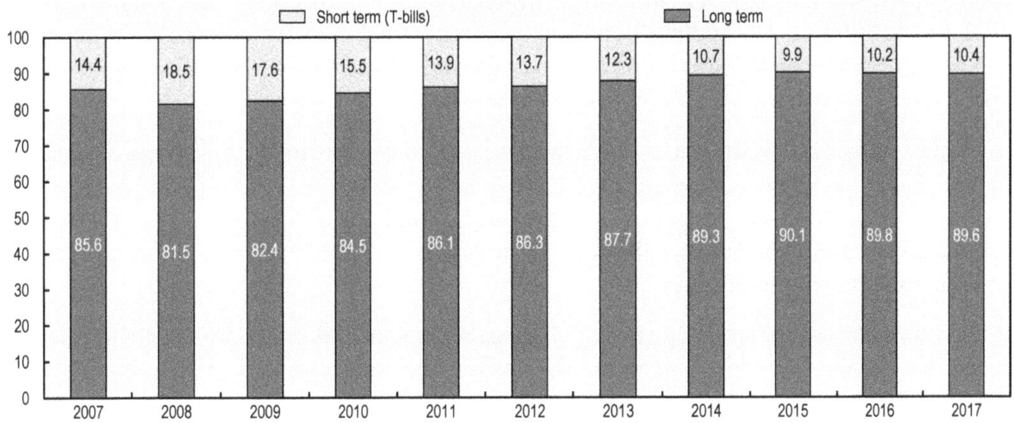

Source: 2016 Survey on central government marketable debt and borrowing carried out by the OECD Working Party on Debt Management; Thomson Reuters, national authorities' websites and author calculations.

StatLink http://dx.doi.org/10.1787/888933474683

Figure 1.11. **Average term-to-maturity of outstanding marketable debt in selected OECD countries**

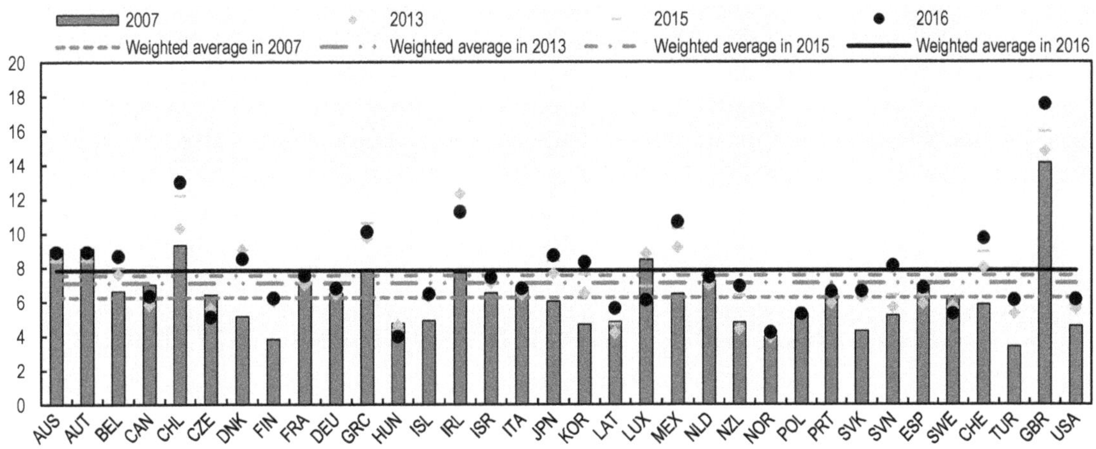

Notes: Average term-to-maturity in years (e.g. 0.5 years correspond to 6 months) of outstanding marketable debt. Data are collected from debt management office and national authorities' websites. Data are not strictly comparable across countries. The average term-to-maturity of outstanding debt might include government holdings (e.g. Norway), might include short-term debt (e.g. Denmark, United Kingdom) or exclude it (e.g. Ireland), include the effect of swaps (e.g. for France and Norway) or exclude that effect. The weighted average was calculated based on the data of all countries for which the average term to maturity was available for 2007, 2013, and 2015. The values of central government marketable debt (without cash) in 2007, 2013, 2015 and 2016, expressed in USD values using the December 2009 exchange rates, were used as weights in constructing the average. Figures for 2016 refer to the latest, publicly available, information.

Source: Surveys on central government marketable debt and borrowing carried out by the OECD Working Party on Debt Management; debt management offices and national authorities' websites and author calculations.

StatLink http://dx.doi.org/10.1787/888933474698

One of the most commonly used measures for refinancing risk is the ATM of outstanding debt, a historical evolution of which is provided in Figure 1.11. The weighted ATM of outstanding marketable debt has increased by 1.5 years compared to the pre-crisis period, reaching historic highs for several countries including Belgium, Mexico, the United Kingdom and the United States.

Higher ATM and duration figures imply a relatively lower pass-through impact of interest rate changes on government interest costs and, correspondingly, more predictability of debt service payments. Although a high ATM figure is often preferable, debt managers are also cautious about extreme levels to be able to benefit from potential lower interest rates in the future.

In a number of countries (including Denmark, Ireland, Mexico, Switzerland and the United Kingdom), ATMs of outstanding marketable debt rose more than three years between 2007 and 2016. One reason for this is the growing issuance of ultra-long bonds, different aspects of which will be discussed in the last part of this chapter.

1.6 Funding strategies and instrument choices

Debt managers often set overall medium and long-term risk targets, and accordingly determine funding strategies which involve the choice of maturities, interest rates and currency types. The funding strategy is formulated principally by cost versus risk considerations. Therefore, expected paths of certain parameters including inflation, interest rates, exchange rates and existing structure of the debt portfolio play an important role in setting up funding strategies.

Against this backdrop, Table 1.2 reflects the funding structures over the past decade, as well as the projections for 2017. As already noted, the data from 2008 to 2015 shows a clear trend in favor of long-term debt issuance. In 2016, the share of long-term instruments fell to 56.1% from 60.1% in 2015. It is expected that this share will drop further to 54.1% in 2017, mainly due to the US Treasury's increased supply of Treasury bills during this period (see Section 1.5). Nevertheless, the ATM of outstanding debt has continued to lengthen partly driven by the growing number of issuances of ultra-long bonds.

Table 1.2. **Funding strategy based on marketable gross borrowing needs in OECD area**

(Percentage)

	2007	2008	2009	2010	2011	2012	2013	2014	2015	2016	2017
Short Term (T-bills)	50.0	55.5	45.9	44.3	45.0	45.0	43.3	40.6	39.9	43.9	45.9
Long Term	50.0	44.5	54.1	55.7	55.0	55.0	56.7	59.4	60.1	56.1	54.1
Fixed rate	43.7	39.4	49.9	51.3	50.2	50.5	51.2	52.0	53.2	49.7	47.9
Index linked	3.3	2.5	1.8	2.3	2.9	3.2	3.7	4.0	3.7	3.1	2.9
Variable rate	1.5	1.0	1.0	0.9	0.7	0.3	0.9	2.6	2.3	2.4	2.4
Other	1.3	1.0	1.2	1.0	0.9	0.7	0.7	0.6	0.5	0.4	0.4
Of which:											
Local currency	49.6	43.4	53.1	55.1	54.3	54.2	55.9	58.5	58.6	55.2	53.0
Foreign currency	0.2	0.5	0.7	0.5	0.4	0.6	0.6	0.7	0.7	0.6	0.6

Source: 2016 Survey on central government marketable debt and borrowing carried out by the OECD Working Party on Debt Management; Thomson Reuters, national authorities' websites and author calculations.

In terms of the interest-rate composition of long-term debt, which is important for assessing re-fixing risk[8] exposure, fixed rate instruments dominate funding strategies with an average share of 90% between 2007 and 2017, albeit a gradual increase in the share of floating debt instruments in recent years. Inflation-indexed bonds, which gained in popularity particularly during the post-crisis period, have a diminishing share in total gross financing since 2015.

1.7 Growing issuance of ultra-long government bonds

The history of ultra-long bonds goes back to the 18th Century when the United Kingdom borrowed through issuance of "undated" gilts. More than two centuries later, the last undated bonds in the United Kingdom gilt portfolio were completely redeemed, in 2015. Globally, sovereign bonds with maturities of more than 30 years were a rarity until a decade ago. In recent history, just two sovereigns have issued 100-year bonds: China in 1996 and the Philippines in 1997. The change in the playing field was triggered by low and sometimes even negative interest rates.

In recent years, governments are extending the average length of their public debt and locking in low borrowing rates in a historically low interest-rate environment. Figure 1.12 reflects aggregate figures for government issuance of ultra-long bonds. Compared to pre-crisis years, government ultra-long bond issuances have increased significantly since 2009 as a result of increased borrowing requirements as well as maturity choice in issuance strategy. Specifically, the annual volume of ultra-long bond sales has almost tripled from 2006 to 2016, as the number of issues doubled in the same period. In recent years, several countries including Australia, Austria, the United Kingdom,[9] the United States, Japan, France, Italy, Spain, Canada and Switzerland have issued a number of securities maturing in 30 to 70 years. Mexico, Belgium and Ireland have sold 100-year bonds, which are called "century bonds". As a result, not only the volume, but also the average maturity of ultra-long bond issues has significantly increased.

Figure 1.12. **Issuance of government bonds with maturities of 30 years or more**

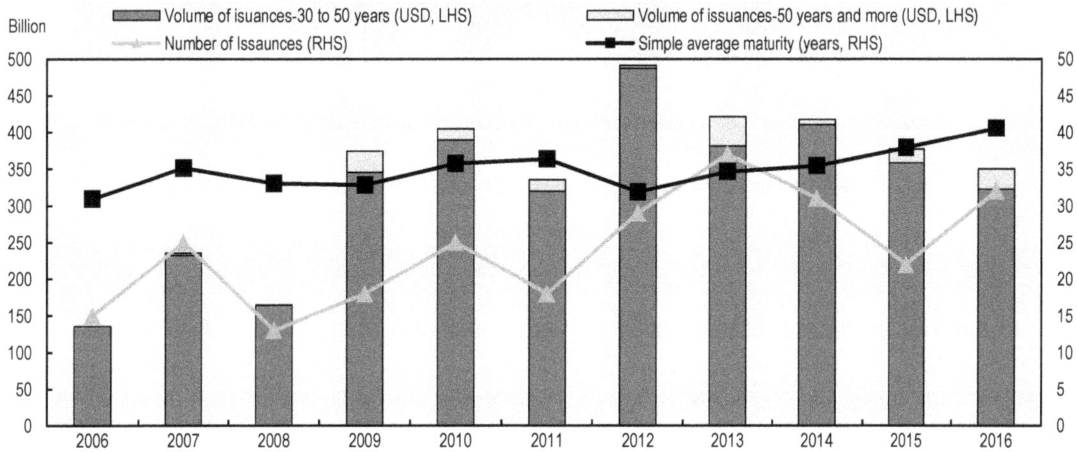

Notes: As of December 2016 for OECD countries only, volume is based on issuance amounts using flexible exchange rates.

Source: Thomson Reuters, national authorities' websites, OECD Economic Outlook No. 100 and author calculations.

StatLink http://dx.doi.org/10.1787/888933474700

As of December 2016, the outstanding stock of ultra-long bonds issued since 2006 has reached USD 3.7 trillion which comprises 9% of the central government marketable debt. While ultra-long bonds are still a small component of the government debt market, they are a fast-growing maturity segment. In 2016, six sovereigns sold 50-year bonds and two sovereigns sold 100-year bonds with a total volume of USD 27.6 billion (Figure 1.13). Various aspects of these issues were discussed during the last annual meeting of the OECD Working Party on Public Debt Management (WPDM) held on 7-8 November in 2016. Debt managers acknowledged potential benefits and risks associated with issuance of ultra-long bonds. Long-term debt issuance, and ultra long-term debt in particular, provides predictability of redemptions over decades in advance. Debt managers benefit from long-term bond issuances to diversify a government's debt portfolio and reduce maturity mismatches on the sovereign balance sheet,[6] as well as to mitigate refinancing risk of the outstanding debt. Hence, for several large issuers including the United States, the United Kingdom, Japan and Italy, 30-year bonds have long been a part of their regular borrowing programs as a result of strong and sustained investor demand. The majority of issuers noted that bonds with longer than 30-year maturities are tactical decisions to lock in historically low interest rates and rapidly reduce re-financing risk.

Figure 1.13. **Issuance of government bonds with maturities of 50 years or more**

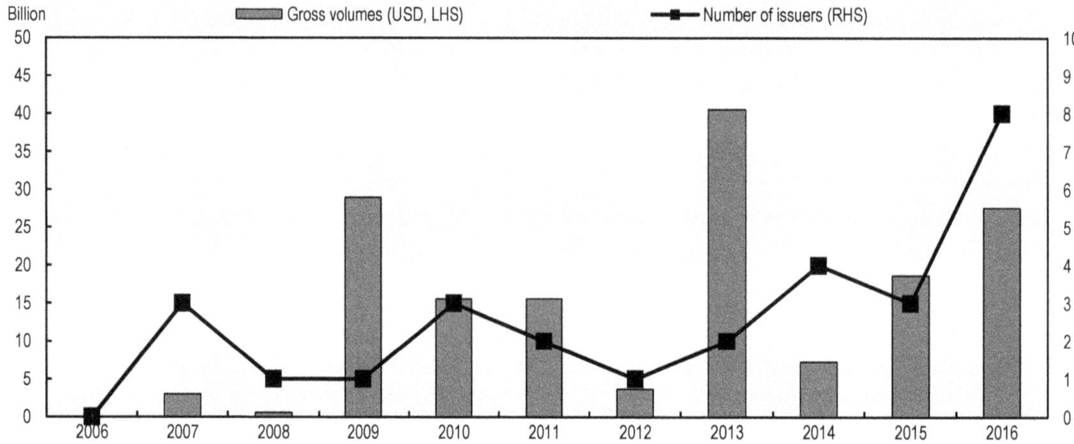

Notes: As of December 2016, for OECD countries only, volume is based on issuance amounts using flexible exchange rates.

Source: Thomson Reuters, national authorities' websites, OECD Economic Outlook No. 100 and author calculations.

StatLink http://dx.doi.org/10.1787/888933474717

In addition to the advantages, debt managers also consider potential risks related to fixing the rate of interest payable on debt over such a long period. In this context, some countries, including the United Kingdom, Denmark and Sweden, highlighted "regret risk" i.e., being cautious about assuming current rates as unique. Anecdotal evidence suggests that ultra-long bonds were issued in the past when borrowing costs were thought to be at their lowest level, only to see rates fall further. A potential future downside to the risk of locking into a high quantum of long-term borrowing is that it turns out to be unnecessary and/or costly after the fact (OECD, 2011). Several countries, including the United States, Sweden and Turkey, stressed that, in the absence of continued demand, ultra-long issuance might be opportunistic and inconsistent with regular and predictable financing policies. Against this backdrop, debt managers agreed that careful consideration needs to be given to the depth and sustainability of investor demand for such instruments and the potential impact of issuance on the long-term functioning of the government bond market, including the risk of fragmenting market liquidity at the long end of the yield curve, as well as the potential impact of supply on the shape of the yield curve.

With regard to investor type, the main buyers of these securities are insurance companies and pension funds as they need to match liabilities that span decades. Therefore, these bonds are expected to have lower secondary market liquidity compared to conventional maturity segments. In addition to liability-driven investors, much of the demand for long-term bonds is driven by a broader spectrum of investors searching for positive yields in recent years. Also, portfolio managers who are specifically aiming to protect against a sudden decline in yields, invest in these bonds as they exhibit positive convexity.[10]

In countries where 30-year bonds are already part of financing programs, auctions are the primary distribution method. As these bonds are often regularly issued and re-opened after the initial issuance, their outstanding volume and trade levels in the market are adequate for an efficient price formation of new issues through auctions. For a debut issue of a longer dated bond, several debt management offices (DMOs) prefer syndications while a few small issuers use private placements (Appendix A). With these approaches and in the absence of a benchmark bond, issuers get a better sense of borrowing costs and demand before committing to a sale. These methods enable debt managers to retain flexibility in aligning demand with supply as each syndication is placed according to the size and quality of investor demand.

1.8 Recent developments in markets for index-linked bonds

Given the currently high sovereign debt levels, low interest rates and weak real activity growth outlook, the idea of governments issuing financial instruments whose repayments are indexed to domestic GDP has received renewed attention. Fuelling that debate, a recent paper with contributions from several central banks,[11] argues that, in theory, the case for issuing such forms of state-contingent debt might be particularly strong now.[12] The paper argues that GDP-linked bonds offer additional fiscal space in downturns and an alternative way of delevering from high debt levels, which implies that the benefits from issuing such instruments are likely to be largest when debt levels are already high relative to GDP and there is an attempt to minimize the probability of debt reaching an unsustainable trajectory.

Issuing debt instruments whose payments are indexed to economic variables such as domestic GDP, consumption or inflation is not a new idea, although historical examples are rare. A widely- quoted early example of a type of inflation-indexed bond is a “depreciation note”, indexed to a basket of goods including corn, beef, wool and leather, by the State of Massachusetts in 1780. Following the debt crises of the 1980s, interest in the idea of sovereigns issuing bonds whose service or repayments would be linked to measures of the debtors’ payment capacity, exports or commodity prices rose, although the discussion remained mostly academic. Numerous proposals were made during the late 1980s and 1990s for making promised payments contingent on some form of index. Concerns were expressed about the possibility of moral hazard on the part of the debtor, which is why indices were thought preferable as they are less directly influenced by debtors’ actions. One form of debt instrument with indexed payments that has met with some success, in terms of actual proliferation of instruments, are inflation-indexed bonds.

Many OECD countries issue bonds that are linked to inflation-indices. The United Kingdom established an inflation-linked government bond program in 1981. Among OECD countries, this issuance choice was followed by Australia in 1985, Canada in 1991, Sweden in 1994, the United States in 1997, France in 1998, Italy in 2003, Japan in 2004, and Germany in 2006. As shown in Table 1.2 above, the issuance of index-linked bonds which fell during the global financial crisis, fell again after having increased from 2011 to 2014 and is currently standing at levels around those observed before the global financial crisis. Around 3% funding of gross borrowing needs in the OECD area in 2016 and 2017 is in the form of index-linked debt. Today, the United States Treasury Inflation-Protected Securities (TIPS) programme accounts for 39% of the outstanding sovereign linkers in the OECD area. This is followed by the United Kingdom (19%) and Italy (12%).

An important aspect of such issuances is the choice of inflation index. Several countries, including the United States, Japan, Canada, Sweden and Turkey, use the consumer price index (CPI), while the United Kingdom uses the retail price index (RPI). In the Eurozone area, France and Italy issue bonds which are linked to the national consumer price index excluding tobacco, as well as bonds that are linked to the Eurozone harmonised index of consumer prices excluding tobacco (HICP ex-tobacco). Bonds tend to have guaranteed redemption at par, which implies that the redemption amount will be equal to the face value of the bond in case of deflation, rather than inflation, during the lifetime of the bond. Tax regimes and perceived credit quality differ depending on the issuing country.

Further discussion of inflation-linked government bonds is provided in the Chapter 3 of this *Outlook*.

Notes

1. The cut-off date for data collected through the Survey on central government marketable debt and borrowing carried out by the OECD Working Party on Debt Management was mid-November 2016 and the cut-off date for other data considered in this chapter was December 2016.
2. This assessment is based on estimates of OECD aggregates using the assumption of exchange rates that are fixed as of 1 December 2009 when converting national values to USD equivalents.
3. One of the key determinants of government debt dynamics is the differential between interest rate paid to service government debt and the growth rate of the economy (r-g). Simply, higher interest rates imply higher interest payments to service government debt so adversely influencing debt dynamics, whereas higher nominal GDP growth rate reduces the debt burden by increasing the denominator. In this context, an interest rate-growth differential of lower than zero reduces debt-to-GDP ratio, for a given primary budget balance. Public debt sustainability frameworks suggest that debt stock grows by the existing debt stock (d) multiplied by r-g, less the primary budget balance (pb): Δdt = - pbt + (rt – gt) dt-1. Hence, for a given primary balance and initial net debt ratio, the rate of increase in the debt-to-GDP ratio is positively related to the interest-rate-growth differential (Spinelli and Turner, 2011).
4. General government debt is a wider concept than the central government debt considered in the previous sub-sections.

5. Sovereign debt managers face a cost-risk trade-off in the choice between short and long duration debt when determining how to finance the government's borrowing requirements. A normal (positive) yield curve indicates that reducing cost implies issuing short-term debt while reducing rollover risk implies issuing long-term debt. Since the government debt entails interest-rate risk because future debt financing and debt costs are subject to future unknown interest rates, short-duration debt (short-term or floating) is usually considered more risky than long duration (long-term, fixed-rate) debt (OECD, 2005).

6. From a sovereign asset liability management perspective, correlation between the interest and maturity structure of the balance sheet may decrease the volatility of the balance sheet against demand and supply shocks, and contributes to reduce budget risk. Since non-financial assets on the government balance sheet are usually long-lived assets, such as lands and buildings, an attempt to match maturity profile of government liabilities with that of assets implies lengthening the average maturity of borrowing (Koc 2014).

7. In May 2015, the United States Treasury Borrowing Advisory Committee of the Securities Industry and Financial Markets Association announced the increase of its minimum cash balance to USD 150 billion - an amount of cash necessary for approximately one week - in case of a market disruption, and to maintain a higher cash balance to mitigate risks associated with the temporary loss of market access. The Committee agreed that Treasury should issue additional bills to support a higher cash balance framework and to meet increased market demand for short-dated high quality assets. It was also noted that increasing Treasury bills would be consistent with Treasury's goal of funding government at the lowest cost over time and that this recommendation should not be viewed as a change to the strategy of extending the weighted average maturity of the debt (US Department of the Treasury, 2015).

8. Re-fixing risk refers to the risk that debt servicing costs are higher than expected because interest rates, when interest rate is re-fixed, are higher than expected.

9. The UK government real yield curve has an inverted shape; this situation supports the assumption of a 'negative' term premium existing in long-dated real yields due to heavy demand from institutional investors, particularly pension funds. As a result, the UK DMO adopted its funding strategies to capture this premium through issuance of long-dated index-linked gilts (OECD, 2011).

10. Convexity refers to the second derivative of the price of a bond. Convexity is a measure of the curvature of the price/yield relationship of a bond and provides an approximation of the part of the price change of a bond for a given change in yield that is not captured by modified duration. A bond with positive convexity will have larger price increases due to a decline in yields than price declines due to an increase in yields.

11. Prepared by Bank of England staff, with contributions from the Banco Central de la República Argentina and the Bank of Canada.

12. Such debt could be issued as part of debt restructurings, although the focus here is on the proposal for issuance of such bonds in normal times.

References

Altavilla, C., G. Carboni and R. Motto (2015), "Asset purchase programmes and financial markets: lessons from the euro area", ECB Working Paper No 1864, November; https://www.ecb.europa.eu/pub/pdf/scpwps/ecbwp1864.en.pdf?9f482224ba19759047b2c7f85670b0d3.

Antolin, P., Sebastian Schich and Juan Yermo (2011), "The Economic Impact of Protracted Low Interest Rates on Pension Funds and Insurance Companies", *OECD Journal: Financial Market Trends*, Vol. 2011/1. http://dx.doi.org/10.1787/fmt-2011-5kg55qw0m56l.

Arslanalp, S. and Y. Liao (2015), "Contingent Liabilities from Banks: How to Track Them?", IMF Working Paper WP/15/255, December; www.imf.org/external/pubs/ft/wp/2015/wp15255.pdf.

Assekurata Assekurnz Rating-Agentur GmbH (2016), Marktausblick zur Lebensversicherung 016/2017, June, www.assekurata.de/fileadmin/mediendatenbank/Dokumente/Publikationen/Marktausblick/2016/Leben/Assekurata_Marktausblick_Lebensversicherung_2016_2017.pdf.

Bean C., C. Broda, T. Ito and R. Kroszner (2015), "Low for Long? Causes and Consequences of Persistently Low Interest Rates", The 17th Geneva Report on the World Economy, CEPR, London, 23 October; www.voxeu.org/content/low-long-causes-and-consequences-persistently-low-interest-rates.

Bank of England (2015a), *Inflation Report*, November 2015; www.bankofengland.co.uk/publications/Pages/inflationreport/2015/nov.aspx.

Bank of England (2015b), *Financial Stability Report*, Issue No. 38, December 2015; www.bankofengland.co.uk/publications/Documents/fsr/2015/dec.pdf.

BIS (2015), "Is the unthinkable becoming routine?", Chapter 1 of 85th Annual Report 2014/15, 28 June 2015; https://www.bis.org/publ/arpdf/ar2015e1.htm.

Blix-Grimaldi, M., J. Hofmeister, S. Schich, and D. Snethlage (2016), "Estimating the size and incidence of bank resolution costs for selected banks in OECD countries", OECD *Financial Market Trends*, Volume 2016-Issue 1 http://dx.doi.org/10.1787/fmt-2016-5jlvbslktw7j.

Bloch, D. and F. Fall (2015), "Government debt indicators: Understanding the data", *OECD Economics Department Working Papers,* No. 1228, OECD Publishing, Paris. http://dx.doi.org/10.1787/5jrxv0ftbff2-en.

Blommestein, H.J. and P. Turner (2012), "Interactions Between Sovereign Debt Management and Monetary Policy Under Fiscal Dominance and Financial Instability", *OECD Working Papers on Sovereign Borrowing and Public Debt Management*, No. 3, OECD Publishing, Paris. http://dx.doi.org/10.1787/5k9fdwrnd1g3-en.

Cariboni, J., A. Fontana, S. Langedijk, S. Maccaferri, A. Pagano, M. Petracco Giudici, M. Rancan, and S. Schich (2016), "Reducing and sharing the burden of bank failures", OECD *Financial Market Trends*, Volume 2016-Issue 1 http://dx.doi.org/10.1787/fmt-2015-5jm0p43ldl30.

Committee on the Global Financial System (CGFS, 2014), "Market-making and proprietary trading: industry trends, drivers and policy implications", CGFS Paper No. 52, November 2014; www.bis.org/publ/cgfs52.htm .

Domanski, D., H.S. Shin, and V. Sushko (2015), "The hunt for duration: not waving but drowning?", BIS Working Paper No. 519, October; www.bis.org/publ/work519.pdf.

Grunfeld, A. (2016), "Global Pension Underfunding Concerns - An Issue Brief", MSCI, October, https://www.msci.com/documents/10199/904da30f-d851-4c48-bcfc-5e5f76d3335b.

Hannoun, H. (2015), "Ultra-low or negative interest rates: what they mean for financial stability and growth", remarks at the Eurofi High-Level Seminar, Riga, 22 April 2015, http://www.bis.org/speeches/sp150424.pdf.

Jackson, H. (2015), "The International Experience with Negative Policy Rates", Bank of Canada, Staff Discussion Paper 2015-13, November; www.bankofcanada.ca/2015/11/staff-discussion-paper-2015-13/.

Koc, Fatos (2014), "Sovereign Asset and Liability Management Framework for DMOs: What Do Country Experiences Suggest?", UNCTAD, Geneva; http://unctad.org/en/PublicationsLibrary/gdsddf2014misc1_en.pdf.

McLaren, N., Banerjee, R.N., and Latto, D., (2014) "Using changes in Auction Maturity Sectors to help identify the impact of QE on Gilt Yields", *The Economic Journal*, Vol. 124(576), 453-479; http://onlinelibrary.wiley.com/doi/10.1111/ecoj.12141/abstract.

Meaning, J. and F. Zhu (2012), "The impact of Federal Reserve asset purchase programmes: another twist, BIS Quarterly Review, March, pp.23-30; www.bis.org/publ/qtrpdf/r_qt1203e.pdf.

OECD (2011), "Principles and Trade-Offs When Making Issuance Choices in the UK: Report by the United Kingdom Debt Management Office", *OECD Working Papers on Sovereign Borrowing and Public Debt Management, No. 2,* OECD Publishing, Paris. http://dx.doi.org/10.1787/5k9gz2mmx0vh-en.

OECD (2016a), *OECD Economic Outlook, Volume 2016 Issue 2*, OECD Publishing, Paris; http://dx.doi.org/10.1787/eco_outlook-v2016-2-en.

OECD (2016b), *OECD Pensions Outlook 2016*, OECD Publishing, Paris; http://dx.doi.org/10.1787/pens_outlook-2016-en.

OECD (2016c), *OECD Sovereign Borrowing Outlook 2016, OECD Publishing, Paris;* http://dx.doi.org/10.1787/sov_b_outlk-2016-en.

OECD (2014), *OECD Sovereign Borrowing Outlook 2014,* OECD Publishing, Paris; http://dx.doi.org/10.1787/sov_b_outlk-2014-en.

OECD (2013), *OECD Sovereign Borrowing Outlook 2013,* OECD Publishing, Paris; http://dx.doi.org/10.1787/sov_b_outlk-2013-en.

OECD (2005), *Advances in Risk Management of Government Debt*, OECD Publishing, Paris; http://dx.doi.org/10.1787/9789264104433-en.

Pescatori, A. and J. Turunen (2015), "Lower for Longer: Neutral Rates in the United States", IMF Working Paper WP/15/135; https://www.imf.org/external/pubs/ft/wp/2015/wp15135.pdf.

Saiki, A. and J. Frost, "Does Unconventional Monetary Policy Affect Inequality? Evidence from Japan", CEP Council on Economic Policies Working Paper 2014/2, October 2014; www.cepweb.org/wp-content/uploads/CEP_WP_Unconventional_Monetary_Policy_and_Inequality.pdf.

Schich, S. and Y. Aydin (2014), "Measurement and analysis of implicit guarantees for bank debt: OECD survey results", *OECD Journal: Financial Market Trends*, Vol. 2014/1. http://dx.doi.org/10.1787/fmt-2014-5jxzbv3r9rf4.

Turner, D. and F. Spinelli (2011), "Explaining the Interest-Rate-Growth Differential Underlying Government Debt Dynamics", *OECD Economics Department Working Papers*, No. 919, OECD Publishing, Paris. http://dx.doi.org/10.1787/5kg0k706v2f3-en.

The UK Debt Management Office (2012), "Super-long and perpetual gilts, Consultation Papers, 5 December 2012 www.dmo.gov.uk/documentview.aspx?docname=publications/giltsmarket/consultationpapers/cons20121205.pdf&page=Gilts/Consultation.

The UK Debt Management Office (2005), "Issuance of ultra-long gilt instruments", Consultation Papers, 16 March 2005 www.dmo.gov.uk/documentview.aspx?docname=publications/giltsmarket/consultationpapers/cons160305.pdf&page=Gilts/Consultation.

US Department of the Treasury (2015), "Minutes of the Meeting of the Treasury Borrowing Advisory Committee of the Securities Industry and Financial Markets Association"on 5 May 2015; https://www.treasury.gov/press-center/press-releases/Pages/jl10043.aspx.

ANNEX 1.A1.

Methods and sources

Regional aggregates

- Total OECD area denotes the following 35 countries: Australia, Austria, Belgium, Canada, Chile, Czech Republic, Denmark, Estonia, Finland, France, Germany, Greece, Hungary, Iceland, Ireland, Israel, Italy, Japan, Korea, Latvia, Luxembourg, Mexico, Netherlands, New Zealand, Norway, Poland, Portugal, Slovak Republic, Slovenia, Spain, Sweden, Switzerland, Turkey, the United Kingdom and the United States.
- The G7 includes seven countries: Canada, France, Germany, Italy, Japan, United Kingdom and the United States.
- The OECD euro area includes 16 countries: Austria, Belgium, Estonia, Finland, France, Germany, Greece, Ireland, Italy, Latvia, Luxembourg, Netherlands, Portugal, Slovak Republic, Slovenia and Spain.
- In this publication, the Emerging OECD group is defined as including ten countries: Chile, Czech Republic, Estonia, Hungary, Latvia, Mexico, Poland, Slovak Republic, Slovenia and Turkey.
- The Other OECD group includes 15 countries: Australia, Chile, Czech Republic, Denmark, Hungary, Iceland, Israel, Korea, Mexico, New Zealand, Norway, Poland, Sweden, Switzerland and Turkey.
- The euro (€) is the official currency of 19 out of 28 EU member countries. These countries are collectively known as the Eurozone. The Eurozone countries are Austria, Belgium, Cyprus, Estonia, Finland, France, Germany, Greece, Ireland, Italy, Latvia, Lithuania, Luxembourg, Malta, the Netherlands, Portugal, Slovakia, Slovenia, and Spain.

Calculations, definitions and data sources

- Gross borrowing requirements (GBR) as a percentage of GDP is calculated using nominal GDP data from the OECD Economic Outlook No. 100, November 2016.
- To facilitate comparisons with previous Outlooks, figures are converted into US dollars using exchange rates from 1 December 2009, unless indicated otherwise. Where figures are converted into US dollars using flexible exchange rates, the main text refers to that approach explicitly. Source: Thomson Reuters. The effects of using alternative exchange rate assumptions (in particular, fixing the exchange

rate versus using flexible exchange rates) are illustrated in Figures 1.3 and 1.4 of Chapter one of the *Sovereign Borrowing Outlook 2016*.

- All figures refer to calendar years.
- Aggregate figures for gross borrowing requirements (GBR), net borrowing requirements (NBR), central government marketable debt, redemptions, and debt maturing are compiled from the answers to the Borrowing Survey. The Secretariat inserted its own estimates/projections in cases of missing information for 2016 and/or 2017, using publicly available official information on redemptions and central government budget balances.

Chapter 2

Implications of a low interest rate environment for government debt markets

A low interest rate environment seems to have become the norm in OECD countries, reflecting a variety of factors. Among them, central banks in major advanced economies lowered policy rates close to zero, or even below, and several also implemented unconventional policy measures in response to the global financial crisis and deteriorating real activity outlook. While volumes of sovereign debt trading at negative yields surged to record levels in 2016, some sovereign debt management offices were (and still are being) paid for issuing their domestic government bonds.

The persistent ultra-low interest rate environment has had a number of significant effects on volumes and structures of government debt markets in recent years. Lower interest rates have improved debt dynamics and eased funding of government debt. Declining long-term bond yields – reaching negative territory in several OECD countries – have raised concerns about secondary market liquidity. This chapter discusses the potential challenges arising from the ultra-low interest rate environment for government debt markets, as well as developments regarding the investor base and duration risks.

The statistical data for Israel are supplied by and under the responsibility of the relevant Israeli authorities. The use of such data by the OECD is without prejudice to the status of the Golan Heights, East Jerusalem and Israeli settlements in the West Bank under the terms of international law.

2.1. Introduction

The persistent ultra-low interest rate environment has had a number of significant impacts on both primary and secondary government debt markets in recent years. This chapter* elaborates on the implications of the ultra-low interest rate environment for debt dynamics, funding strategies, investor base, and market liquidity.

Key findings

- A low interest rate environment has become the norm in OECD countries; furthermore, negative-yielding government debt increased from USD 2.6 trillion in January 2016 to above USD 10 trillion in November 2016 with Japan, France and Germany accounting for well over two-thirds of that amount.
- As discussed in Chapter 1, prolonged ultra-low interest rates have reduced the cost of borrowing in OECD countries considerably. Since interest rates have declined by more than GDP growth and the decline in interest rates more than offsets the increase in the debt-to-GDP ratio, debt-servicing has been facilitated and debt sustainability concerns have been alleviated in a number of OECD countries.
- Some sovereigns (including France, Germany, the Netherlands and Japan) have issued negative yielding debt and received premiums from these issues. A study examining sovereign bond auctions in 14 OECD countries indicated that the volume of negative-yielding fixed-rate bond issues reached USD 1.25 trillion between 2014 and 2016.
- Funding strategies of many Debt Management Offices (DMOs) have leaned steadily towards long-term local currency financing instruments as the low interest rate environment eases the trade-off between expected cost and risk parameters of different maturity choices. Several OECD DMOs have issued long dated (sometimes ultra-long dated) securities and lengthened redemption profiles, as discussed in Chapter 1.
- Sovereign debt managers have observed a change in investors' appetite and behaviour in response to the negative rate environment. Large central banks and public funds have become dominant holders of sovereign debt in major OECD countries.
- A recent survey of liquidity in secondary government bond markets revealed concerns about market liquidity of government bonds. Reduced liquidity impairs - to some extent - the price discovery process, increases cost of borrowing via a higher risk premia and limits issuers' abilities to tap a variety of investors. In response to these concerns, debt managers in several countries have introduced policy measures such as tap sales, buy-backs and switch operations, and smaller auctions to improve liquidity conditions.

---

* This chapter was prepared by Fatos Koc and Sebastian Schich, Senior Policy Analyst and Principal Administrator respectively, OECD Financial Affairs Division, with research and statistical support from Gary Mills, Statistician, OECD Financial Affairs Division.

Figure 2.1. **Government benchmark interest rates in selected OECD countries, 2006-2016**

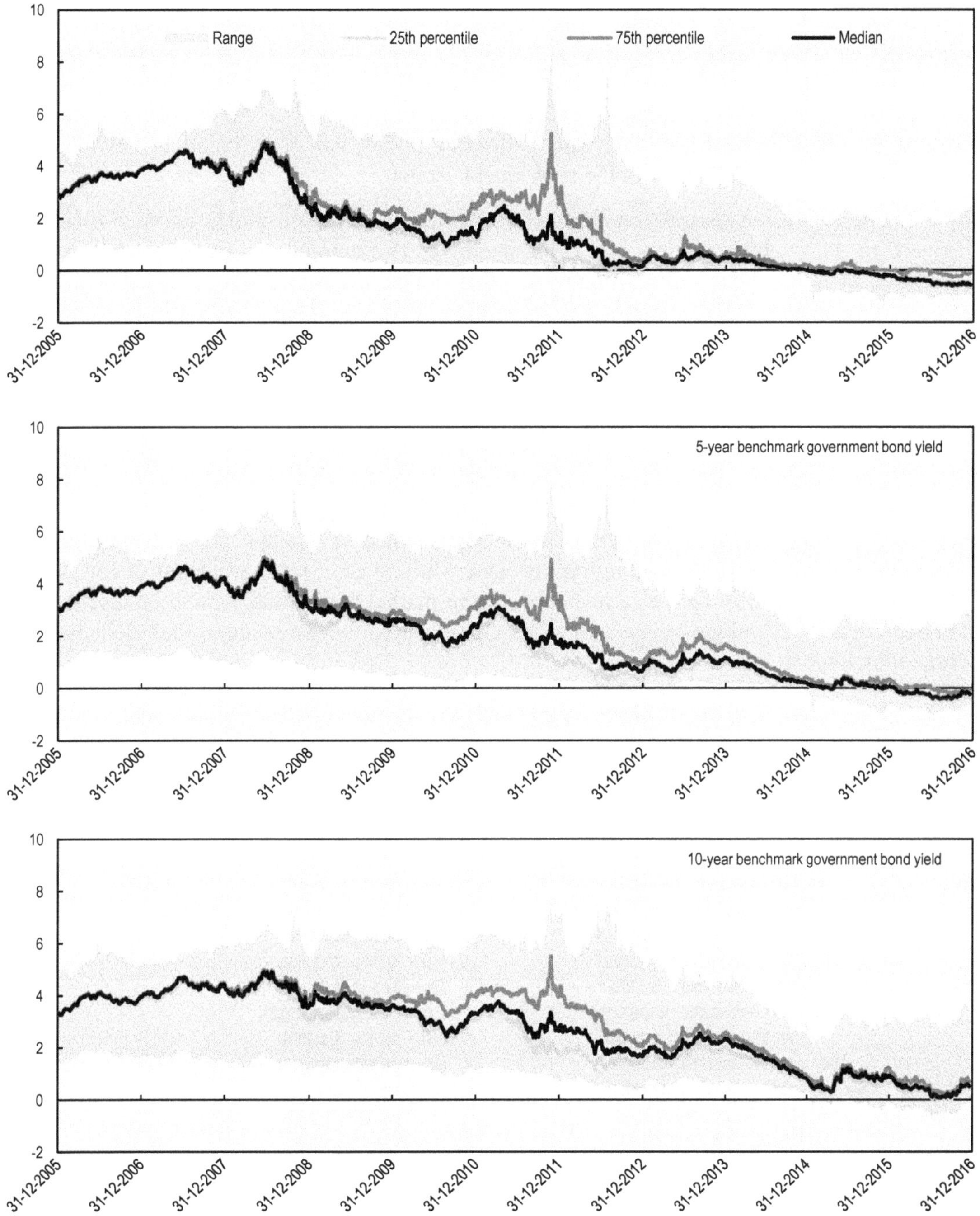

Note: The charts show the evolution of several metrics (minimum, maximum, 25th percentile, 75th percentile, median) of 3-year, 5-year and 10-year benchmark government bond yields, calculated for 14 countries: Austria, Belgium, Czech Republic, Denmark, Finland, France, Germany, Italy, Japan, Netherlands, Poland, Spain, Sweden (5 and 10 year only) and Switzerland. The grey area shows the range of minimum and maximum values among all the included countries.

Source: Thomson Reuters, national authorities' websites and author calculations.

StatLink http://dx.doi.org/10.1787/888933474722

2.2. Government bond yields are low and often negative

A secular decline in sovereign bond yields has characterised much of the OECD area (Figure 2.1). The decline in interest rates observed over the last few years is a continuation of a trend that stretches over several decades, and it reflects reduced inflation expectations, compressed risk and term premia and a decline in (inflation-adjusted) real interest rates. That said, monetary policy has contributed to downward pressures, as will be discussed in the subsequent section.

The downward pressures on rates are reflected in observed yields on high-quality sovereign debt, which are low and often negative. The amount of sovereign debt with negative rates has been growing and exceeded double-digits of trillions of USD in the OECD area (Figure 2.2), amounting to more than 80% of the total outstanding sovereign debt in the case of some countries. In most countries covered in the present sample, the proportion of negative-yielding bonds as a total of outstanding sovereign bonds ranges between 40% to 70%.

United States Treasury bond rates have continued to be positive and risen following the 2016 Presidential election results, but at least part of the maturity spectrum of the debt of several European sovereigns and the Japanese sovereign paid negative interest rates at the end of 2016. Yields on the debt of some highly rated sovereigns can be negative out to more than five years, depending on the issuer. In one case, rates are negative for even more than ten years. In fact, as a result of current market conditions, as will be discussed in Section 2.4, several governments are being paid a premium on some of their debt at the time they issue it.

Figure 2.2. **Negative-yield sovereign bonds are dominant in Europe and Japan**

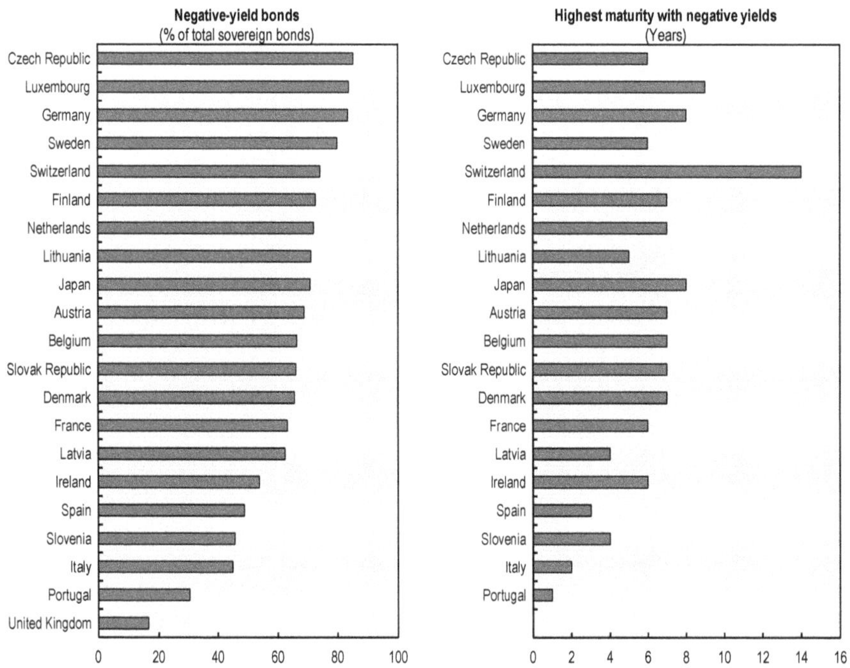

Note: Estimate based on benchmark sovereign bond yields as of end-December 2016. Highest maturity with negative yields was unavailable for the United Kingdom.

Source: Thomson Reuters; Bloomberg; and OECD calculations.

StatLink http://dx.doi.org/10.1787/888933474730

2.3. Unconventional monetary policy has facilitated duration extension

Further to lowering rates to close to zero, or even below, several central banks also implemented policy measures considered unconventional, including outright purchases of large amounts of long-term bonds, in particular government bonds. Such measures were aimed at affecting real activity through several channels, including signalling and portfolio balance channels. The signalling channel takes the following form; by buying long-term bonds, the central bank can be assumed to have an incentive to maintain low interest rates until the bonds mature so as to avoid mark-to-market losses arising from an interest rate increase. To the extent that the signalling is credible, a lower expected path of short-term rates will result, with reduced long-term rates and compressed risk premia due to the reduction in uncertainty. A portfolio balance channel operates via compressions of term premia. As the central bank purchases longer-term securities, it reduces the amount of duration risk in the hands of investors and thus might lead investors to buy assets with even greater duration (or higher credit risk), thus lowering the long end of the yield and encouraging greater credit and other risk-taking. In fact, encouraging additional risk-taking by bond investors is precisely the aim of quantitative easing strategies.

Examples of quantitative easing strategies that have had a direct impact on sovereign debt markets include the United States' Federal Reserve's Large-Scale Asset Purchase (LSAP) Programme introduced in 2008 and the Maturity Extension Programme (MEP) of 2011. As a result of such unconventional monetary policy measures, the Federal Reserve has emerged as an important holder of US Treasuries, especially of long-term US Treasury securities. Most recently, the holdings of outstanding US Treasury securities as of total outstanding US Treasury securities has somewhat declined again, although it is still well above historical norms.

In January 2015, the European Central Bank (ECB) announced its expanded asset purchase programme. The programme, starting in March 2015 until September 2016, initially included purchases of securities worth 60 billion Euro per month, however it was subsequently extended to March 2017 with an increase to 80 billion Euro per month. As a result, securities worth more than 10% of the Euro area GDP would be purchased. The Bank of Japan has been a major buyer of Japanese government bonds for some time now. It expects to continue to buy government bonds for an amount equivalent to around 15% of GDP per year, until the Consumer Price Index (CPI) exceeds the price stability target of 2% and stays above that target in a stable way. As a result of quantitative easing programmes in Japan, the United States and the Euro area, central banks in these regions hold respectively more than a third, a fifth and a tenth of outstanding local government bonds; and central banks have become major investors in local government debt securities (Figure 2.3).

The addition of a major dedicated buyer has been reflected in higher government bond prices and further compressed yields. For example, exploiting the information available from new micro-level data sets on security-level portfolio holdings of major investor sectors in each country of the Eurosystem, Koijen et. al. (2016) finds that, on average, yields of European government bonds have declined by about 13 basis points as a result of purchase programmes.

Figure 2.3. **Central banks' holdings of domestic government bonds**

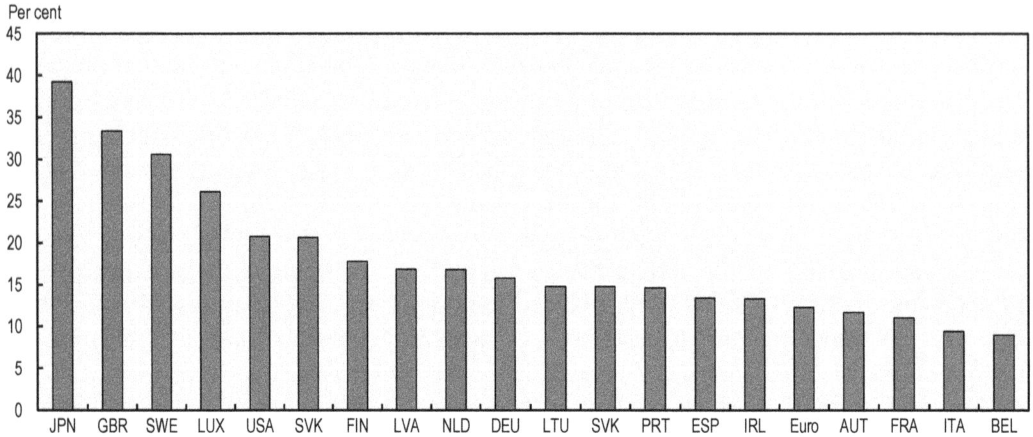

Notes: For the United States, marketable treasury securities, excluding treasury bills, held by the Federal Reserve as a share of outstanding marketable treasury securities excluding treasury bills at market value. For the United Kingdom, Asset Purchase Facility holdings as a share of outstanding gilts (conventional and index-linked), at market value. For Japan, government bonds held by the Bank of Japan as a share of outstanding treasury securities, excluding treasury discount bills and including Fiscal Investment and Loan Program (FILP) bonds, at market value. For the Euro area countries, cumulative net purchases of government bonds in the Eurosystem Public Sector Purchase Programme at book value as a share of outstanding general government bonds at face value. For the Euro area, the numerator and the denominator of the share are sums of respective values for all Euro area countries. For Sweden, it includes the purchase of government bonds (245 billion SEK in 2016) as a share of the outstanding government bonds issued in national currency, at face value.

As of June 2016 for Japan, the United Kingdom and the United States.

Source: Board of Governors of the United States' Federal Reserve System; Bank of Japan; Sveriges Riksbank; Riksgälden; UK Debt Management Office; European Central Bank; and OECD calculations.

StatLink http://dx.doi.org/10.1787/888933474741

Where central banks have become a new committed buyer of domestic government bonds, the implications of this situation for liquidity are not immediately clear. There is empirical evidence that liquidity premiums are reduced as a result of quantitative easing programmes (Christensen and Gillan, 2016). Thus, quantitative easing can improve liquidity, although it does not have to do so under all circumstances (Iwatsubo and Taishi, 2016). Central banks typically apply buy-and-hold strategies, and this observation implies that the increased participation of such investors might, in principle, also decrease secondary bond market liquidity. To address this and other potential issues (such as distorting relative prices), central banks attempt to act as "market neutral" as possible and tend to limit their purchases of specific bond issues to not exceed specific thresholds in terms of percentages held as of the total outstanding. Debt managers also react to such potential issues by intensifying their efforts to achieve more balanced mixes of investors, and are focusing on bringing in new investors with diverse mandates and investment horizons as well as taking other measures to supporting liquidity, as discussed in Section 2.5.

2.4. A number of governments have issued negative-yielding debt

The government bond secondary market developments in OECD countries, described in Section 2.2, are also reflected in primary market developments. Government debt markets have experienced an unprecedented phenomenon over the past couple of years as an increasing number of OECD governments have issued negative-yielding debt.

Figure 2.4 shows the result of an empirical study that examines fixed rate sovereign bond auctions in 14 OECD countries between 2014 and 2016. The methodological approach and sources of this study are provided in Annex 2.1A. The figures indicate that the volume of negative-yielding bond issues has surged from about USD 23 billion in 2014 to just over USD 1 trillion in 2016, as the total number of such issues, including re-openings, has exceeded 200. It is important to highlight that this study excludes Treasury-Bills - although the amount and number of negative yielding issues of Treasury-Bills exceeds those of bonds - considering that the purpose of short-term debt issuance varies from country to country (e.g. liquidity management and debt management).

Figure 2.4. **Negative-yielding sovereign bond issues by selected OECD governments, 2014-2016**

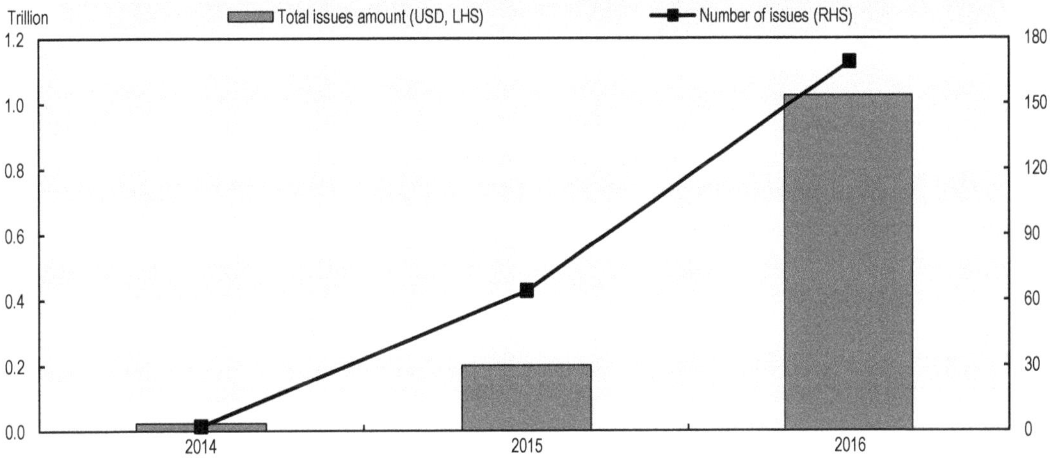

Source: Thomson Reuters, national authorities' websites and author calculations.

StatLink http://dx.doi.org/10.1787/888933474757

In 2014, when the ECB set its first negative deposit rates, only two OECD sovereigns issued negative yielding bonds. The number of countries quickly surged in the following years, as the Bank of Japan and several smaller European authorities adopted a negative interest rate policy (Figure 2.5). Of the 14 selected countries, Japan, Germany and France account for more than 90% of the total negative yielding bonds.

Figure 2.5. **Country compositions of outstanding negative-yielding sovereign bond issues, 2014-2016**

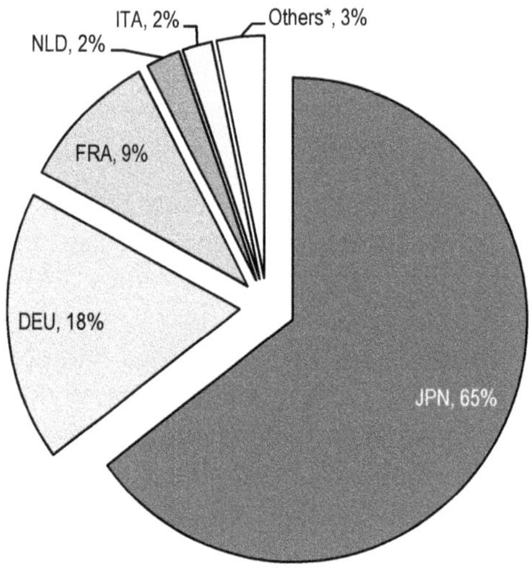

Note: "Others" category includes Austria, Belgium, Czech Republic, Denmark, Finland, Poland, Spain, Sweden, and Switzerland.

Source: Thomson Reuters, national authorities' websites and author calculations.

StatLink http://dx.doi.org/10.1787/888933474762

Governments who issue negative-yielding bonds have received premiums – instead of paying interest costs – for issuing government debt. Calculations reveal that total premiums received reached almost USD 9 billion via a total of USD 1.25 trillion negative yielding sovereign bond issues in 14 selected countries between 2014 and 2016 (Figure 2.6), split unequally between different countries. It is important to note that the maturity of negative-yielding issues can go out to 10 years, as is the case in Japan, Germany and Switzerland.

Figure 2.6. **Premiums received via negative-yielding sovereign bond issues, 2014-2016**

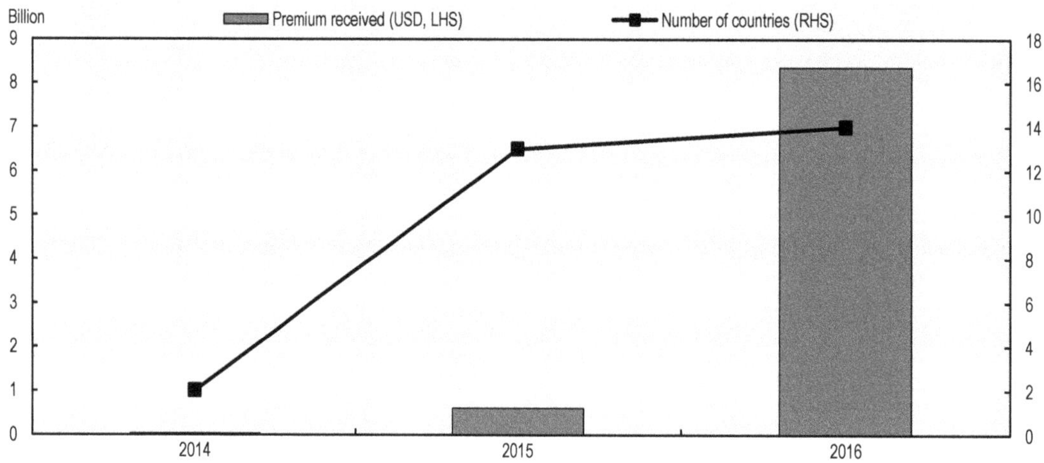

Source: Thomson Reuters, national authorities' websites and author calculations.

StatLink http://dx.doi.org/10.1787/888933474778

2.5. Liquidity concerns and measures taken by sovereign debt managers

Market liquidity of sovereign bonds is an important element for debt managers, as investors pay lower prices and demand higher returns from less liquid securities than from otherwise similar more liquid securities. This liquidity premium contributes to borrowing costs at issuance of each security. Therefore, sovereign debt managers often monitor market liquidity indicators diligently and try to enhance it.

Against this backdrop, a survey of debt managers undertaken since 2013, from the OECD Working Party on Debt Management (WPDM) group on secondary market liquidity, reveals important policy information. Country responses to the 2016 edition of the OECD Liquidity Survey are provided in Appendix B. In parallel to previous editions of the survey, more than half of the respondents (including the United Kingdom, Switzerland, Germany, Italy and Spain) to the current survey have observed deterioration in liquidity conditions in their local currency debt market – in terms of bid-ask spread, trading volumes, etc. – in recent years (Figure 2.7)

Figure 2.7. **Observations of changes in liquidity conditions of domestic sovereign bonds in recent years**

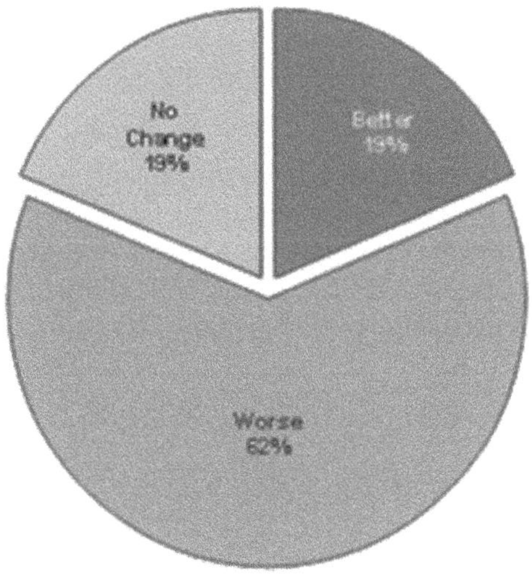

Source: OECD Survey on Liquidity in secondary government bond markets (2016).

StatLink http://dx.doi.org/10.1787/888933474786

One of the jurisdictions where secondary market liquidity has not been a concern is the United States Treasury market. A recent study which considers measures, including daily trading volumes, bid/ask spreads, trade size, price impact and market depth, shows that "current liquidity conditions are broadly similar to levels that have prevailed since 2010 (Clark et al., 2016). The policy note also presents a historical analysis of "G-Spread" which helps to compare liquidity of on-the-run and off-the-run issues. The results show that G-spreads for 10-year Treasuries are also in line with historical trends.

Survey results revealed enhanced liquidity conditions in a few countries (Figure 2.7). In this regard, a notable comment is provided by the Ireland National Treasury Management Agency (NTMA) concerning a considerable improvement in market liquidity of the Irish sovereign bond since exiting the EU/IMF Programme of financial assistance at end-2013 returning to regular scheduled market issuance. It was noted that, as investor sentiment improved along with Credit Rating Agency ratings upgrades[1] and ECB bond purchasing activity, regular market access has increased turnover ratios, and allowed dealers to improve bid-offer spreads. During this period, the NTMA has undertaken measures to assist with liquidity by providing repos and switches for Primary Dealers when required.

Debt managers highlighted several factors affecting liquidity conditions among which regulatory changes, central banks purchasing programmes and low interest rates are the most frequently mentioned (Table 2.1). Moreover, in countries where funding needs are decreasing, (including Sweden, the Netherlands, Iceland and Canada), reduced government borrowing has also played a role in deteriorated liquidity (Appendix B).

Fourteen respondent countries stated that declining involvement of banks as "market-makers" due to regulatory reforms is an important factor affecting liquidity. The regulatory reforms (Basel III, Solvency II, CACs, MiFID II, Dodd-Frank Act, etc.) implemented since the financial crisis, require more capital and impose restrictions on banks leverage. Although it is fairly difficult to quantify the full impact of new regulations on market liquidity empirically, several debt managers observed that these balance sheet constraints increase banks' cost of warehouse stock and diminish their allowable holding periods of bonds. Australia, Denmark, Germany, Italy and the United Kingdom experienced an overall reduction in the amount of principal-based market making activities.

Beside the new regulations, debt managers also underlined the impact of central bank policies, in particular bond purchasing programmes, and the low interest rate environment in secondary market liquidity. As discussed in section 2.3, central banks - characterised as buy-and-hold type of investors - in Japan, the United States and the Euro area have become major investors in local government debt securities due to quantitative easing programmes. Several DMOs highlighted that increased holdings of domestic and foreign central banks have had an impact on liquidity, as they have reduced the total stock of debt securities available to purchase in the market. In some cases, this has been exacerbated by strong demand from foreign central banks, as in the case of Canada and Switzerland.

Table 2.1 **DMOs views on the main reasons affecting liquidity**

	Number of answers[1]					
	New regulations[2]	Central bank policies	Low interest rate environment	Investor base	Credit ratings	Market infrastructure developments
What are the main reasons affecting domestic liquidity conditions?	14	13	9	7	6	3

Notes:

1. 23 countries' responses. A country might give more than one reason.
2. Regulatory changes in the financial system including Basel III, Solvency II, CACs, MiFID II, Dodd-Frank Act, etc.

Source: OECD Survey on Liquidity in secondary government bond markets (2016).

It is important to note that advances in technology have had an impact on market structures in recent years by changing registration, clearing, settlement, payments, reporting and monitoring operations in financial markets. As electronic trading enables quicker, safer and cheaper financial transactions, the share of electronic trading has increased (BIS, 2016). Given its growing importance, the benefits and risks associated with electronic trading were discussed during the last annual meeting of the OECD Working Party on Public Debt Management (WPDM) held on 7-8 November 2016. Debt managers acknowledged that the fixed-income market landscape is changing as electronic platforms (e.g. Direct Streams, BrokerFee Direct, and Liquidity Direct) are emerging to provide a continuous two-way market, via the web or special software and bypassing the retail broker. They enable investors to make ultra-fast executions at lower cost. Debt managers also indicated that electronic trading, in particular automated and high-frequency trading, may become a source of volatility. One example is the flash-crash in the United States Treasury market in October 2014, where the role of computer-driven trading on historical intraday changes in 10-year bond yields has been confirmed (US Treasury joint staff report, 2015). BIS (2016) also highlights that electronic trading, beside its benefits, poses a number of challenges to policymakers, including the need to monitor its effect on market liquidity and functioning and to ensure appropriate governance of automated trading.

From a debt managers' perspective, liquidity in financial markets is important for the cost and stability of funding. Illiquid sovereign bonds are more sensitive to market risks than more liquid sovereign bonds. Therefore, reduced liquidity impairs - to some extent - the price discovery process, increases the cost of borrowing via higher risk premia[2] and limits issuers' abilities to tap a variety of investors. In response to recent low liquidity concerns, debt managers in several countries have followed various policy measures as summarized below:

- *Building key benchmark bonds:* It is a common strategy among DMOs to aim at regular issuance across the maturity spectrum throughout the financial year and build up benchmarks at key maturities, in particular 3-, 5-, 10-, and 30-year maturity segments. In countries where funding needs are small or decreasing (including Sweden, Netherlands, Canada), debt managers find it useful to raise decreased funding requirements through key benchmark bonds to achieve a benchmark premium. Table 2.2 shows the survey responses on the number of domestic currency bond lines by country.
- *Tap sales and re-opens*: Both large and small issuers including Germany, Japan, Austria, Latvia, and Slovenia use tap sales and re-opens to support existing lines of key benchmark bonds.
- *More frequent and smaller auctions:* Some DMOs, including those of the United Kingdom and Sweden, have adopted more frequent and smaller sized auctions to enhance market liquidity of government bonds.
- *Separate Trading of Registered Interest and Principal of Securities (STRIP) Programmes:* STRIPs provide for the separation of the interest and principal payments on a bond into single-payment, or "zero-coupon" obligations. The United States Treasury STRIP programmes, both for fixed and inflation-linked securities, introduced in early 1985, have been very successful in enhancing market liquidity. Other countries that have adopted STRIP programmes are Germany, Mexico, Korea and Israel.

- *Buy-backs and switch operations:* The most recently issued (on-the-run) bonds are more liquid than older bonds. Through buy-back and switch operations, DMOs aim to increase the size of on-the-run bonds at the expense of off-the-run bonds. It is a common exercise among OECD countries through which bonds with certain remaining life to maturity (e.g. less than 12 months) are repurchased from investors continuously (e.g. Belgium, Denmark, Turkey) or discretionary (e.g. Austria, France, Canada, Italy, Spain).
- *Repurchase agreements (Repos) and reverse repos:* Repurchase agreements (repos) enable financial market participants to borrow while reverse repos enable participants to lend securities from/to DMOs. Some DMOs, including those of the Netherlands, Sweden, Finland and Canada, act as a lender of last resort and offer repo facility to reduce the risk of shortages, and in turn enhance the liquidity in government debt markets. This facility is generally available for primary dealers regardless of a government's borrowing limits.
- *Changes to the primary dealership (PD) system:* A few DMOs have imposed new requirements on market-makers in their provision of liquidity in recent years. For example, the Turkish Treasury changed PD obligations by decreasing the maximum spread between bid and offer rates of benchmark securities. The United Kingdom DMO has encouraged primary dealers to participate more fully in the price formation process by setting an expectation of a minimum bid of 5% of each auction averaged over a rolling 6-month period. The Finnish DMO has introduced a maturity weighting in ranking the primary dealers' secondary market trades.

Table 2.2 **Structure of domestic currency bond lines by country**

	Number of domestic currency bond lines	More than USD 5 billion on issue?	More than USD 10 billion on issue?
Australia	22 domestic currency bond lines	20	14
Austria	23 domestic currency bond lines	21	11
Belgium	29 domestic currency bond lines	25	19
Canada	50 bond lines are outstanding, covering the 2, 3, 5, 10, 30, and 50-year sectors.	43	16
Chile	37, but a liability management program was implemented, in order to strengthen 8 lines, selected as benchmark bonds (4 in inflation-linked and 4 in nominal curve, with maturities in approx. 5, 10, 20 and 30 years). Through this program, these 8 bonds were issued, accepting other existing bonds as payment (cash was not acceptable). Due to this, these 8 benchmark bonds have greater stocks in comparison with the others.	4	0
Czech Republic	25 (excl. 16 lines of savings bonds)	0	0
Denmark	11 (plus 2 T-bills lines)	9	4
Finland	16 domestic currency bond lines	13	0
France	68 lines (nominal + inflation-linked).	64	58

Table 2.2. **Structure of domestic currency bond lines by country** (cont.)

	Number of domestic currency bond lines	More than USD 5 billion on issue?	More than USD 10 billio n on issue?
Germany	Number of domestic currency bond lines" was 65, including 59 nominal bonds (Bunds, Bobls, Schaetze) and 6 inflation-linked securities.	63	60
Greece	57 domestic currency bond lines	0	0
Hungary	25 (wholesale only)	0	0
Iceland	There are 7 market making series and 5 non-market making, total of 12.	0	0
Ireland	13 fixed-rate, 10 amortising and 7 floating rate	15	3
Israel	31 domestic currency bond lines	1	0
Italy	121 lines: 18 lines of bills, 69 lines of bonds, 11 lines of floaters, 12 lines of linkers, 4 lines of zero coupon bonds, 7 lines of linkers tailored to retail investors.	119	91
Japan	Number of domestic currency bond issues: 502	340	262
Korea	There are 47 bond lines. Among them, 41 of them are fixed bonds, and 6 of them are inflation-indexed bonds.	37	24
Latvia	There are 13 domestic and 6 international with an International Securities Identification Number (ISIN) outstanding in EUR.	0	0
Luxembourg	6 domestic currency bond lines	0	0
Mexico	19 lines in the Bonos M market (Fixed Rate Bonds) and 8 lines in the Udibonos market (Inflation-Linked Bonds).	23	5
Netherlands	26 domestic currency bond lines	24	21
New Zealand	11 domestic currency bond lines	4	0
Norway	7 domestic currency bond lines	5	0
Poland	31 domestic currency bond lines.	15	0
Portugal	21 domestic currency bonds. However, if we take only into consideration the PGB curve, we have 14 bonds.	11	5
Slovak Republic	20 domestic currency bond lines	0	0
Slovenia	There are 21 domestic currency government bonds.	0	0
Spain	There are 47 lines of coupon bonds plus 12 lines of zero-coupon bills. 47 lines of coupon bonds include 4 lines linked to Euro Area Harmonised Index Consumer Price HICP (excl. Tobacco). This excludes assumed debt originally launched by a different public issuer.	42	36
Switzerland	We have 23 outstanding bond lines.	4	0
Turkey	There are 53 different bonds in domestic debt stock.	15	10
United Kingdom	41 nominal lines, 28 inflation-linked.	67	66
United States	U.S. Treasury has 386 existing domestic currency bond lines.	386	374

Notes: Estonia has no outstanding government bonds.

Source: OECD Survey on Liquidity in secondary government bond markets (2016).

2.6 Long-duration government bonds carry duration risk

From an investor perspective, the strategy of investing in long-term and ultra-long-term bonds has been successful in the sense that long-term bonds, as an asset class, have been profitable in many markets over the past few years. That said, such a strategy obviously also carries risks, especially if central banks were to raise rates faster than expected by market participants. As a rule of thumb, a one percentage-point change in interest rates implies a change in the bond's price equal to its duration. Looking at the currently outstanding bonds issued by OECD governments, duration is high by historical standards. For example, Figure 2.8 illustrates that, based on a large sample of outstanding G7 government debt securities (around USD 30 trillion), a 1% increase in interest rates would imply an approximate loss potential equivalent to about USD 1.9 trillion. This illustration abstracts from any potential hedging through derivatives or otherwise.

Figure 2.8. **Potential mark-to-market losses on outstanding G7 government bonds for a 1% yield increase**

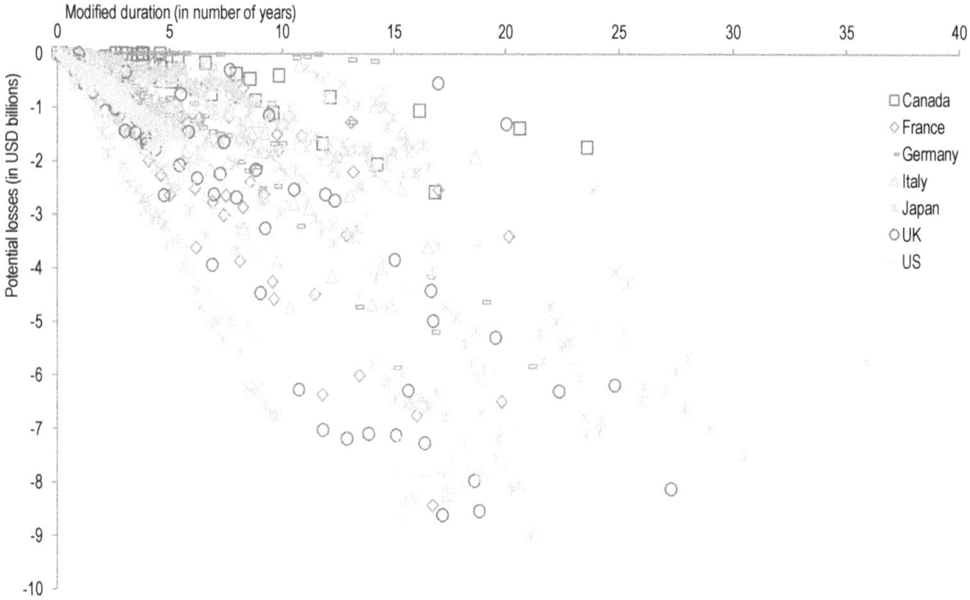

Note: Approximate losses on government bonds issued by G7 governments in G7 markets for an assumed market interest rate increase by 1% (vertical axis, in USD billion), based on bond-specific estimates of modified duration (horizontal axis, in years) multiplied by the market value of the amount of bond outstanding. Not considering exchange rate changes. Considering only bonds with a reported market price strictly greater than zero, the sample is equal to 1 084 bonds, representing an outstanding amount of USD 28.1 trillion. Total accumulated losses for a 1% yield increase on that sample is equal to USD 1.9 trillion. Excludes short-term securities, data as of December 2016.

Source: Thomson Reuters, and author calculations.

StatLink http://dx.doi.org/10.1787/888933474791

While the interest rate outlook does not suggest a rapid increase in rates across the OECD area, the interest rate outlook differs from country to country, and it is a relevant question to ask who might be exposed to duration risk. The capacity of different types of investors to manage duration risk differs, depending in particular on the nature and duration of their own liabilities. In this context, Domanski et. al. (2015) drew attention to the possibility that financial intermediaries that accumulate savings to finance retirement incomes might have contributed to the downward pressure of interest rates, in the process of attempting to better match the duration of their assets and liabilities by increasing the duration of their assets.

Exposure of pension funds and life insurance companies to domestic government debt differs from country to country. In the United States, exposure of private pension funds and insurance companies to US Treasury debt securities currently stands at 3% and 6%, respectively, of the total outstanding US Treasuries. While the measured exposure has not changed much over recent years, it has been lower as compared to the 1990s. Exposure by pension funds, including public ones, to domestic government debt is very high in Japan. For example, the large Government Pension Investment Fund reportedly had nearly 60% of its portfolio invested in Japanese government debt during 2014 before it reduced the exposure to 35% more recently.[3] In Europe, some analysts have distinguished between "vulnerable" (Italy, Spain, Portugal, Ireland, Greece and Cyprus) and "non-vulnerable" countries (other Eurosystem countries). For example, Koijen et. al. (2016) finds that the "home bias" varies mostly geographically and less by type of investor and they find pension funds and insurance companies in "vulnerable" countries to be relatively more exposed to their domestic sovereign debt than similar investors in "non-vulnerable" countries. They conclude that a potential negative feedback loop (which received much supervisory attention in the case of banks) might also exist in the case of pension funds and insurance companies.

Notes

1. Ireland was the first country in the Eurozone to officially enter a recession related to the financial crisis of 2008. The country's credit rating was first downgraded to "AA-" by Standard & Poor's in August 2010, followed by several subsequent downgrades until 2013 (BBB from S&P and Ba1 from Moody's) due to the cost of recapitalising the banks and weakening of the fiscal flexibility over the medium-term. Ireland exited an EU/ECB/IMF bailout programme and the Irish economy began to recover in the second half of 2013. In turn, its credit rating has picked up quickly and reached A+ of S&P and A3 of Moody's as of December 2016.
2. A liquidity premium emerges due to the lower level of liquidity in some bonds or maturities, which restricts investors' ability to buy and sell easily at its fair market value. In general, in addition to liquidity premium, a risk premium may have several components, including: (i) a premium which compensates investors for duration risk that increases for longer maturity investments; (ii) a credit and default risk premium; and (iii) an inflation risk premium to compensate investors in nominal bonds for uncertainty due to inflation.
3. See www.gpif.go.jp/en/fund/pdf/annual_report_fiscal_year_2015.pdf.

References

Andrade, OP., J. Breckenfelder, F. De Fiore, P. Karadi, O. Tristani (2016), "The ECB's asset purchase programme: an early assessment"; European Central Bank – Eurosystem Working Paper Series No. 1956, September; https://www.ecb.europa.eu/pub/pdf/scpwps/ecbwp1956.en.pdf

Christensen, Jens H.E., and James M. Gillan (2016). "Does Quantitative Easing Affect Market Liquidity?" Federal Reserve Bank of San Francisco Working Paper 2013-26; www.frbsf.org/economic-research/publications/working-papers/wp2013-26.pdf.

Clark J. and Gabriel Mann (2016), "A Deeper Look at Liquidity Conditions in the Treasury Market "May 2016, US Treasury Notes; https://www.treasury.gov/connect/blog/Pages/A-Deeper-Look-at-Liquidity-Conditions-in-the-Treasury-Market.aspx.

Domanski, D., H.S. Shin, and V. Sushko (2015), "The hunt for duration: not waving but drowning?", BIS Working Paper No. 519, October; www.bis.org/publ/work519.pdf

European Systemic Risk Board (2016), "Market liquidity and market-making", October 2016; https://www.esrb.europa.eu/pub/pdf/reports/20161005_market_liquidity_market_making.en.pdf.

Iwatsubo, K. and T. Taishi (2016), "Quantitative easing and liquidity in the Japanese government bond market", Kobe University Graduate School of Economics Discussion Paper No.1623, September.

Koijen, R.S.J., F. Koulischer, B. Nguyen, and M. Yogo (2016), "Quantitative easing in the euro area: The dynamics of risk exposures and the impact on asset prices", Banque de France Document de Travail No. 601, September.

Markets Committee (2016), "Electronic Trading in Fixed Income Markets" Markets Committee Publications No 7, Bank of International Settlement, Basel; www.bis.org/publ/mktc07.htm.

US Department of Treasury joint staff report (2015), "The U.S. Treasury market on October 15, 2014", U.S. Department of the Treasury, Board of Governors of the Federal Reserve System, Federal Reserve Bank of New York, U.S. Securities and Exchange Commission and U.S. Commodity Futures Trading Commission July 13 2015, Washington DC; https://www.treasury.gov/press-center/press-releases/Documents/Joint_Staff_Report_Treasury_10-15-2015.pdf.

ANNEX 2.A1

Methods and sources

Calculations, definitions and data sources

- For the negative yields analysis in section 2.4, we used simple search criteria within Thomson Reuters data to first identify those countries which had issued negative yielding securities between 2014 and 2016. This simplified selection criteria was as follows:
  - Country within the OECD
  - All securities classified as issued by Government; active or inactive
  - Securities issued between 1 January 2014 and end of November 2016
  - Excluded STRIPS
  - Simplified negative yielding definition - securities with zero coupons and issue prices strictly above 100.
- These search criteria produced a list of 15 countries for which we then collected auction results directly from the sovereign's websites for a more detailed analysis. The countries identified in the initial search were: Austria, Belgium, Czech Republic, Denmark, Finland, France, Germany, Italy, Japan, Netherlands, Poland, Portugal, Spain, Sweden and Switzerland.
- For a more detailed analysis we chose to look at all sovereign auction results from 2014 to 2016 with coupon values which still resulted in negative yields. In order to be sure that no securities issued for cash management purposes were included, we focussed only on long-term instruments. Focussing only on long-term securities resulted in Portugal issuances being excluded from the analysis.
- To estimate the monetary value in this analysis, we used flexible currency rates from the OECD Economic Outlook No. 100 to convert all currencies into US dollars.

Chapter 3

The outlook for inflation-linked bonds

This chapter provides an overview of inflation-linked sovereign debt which has grown significantly in OECD countries since the early 1980s, with currently USD 3 trillion bonds outstanding. First, it examines the historical trend of sovereign issuance of inflation-linked debt, along with strategic perspectives from investors and policymakers. It then discusses potential implications of changes in market conditions for inflation-linkers, including liquidity premium and potential impacts of relatively lower current break-even inflation rates in several jurisdictions. The principal conclusion of this study is that there is, and will continue to be, an important place for linkers in debt portfolios, as these securities offer advantages for issuers and investors even in a low-yield and low-inflation environment. However, there may be opportunities to innovate at the instrument level to enhance the desirability and liquidity of linkers from the perspective of investors.

The statistical data for Israel are supplied by and under the responsibility of the relevant Israeli authorities. The use of such data by the OECD is without prejudice to the status of the Golan Heights, East Jerusalem and Israeli settlements in the West Bank under the terms of international law.

3.1 Introduction

Inflation-linked ("index-linked" or "linkers')[1] debt, which offers a number of benefits for issuers and investors, is an important part of sovereign debt management strategies in several countries. The increase in global supply and number of issuers during the past decade has resulted in inflation-linked bonds becoming a global asset class. This chapter* examines the historical trend in inflation-linked bond issuance and current policy discussions including liquidity premium and potential impact of a low interest rate environment on supply and demand for these securities.

Key findings

- The OECD Working Party on Debt Management survey of central government marketable debt and borrowing reveals that the outstanding volume of inflation-linked debt in OECD area more than doubled between 2007 and 2015, and is expected to exceed USD 3 trillion in 2017.
- While the long-term trend has mainly been determined by the group of G7 countries in parallel to the change in funding strategies and borrowing needs in these countries, regional aggregates also indicate an increasing popularity of linkers in Emerging Markets (EMs) where near-term inflationary pressures are arguably more of a concern.
- Inflation-linked bonds offer a win-win situation both for investors and sovereign issuers as they offer a number of benefits including portfolio diversification and protection against inflation, as well as important information concerning inflation expectations.
- There are also complications concerning the inflation-linked bonds including measurement of cost-effectiveness, a relatively high liquidity premium compared to conventional bonds and lower break-even inflation rates in several jurisdictions.
- Looking ahead, while the structure of financial markets continues to evolve and bring new challenges along with new opportunities, sovereign issuers remain committed to maintaining a well-functioning market for inflation linkers by use of flexibility in market operations and by communicating with investors and other stakeholders.

3.2 Historical trends in inflation-linked sovereign bonds

Inflation-linked sovereign bonds have a distinctive feature: they offer a nearly perfect hedge for investors against inflation. The history of inflation-linked issues goes back to the 18th century in the US when the Massachusetts state government discovered a significant financial innovation to manage severe wartime inflation: The so-called "depreciation notes" were issued to soldiers as delayed compensation for their services

* This chapter was prepared by Fatos Koc and Sebastian Schich, Senior Policy Analyst and Principal Administrator respectively, OECD Financial Affairs Division, with research and statistical support from Gary Mills, Statistician, OECD Financial Affairs Division.

and discontinued afterwards (Shiller, 2004). Largely forgotten for many years, in recent history they were introduced by the government of Finland in 1945 and then by the government of Israel in 1955. Issuance of inflation-linked bonds became a part of the regular funding programme of a sovereign for the first time when the UK Treasury announced its marketable indexed Guilt programme in 1981 (HM Treasury Note, 1981). This was followed by other advanced economies: Australia in 1985, Canada in 1991, Sweden in 1994, the United States in 1997, France in 1998, Italy and Japan in 2003, and Germany in 2006. Today, inflation-linked sovereign bonds are an important part of sovereign borrowing strategies in 21 OECD countries.

Figure 3.1 provides an overview of index-linked issuance in the OECD area, based on data collected through a survey on central government marketable debt and borrowing by the OECD Working Party on Debt Management and includes OECD staff projections for 2017. The figure indicates the outstanding volume of index-linked debt increased by about two-and-a-half times between 2007 and 2015. Nevertheless, the volume has remained stable since 2015 and is expected to exceed USD 3 trillion in 2017. Consequently, the share of indexed debt in central government debt has risen from 5.5% to above 7% during the same period. Clearly, the trend has been mainly determined by the change in sovereign borrowing needs and funding strategies in OECD countries (See Chapter 1 of this *Sovereign Borrowing Outlook* for a more detailed discussion of developments in sovereign borrowing needs and funding structures in OECD countries).

Figure 3.1. **Index-linked debt in OECD countries, 2007-2017**

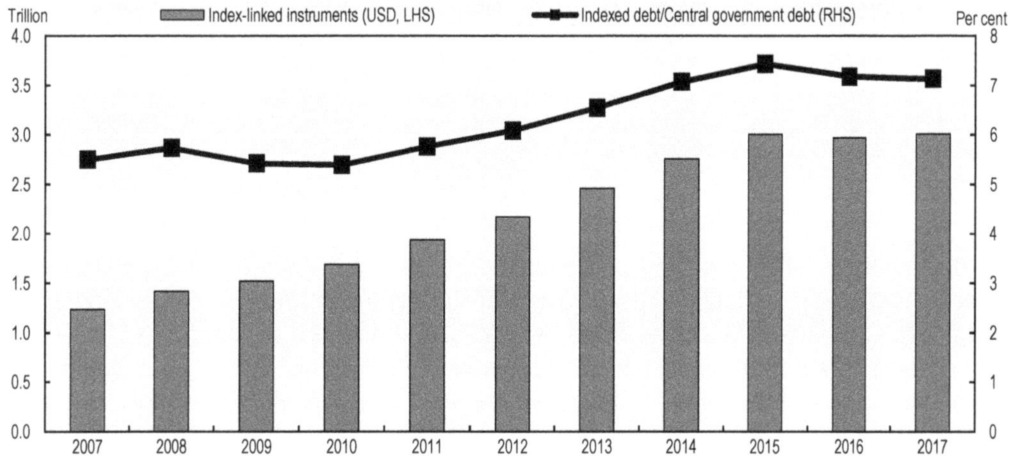

Notes: Values of marketable index-linked debt and total central government marketable debt have been aggregated by using fixed exchange rates, as of 1st December 2009, for all years.

Source: 2016 Survey on central government marketable debt and borrowing carried out by the OECD Working Party on Debt Management; OECD Economic Outlook No. 100; Thomson Reuters, national authorities' websites and author calculations.

StatLink http://dx.doi.org/10.1787/888933474800

Amongst selected OECD country groupings, the group of G7 countries dominates the aggregate inflation-linked bonds as they comprise more than 85% of the outstanding total (Figure 3.2). Specifically, the United States was the largest issuer of linkers, followed by the United Kingdom, Italy and France as of 2016 (Figure 3.3). Regional aggregates also indicate an increasing popularity of linkers in Emerging Markets (EMs). Figure 3.2 shows a significant rise of indexed-linkers from USD 28.4 billion in 2007 to USD 205 billion in EMs where near-term inflationary pressures are arguably more of a concern.

Figure 3.2. **Outstanding index-linked bonds, regional aggregates, between 2007-2017**

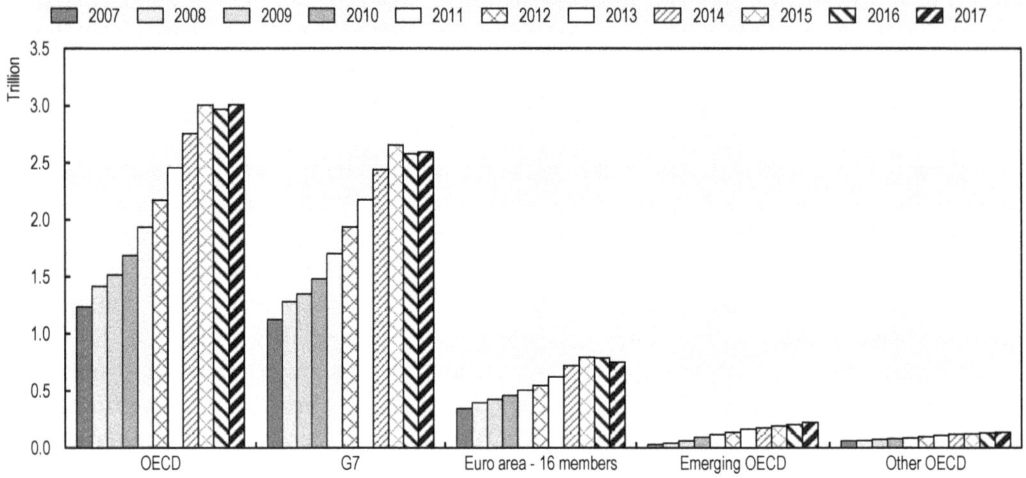

Notes: Values of marketable index-linked debt have been aggregated by using fixed exchange rates, as of 1st December 2009, for all years. "Euro area - 16 members" includes the following OECD countries: Austria, Belgium, Estonia, Finland, France, Germany, Greece, Ireland, Italy, Latvia, Luxembourg, Netherlands, Portugal, Slovak Republic, Slovenia and Spain. "Emerging OECD" include Chile, Czech Republic, Estonia, Hungary, Latvia, Mexico, Poland, Slovak Republic, Slovenia and Turkey. "Other OECD" includes Australia, Denmark, Iceland, Israel, Korea, New Zealand, Norway, Sweden and Switzerland.

Source: 2016 Survey on central government marketable debt and borrowing carried out by the OECD Working Party on Debt Management; OECD Economic Outlook No. 100; Thomson Reuters, national authorities' websites and author calculations.

StatLink http://dx.doi.org/10.1787/888933474816

In a sovereign debt portfolio, index-linked bonds are usually part of a wider set of issuance choices, including fixed-coupon bonds, floating rate notes (FRNs) and short-term paper (Treasury bills or sovereign commercial paper). Most commonly, the linkers are complementary but of secondary importance in funding strategies compared to traditional nominal long-term funding instruments. As discussed in Chapter 1 of this *Sovereign Borrowing Outlook*, in terms of interest-rate composition of funding strategies, fixed-rate instruments dominate long-term debt with an average share of 90% between 2007 and 2016 to mitigate re-fixing risk exposure. Nevertheless, the indexed-linked bonds have gained in popularity during the post-crisis period while the volume of variable-rate instruments mainly remained unchanged. Figure 3.4 suggests that during the post-crisis period, debt managers have preferred to raise a part of additional funding needs through inflation-linked bonds, concentrated at the long end of the yield curve, rather than variable-rate instruments such as FRNs. Since inflation-linked products generally have a longer duration, their higher share in the debt portfolio has positive cost-risk implications over the long term.

Figure 3.3. **Country breakdown of outstanding index-linked bonds in 2016**

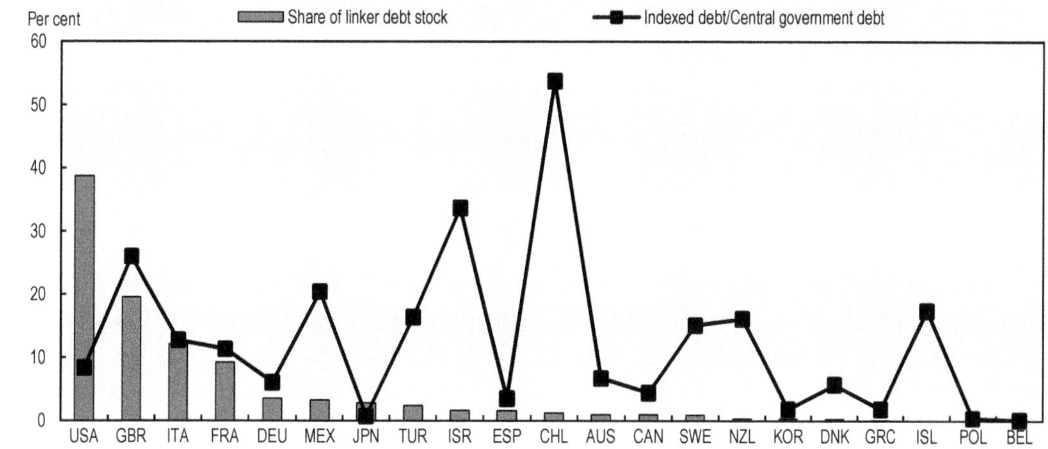

Notes: Values of marketable index-linked debt and total marketable debt have been aggregated by using fixed exchange rates, as of 1st December 2009.

Source: 2016 Survey on central government marketable debt and borrowing carried out by the OECD Working Party on Debt Management; OECD Economic Outlook No. 100; Thomson Reuters, national authorities' websites and author calculations.

StatLink http://dx.doi.org/10.1787/888933474821

Figure 3.4. **Long-term trends of index-linked debt vs variable debt**

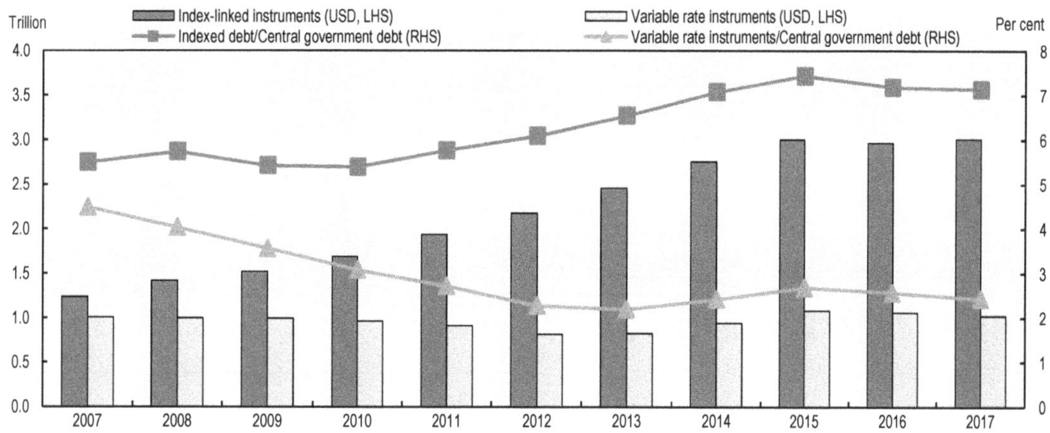

Notes: Values of marketable index-linked instruments and variable rate instruments have been aggregated by using fixed exchange rates, as of 1st December 2009, for all years.

Source: 2016 Survey on central government marketable debt and borrowing carried out by the OECD Working Party on Debt Management; OECD Economic Outlook No. 100; Thomson Reuters, national authorities' websites and author calculations.

StatLink http://dx.doi.org/10.1787/888933474837

Historical trends show that the share of linkers in government debt in OECD countries has gradually increased from 5.5% in 2007 to 7.2% in 2016 (Figure 3.4). Inflation-linked debt comprises a notable share of total marketable debt in several OECD countries, which indicates a strong commitment by sovereign debt managers to establish a liquid market for linkers. For example, in some of the large issuers such as the United Kingdom, Italy and France, the share of linkers comprises a significant portion of outstanding long-term debt, currently 27.4%, 13.5% and 12.4% respectively (Figure 3.3). Also, inflation linkers have become an important part of the funding programme in some EMs including in Chile,[2] Mexico and recently Turkey. Specifically, the share of linkers in total marketable debt in 2016 was 54% in Chile, 23% in Mexico and 16% in Turkey (Figure 3.3).

3.3 Linker-markets in EMs are progressing from their niche status

Historically, EMs tend to have significantly higher and more volatile inflation rates than developed economies. Figure 3.5 shows that the spread of Consumer Price Index (CPI) inflation rates of Brazil, Chile, Mexico, Poland, South Africa and Turkey have been persistently higher compared to the group of G7 countries over the past few decades, although the inflation risk has been significantly alleviated in these countries after the adoption of an inflation targeting regime, respectively by Brazil and Chile in 1999, South Africa in 2000, Mexico in 2001 and Turkey in 2006 (*Ebeke C. et al, 2015)*.

Figure 3.5. **Monthly CPI in selected EMs and G7 countries, between 1991 and 2016**

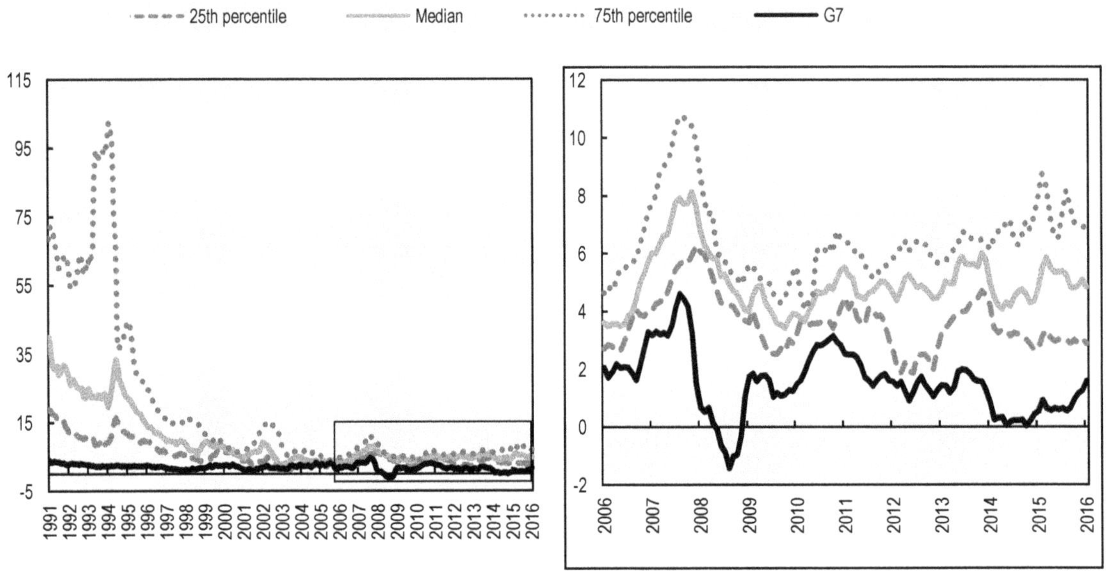

Notes: The charts show the evolution of several metrics (25th percentile, 75th percentile, median) of monthly CPI, with calculations based on 6 emerging countries: Brazil, Chile, Mexico, Poland, South Africa, and Turkey.

Source: OECD Economic Outlook No. 100.

StatLink http://dx.doi.org/10.1787/888933474841

In countries where high and volatile inflation rates prevailed for a prolonged period, local investors, particularly insurance companies and pension funds, tend to give greater priority to protecting the future real value of savings. This generates a strong appetite for inflation-linked securities. In fact, an increasing number of EMs, including Brazil, India, Mexico, South Africa, Turkey, and Uruguay have introduced inflation-linked bonds to eliminate the risk of inflation uncertainty over the total return on investment. Figure 3.6 provides the share of indexed-bonds in government funding strategies of Chile, Mexico, and Turkey from 2007 to 2017 (derived from the 2016 survey on central government marketable debt and borrowing by the OECD Working Party on Debt Management). Sovereign funding strategies in these countries clearly indicate a sustained commitment to the market. In fact, benchmark yield curves for indexed bonds have been developed in these countries to complete the market. Specifically, Chilean "UF[3]-denominated bonds" are issued at maturities of 2, 5, 10, 20, and 30 years, Mexican "Udibonos" at 3, 10, and 30 years, and Turkish linkers at 5 and 10 years.

Figure 3.6. **Share of indexed-linked bonds in central government in Chile, Mexico and Turkey, 2007-2017**

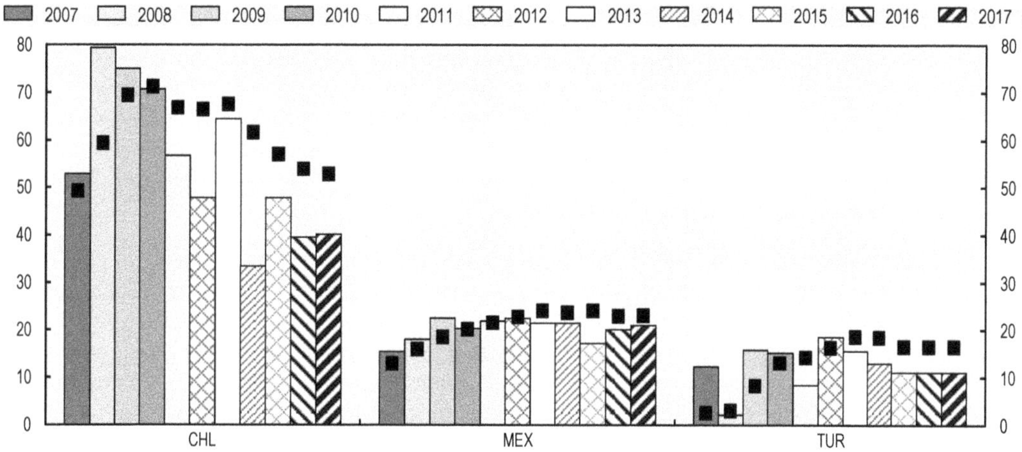

Notes: Bars represent index-linked borrowing as a percentage of total long-term borrowing. Squares represent index-linked debt as a percentage of outstanding long-term debt.

Source: 2016 Survey of central government marketable debt and borrowing carried out by the OECD Working Party on Debt Management; OECD Economic Outlook No. 100; national authorities' websites and author calculations.

StatLink http://dx.doi.org/10.1787/888933474859

Against this backdrop, government securities markets for indexed debt in several EMs such as Brazil, Chile, Mexico, South Africa, and Turkey have evolved into a dynamic and significant segment of bond markets in recent years. Although the share of indexed-linked bonds varies significantly across emerging market countries, these bonds comprise a minimum of 15% of outstanding central government debt in 2016. Indexed-linked bonds are often less liquid compared to nominal bonds, as local pension funds, insurance companies and public funds dominate linkers' investors in most of these countries. Against this backdrop, linker markets in EMs are evolving from this niche status, as demand from foreign investors has gradually been gaining momentum in recent years. Indeed, creations of emerging market dedicated benchmark indices (including Barclays' Emerging Markets Government Inflation-Linked Bond index (EMGILB) and Emerging Markets Tradable Government Inflation-Linked Bond index (EMTIL); CITI's Emerging Markets Inflation-Linked Securities Index (EMILSI) and S&P Global Emerging Sovereign Inflation-Linked Bond Index have played a large role in increasing foreign flows into these securities.

Box 3.1. A brief summary of product design and issuance methods in OECD countries

- **Indexation Methods:** Both the coupons and the principal payments of inflation-indexed bonds are adjusted based on accrued inflation since issuance. In several countries (e.g. Canada, Turkey, and the United Kingdom), inflation compensation calculations are based on principal and payable at maturity and a coupon interest is calculated based on principal and accrued inflation compensation. In terms of coupon frequency, Canada, Chile, Italy, the United Kingdom and the United States pay coupons semi-annually and Sweden, France and Germany pay coupons annually.
- **Indexation Lag:** Indexation lag means the time difference between measuring the price index (inflation value announcement) and adjusting the cash flow of the bond. Several countries (e.g. Canada, the United States, France, Japan, Italy, Germany and Sweden) use a three-month indexation lag methodology. In the United Kingdom, index-linked gilts first issued prior to 2005 have an eight-month indexation lag, while all those issued from 2005 onwards use a three-month indexation lag.
- **Reference Index Choices:** Inflation-linked bonds are contractually linked to a nationally recognized inflation measure. Most OECD countries (e.g. the United States, Canada, Chile, Israel, Korea and Turkey) use a non-seasonally adjusted CPI, mostly headline figures. The United Kingdom's indexed-gilts are linked to the Retail Price Index (RPI). Euro area countries employ the European Harmonised Index of Consumer Prices (HICP) ex-tobacco. In addition, France and Italy also issue bonds indexed to their respective national CPI ex-tobacco.
- **Floor Protection:** In theory, a period of deflation could reduce the nominal value of the inflation-linked bonds below 100. Therefore, in practice several DMOs (e.g. the United States, France, Germany, Italy, Sweden, Australia and Korea) offer deflation floors at maturity to mitigate this risk. In the case of deflation, a holder of an inflation-linked bond with floor protection would still receive the full par amount at maturity. In the United Kingdom, Brazil, Canada, Chile, Mexico and Japan, design of sovereign linkers does not include a floor protection.
- **Auction method:** A recent survey of debt managers from the OECD Working Party on Debt Management (WPDM) group on auction mechanisms (Annex C) shows that ten respondent countries -namely Canada, Chile, Denmark, Iceland, Italy, Japan, Mexico, Poland, the UK and US - use single price auctions while Australia, France, Germany, Israel, New Zealand, Spain, Sweden and Turkey employ multiple-priced auctions in issuance of inflation-indexed bonds. While the majority of issuers use the auction method, non-regular and first time/line issuers prefer a syndication technique to simplify the demand and price formation process (e.g. Australia in 2009).
- Those countries using single-price auctions note that pricing of an inflation-indexed bond can be a complex exercise, and also that the secondary market for linkers –where for the most part, securities are held to maturity– is relatively illiquid and can be volatile around auction time. This situation increases the uncertainty associated with index-linked auctions and increases the risk of the "Winner's Curse" for successful bidders. The single-price auction format incentivises auction participants to bid aggressively at auctions as no penalty is incurred as a result of potentially aggressive bidding behaviour.

Source: Responses to 2016 Survey on Auction Methods carried out by the Japanese Delegation to the OECD Working Party on Debt Management and national authorities' websites.

3.4 Perspectives from investors and policymakers

While originally inflation-linked bonds were created to deal with the impact of high inflation rates on investors, today investors and policymakers have a number of other strategic rationales which favour their use. In fact, a significant portion of the inflation-linked bonds today are issued by countries characterised both by low inflation rates and price stability, including the United Kingdom and euro area countries.

Against this backdrop, sovereign debt management policymakers decide to issue linkers after carefully considering the following factors: *i)* maintaining a balanced portfolio of nominal and index-linked debt; *ii)* impact on strategic cost-risk indicators; *iii)* strong and sustainable demand; *iv)* investor base diversification; *v)* improving the credibility of anti-inflationary policies; and *vi)* smoothing budget volatility.

Sovereign funding strategies entail decisions on how borrowing needs are going to be financed using different instruments (e.g. fixed-coupon bonds, FRNs, indexed and Treasury-bills etc.). Of the funding instruments, fixed-coupon bonds typically account for the largest part of sovereigns' issuance programmes. In this regard, sovereign debt managers consider inflation-linked bonds as instruments to diversify the interest-rate structure of a debt portfolio, and in turn, to obtain a balanced portfolio composition.

Specifically, the decision on sovereign funding strategies is usually made based on medium-long-term cost and risk parameters of different strategies. In this regard, inflation-linked bonds are used to optimize the cost-risk structure of debt portfolios. Issuance of inflation-linked bonds by a government can allow it to reduce its cost of financing. In particular, if investors are willing to pay a premium for protection against inflation, then this premium will be reflected in a lower yield paid by the government on debt instruments that provide such protection. Sovereign issuers have put forward this argument to justify their decisions to issue inflation-linked bonds and, in several instances, issuance of inflation-linked bonds effectively appears to have generated ex-post savings in the real cost of financing by these governments. In terms of risk structures of potential borrowing strategies, inflation-linked securities generate a similar cost pattern to short-term nominal bonds and FRNs with a lower refinancing risk due to their longer average maturity, and therefore are assessed as good alternatives to these instrument choices.

One challenging question of increasing importance to sovereign debt managers is how to assess the cost effectiveness of inflation/index-linked bonds relative to other financing options. The 2014 edition of *Sovereign Borrowing Outlook* provides a robust methodology for conducting such an analysis by using break-even inflation rates and the rationale behind it. The study suggests that if the break-even inflation rate on an index-linked bond is higher than the actual inflation rate over the life of the bond, then issuance of an inflation-linked bond will have been more cost effective than a fixed-coupon bond with same maturity. That said, cost savings are path dependant and will change as implied inflation changes. Therefore, an accurate cost assessment can only be made for matured indexed bonds.

A decision on the issuance of a new instrument requires careful consideration concerning the depth and sustainability of investor demand and the potential on market liquidity of existing bonds (market fragmentation risk). Indexed bonds are of particular interest to pension funds[4] and insurance companies, whose future obligations are linked to nominal developments because of the price or wage indexation of pension benefits. Investing in inflation-linked bonds offers them the opportunity to match liabilities with nominal claims, thus reducing mismatches in the growth of assets and liabilities due to inflation. Obviously, inflation-linked bonds provide a hedge against the risk of inflation. There are other means for investors to hedge themselves against unanticipated fluctuations in prices, such as investing in foreign currency debt or real assets (e.g. real estate), but there is a growing consensus in the literature that domestic inflation-linked sovereign bonds provide the most effective and stable hedge, if viewed over long periods of time.

As regards issuance, one observation is that despite the recently observed reduction of break-even inflation rates, issuance of inflation-linked bonds did not falter as a consequence of the demand from pension funds and insurance companies which remained strong even in the current low inflation environment. The 2016 edition of the *OECD Pensions Outlook* examines the potential impact of prolonged low interest rates and falling inflation rates and points out that this situation poses serious challenges to insurance and pension systems and, in particular, to defined benefit pension funds and life insurance companies offering long-term financial promises. Furthermore, it finds that the adverse effect of low interest rates is larger where the liabilities of these institutions consist of a fixed investment return which, in turn, implies a growing need for high quality long-dated indexed debt from pension systems.

The diversification argument is one of the key factors why sovereign debt issuers retain strong long-term commitment to linker markets, even in the face of increased market volatility and much lower break-even inflation rates. For sovereign debt managers, supporting the growth and development of the linker market is entirely consistent with a broader investor diversification strategy. That said, attracting a broad investor base with as many different categories of domestic and foreign investors as possible (e.g. reserve managers, pension funds, insurance managers and hedge funds) to government security markets, is at the core of building resilience into the long-term funding base and managing funding risk. Linkers have an important role to play in this regard. They typically attract a different class of investor to nominal securities and are part of the suite of products that issuers can offer to support more productive engagement in investor relation activities.

In addition to portfolio-based cost-risk considerations and diversification reasons, somewhat wider economic policy rationales exist to support the issuance of inflation-linked debt. First is the deficit smoothing approach: Inflation-linked bonds help mitigate the budgetary impact of negative demand side shocks by enabling interest payments to move suitably and help minimize budget disturbances. This would support a stable public debt to gross domestic product (GDP) ratio (Missale A., 1997). Another reason is mainly related to their information content on future inflation via break-even inflation rates and enhancing the credibility of central banks in controlling inflation. This is particularly the case during high inflation periods.[5]

From an investor perspective, inflation-linked sovereign bonds provide multiple benefits: First of all, as the origins of the linkers suggest, these bonds offer a security that would enable them to hedge portfolios against inflation. Inflation protection is particularly relevant for insurance companies and pension funds whose liabilities are linked to changes in inflation and wages (e.g. defined benefit pension plans); hence, linkers are an ideal asset class for this group of investors. Also, for a wider investor group, these securities bring along diversification advantages in portfolio management together with conventional bonds, the real value of which falls when actual inflation exceeds the "expected rate" of inflation. Secondly, of relevance for broader financial market participants, the prices of inflation-linked bonds give important insight into how investors view the outlook for future inflation.

Box 3.2. **Considerations regarding GDP-indexed bonds**

- The costs and risks of debt management are the guiding posts for the funding strategy of debt management offices. While formal mandates can also include references to macroeconomic objectives, including the need to ensure broad consistency with macroeconomic policy objectives, such mandates typically have a clear microeconomic focus. That said, funding strategies do not operate in a vacuum and they take into account the broader set of current policy challenges. In this context, debt management offices are considering proposals for issuing new types of index-linked bonds. For example, given currently high sovereign debt levels, low interest rates and weak real activity growth outlooks, the idea of governments issuing financial instruments whose repayments are indexed to domestic GDP has received renewed attention.
- Issuing debt instruments whose payments are indexed to economic variables such as GDP, consumption or inflation is not a new idea but historical examples have been rare. A widely quoted early example of a type of inflation-indexed bond is a "depreciation note", indexed to a basket of goods including corn, beef, wool and leather, by the State of Massachusetts in 1780. Following the 1980's debt crises, there was growing interest in the idea of sovereigns issuing bonds whose service or repayments would be linked to measures of the debtors' payment capacity, exports or commodity prices. Many academic proposals were made, although the role of moral hazard on the part of the debtor was recognised as a potential major impediment. As a general rule, indices were thought preferable to the extent that they were less directly influenced by debtors' actions. One form of debt instrument with indexed payments that has met with some success, in terms of actual proliferation of instruments, is inflation-indexed bonds.
- A related type of debt, GDP-indexed debt, is not been issued by OECD governments. The main advantage of this kind of debt would be to limit the variation of the debt-to-GDP ratio, and thus limit the risk of a debt crisis. In a recession, when tax revenues are relatively low, GDP-indexed bonds would only pay a low interest rate, and thus keep government interest. The argument for the issuance of such debt is currently considered as being fairly strong: OECD public debt levels are at post-World War II highs, as illustrated in Figure 1.6 of the Sovereign Borrowing Outlook 2016, and real economic activity - that would allow a country to grow out of relatively high debt levels - is currently weak. As noted by Benford et. al. (2017), it is useful to distinguish between potential issuance during "normal times" and (periods of) debt restructurings. In normal times, GDP-linked bonds offer additional fiscal space in downturns, another way of deleveraging from high debt levels and a way of preventing solvency crises. These benefits are likely to be largest when debt levels are already high relative to GDP and there is a non-trivial probability of debt reaching an unsustainable trajectory. In debt restructurings, GDP-linked bonds can help by back-loading debt repayments to when recovery is fully underway and help governments insure themselves against subsequent negative growth shocks and having to restructure again. A key issue is uncertainty about GDP developments and the level of the premium charged to compensate for that uncertainty. One suggestion (Benford et. al., 2017) is to "tailor the instrument to buy-and-hold investors, who are less concerned with liquidity and novelty considerations that might otherwise deter asset managers who may need to liquidate positions at short notice." Some progress in preparing the grounds for the issuance of such debt securities has arguably been achieved, although more research is needed to assess the operational viability of GDP-linked bonds.

As the discussion of the inflation outlook has been an increasingly important element in macroeconomic forecasting in recent years, break-even inflation,[6] which is widely-used as a proxy for expected inflation is of great importance to researchers, central bankers and strategists. In this regard, linkers provide a market-based measure of inflation expectations, since it is possible to measure market expectations of inflation by comparing the yields of nominal securities with yields on inflation-protected securities of comparable maturities. This is critical, in the sense that inflation expectations are a major element influencing the inflation process. Nevertheless, it should be noted that, in recent literature, empirical analyses show that break-even inflation rates might change, for some reasons not directly related to changes in expected inflation, such as changes in liquidity premium, investor balance sheets and new regulations. Specifically, Andreasen *et al* (2016) indicate how much the liquidity premium embedded in the prices of these securities has varied over time, and stress that break-even inflation as a measure of inflation compensation should not automatically be equated with investors' inflation expectations. Also, the 2014 edition of *Sovereign Borrowing Outlook* confirms two key factors affecting break-even inflation rates: an illiquidity premium[7] and an inflation risk premium.[8] Obviously, the illiquidity premium on linkers stands as a major caveat concerning the measurement of inflation expectations from break-even inflation rates, as well as the cost-effectiveness of inflation-linked bonds from a sovereign debt management perspective.

3.5 Illiquidity premium on inflation-linked bonds

Liquidity represents a significant risk factor in the pricing of inflation-linked bonds in the market. Given that buyers of linkers are usually buy-and-hold type of investors such as pension funds and insurance companies, these securities are typically less liquid than conventional bonds. Therefore, investors ask a relatively higher liquidity premium on inflation-linked bonds compared to conventional bonds to compensate for poorer liquidity. This, in turn, creates an additional interest cost for issuers.

In spite of the growing market for, and increasing liquidity of, inflation-linked sovereign bonds in several OECD countries, these securities remain less liquid than conventional sovereign bonds. In an attempt to reduce illiquidity premiums on linkers, sovereign debt managers attach a particular importance to the volume of each line. Several debt management offices (DMOs) establish a certain minimum target level for inflation-linked bonds to deal with the illiquidity premium. For example, after an absence of 13 years, the New Zealand DMO resumed inflation-linked bond issuance in October 2012, and made a commitment to the market to increase the outstanding amount to up to 20% of total bond sovereign debt over time. Similarly, the Australian government sought to maintain the indexed share at 10-15% of outstanding long-term debt between 2011 and 2015, as part of the re-entry efforts. Another example is the US Treasury, which also made a public affirmation in 2002 and 2008 of its commitment to the Treasury Inflation-Protected Securities (TIPS) program (Dudley *et al*, 2009). In order to enhance TIPS liquidity, the US Treasury embarked on a series of policy changes to the TIPS program. These changes include lengthening the average maturity of the debt portfolio,[9] adding more auctions to the funding calendar and offering a specific "auction week" each month for TIPS issues as well as increasing the issue sizes of TIPS offerings. TIPS issuance has increased over the years, currently representing almost 40% of the global sovereign inflation-linked bonds and 8% of the US Treasury debt portfolio. In parallel, the illiquidity premium on TIPS after 2004 has been gradually improved compared to the early years of the programme (Gurkaynak *et al*, 2010).

Along with increased size of offerings, there are other policy options to improve linker market liquidity. For example, DMOs execute buyback auctions for off-the-run issues in exchange for on-the-run issues to support overall liquidity. Although this is a more common practice for fixed-rate bonds, it can also be applicable to inflation-linked bonds. Also, debt managers can change auction designs with smaller and more frequent auctions. Another way of supporting liquidity is broadening the investor base, for example, through global bond indices constructed by quantitative investment strategies such as Barclays, PIMCO and BlackRock. Inclusion of a country's bonds into these global benchmark bond indices could significantly increase demand for these securities by indexed portfolios, therefore likely to improve liquidity. Nevertheless, inclusion requires several rules, including minimum markets size, maturity and quality of bonds.

3.6 Potential implications of low break-even inflation rate environment

Closely related to the cost-effectiveness of linkers, the current experience of declining break-even inflation in several jurisdictions has been an issue of discussion among sovereign debt managers. In fact, during the 2016 annual meeting of the OECD Working Party on Public Debt Management (WPDM), members elaborated on the potential implications of this trend for sovereign debt dynamics based on country cases.

Break-even inflation rates on all maturity segments in major advanced economies with relatively large linker portfolios have been on a downward trend in recent years. For example, on average, 10-year break-even inflation rates in Australia, Germany, and Italy have declined by more than 80 basis points since 2010 (Figure 3.7). Regarding potential explanations, debt managers argue that declining break-even inflation can be attributed to factors such as: *i)* changing market expectations of future inflation; *ii)* changes in inflation risk premia; *iii)* poorer liquidity conditions of linkers relative to nominal bonds.

Figure 3.7. **Ten-year break-even inflation rates in selected OECD countries**

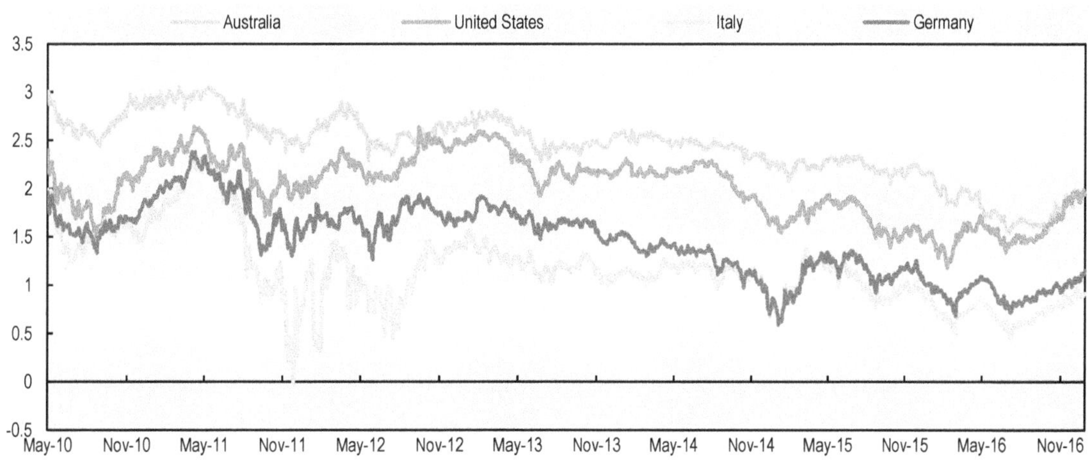

Source: Thomson Reuters and author calculations.

StatLink http://dx.doi.org/10.1787/888933474862

In terms of demand for inflation-linked bonds, debt managers noted that while investors have a range of alternative investment opportunities available to them that offer varying degrees of inflation protection, these alternatives appear unlikely to displace sovereign linkers as an asset class in the foreseeable future. In this regard, linkers are a somewhat unique asset class and are often preferred, by pension funds and insurance companies for example, precisely because of their capacity to provide stable inflation compensated returns with protection from credit risk. Indeed underlying demand for linkers is set to steadily increase as a consequence of aging population demographics and positive trends in life expectancy in most developed countries. With more people requiring low volatility and inflation protecting retirement income products (for longer), pension fund demand for linkers is likely to remain robust.

The principal conclusion from the case studies is that there is, and will continue to be, an important place for linkers in the debt portfolio. Country delegates emphasised that protection against inflation is and will continue to be a main factor of institutional investors' demand as the future level of prices remains uncertain. Also, public benefits of inflation-linked securities, such as promoting public awareness of price increases, are also taken into account – to a certain extent – by sovereign debt managers as part of their broader mission to enhance local currency debt markets.

To be as transparent as possible, debt managers receive regular investor feedback and weigh it against their portfolio management goals and design of securities which influence their desirability among investor groups. That said, closely monitoring market developments and cost effectiveness decisions on maturity segment and issue volumes with regard to issue sizes, auction dates, and tenors have been the key elements of their operational decisions. Looking ahead, as the structure of financial markets continues to evolve it brings new challenges, but at the same time it also brings new opportunities. Sovereign debt managers remain committed to maintaining a well-functioning market for inflation linkers by use of flexibility in market operations and by communicating with investors and other stakeholders on the pros and cons of potential changes of the design of the securities.

Notes

1. In this chapter, the terms "inflation-linked" and "index-linked" bonds are used synonymously. These instruments are also referred to as "linkers" in financial markets.
2. In Chile, pension funds are large and the most important investor of sovereign bonds. They held about two-thirds of government bonds as of October 2016 (Arslanalp S.et al, 2016).
3. A Unidad de Fomento (UF) is an inflation-indexed, Chilean peso-denominated monetary unit that is set daily based on the Chilean CPI of the immediately preceding 30 days, as calculated and published daily by the Central Bank of Chile.

4. This is particularly relevant for defined benefit (DB) plans where the value of accrued benefits is extremely sensitive to inflation, since pension benefits are fixed in nominal terms after retirement (Bodie Z., 1988).

5. In times of high public debt, capital markets might raise a concern that a country could lower its debt commitments by raising inflation. By issuing inflation-linked bonds as a government funding instrument, the fears of inflating away debt could be substantially alleviated, because the government, as the debtor, would not benefit from rising inflation rates due to its impact on overall borrowing costs.

6. The difference between nominal yield on a fixed-coupon bond and real yield on an index-linked bond with similar maturity is known as the breakeven inflation rate. It represents a market-based measure of inflation compensation that is widely used to assess financial market participants' inflation expectations. The Fisher identity can be used to calculate breakeven inflation rates (BEIR):

$$BIER = \left[\frac{1+\frac{y}{2}}{1+\frac{r}{2}}\right]^2 - 1$$

Where:

y = nominal yield on fixed-coupon bond (or nominal yield from yield curve)

r = real yield on index-linked bond (or real yield from yield curve)

7. Liquidity premiums arise when investors require a premium for illiquidity of a security. Index-linked bonds are typically less liquid than conventional bonds, and so investors may require a premium for this illiquidity in order to hold them – this typically causes index-linked yields to be higher relative to fixed-coupon bonds, and the corresponding break-even inflation rate to be lower (OECD, 2014)

8. Inflation premiums arise when investors attach value to protection against inflation risk; they may then be prepared to pay a premium for this protection – this will typically result in lower yields for index-linked bonds relative to fixed-coupon bonds, translating into a higher break-even inflation rate (OECD, 2014).

9. The US Treasury made a decision to discontinue the 20-year TIPS offering and reintroduce the 30-year TIPS in 2010.

References

Andreasen M.M. and J.H.E.Christensen (2016), *"TIPS Liquidity and the Outlook for Inflation" Federal Reserve Bank of San Francisco* (FRBSF), *Economic Letter*, 2016-35 November 21, 2016, San Francisco, www.frbsf.org/economic-research/files/el2016-35.pdf.

Arslanalp S. and Takahiro Tsuda (2016), "Sovereign Investor Base Dataset for Emerging Markets", the Monetary and Capital Markets Department of the International Monetary Fund, Washington D.C., www.imf.org/external/pubs/ft/wp/2014/Data/wp1439.zip.

Benford J., Thomas Best and Mark Joy, Bank of England, with contributions from Mark Kruger, Bank of Canada, and the Research Department, Central Bank of Argentina Bank of England, *Financial Stability Paper* No. 39 – September 2016, www.bankofengland.co.uk/financialstability/Documents/fpc/fspapers/fs_paper39.pdf.

Bodie Zvie (1988), "Inflation, Indexed-linked bonds, asset allocation", NBER Working Paper No. 2793, Boston USA, www.nber.org/papers/w2793.pdf.

Dudley, W.C., R. Roush and M.S. Ezer (2009), "The Case for TIPS: An examination of the costs and benefits", Reserve Bank of New York Economic Policy Review, No. 10(1), pp. 47-63, https://www.newyorkfed.org/medialibrary/media/research/epr/09v15n1/0907dudl.pdf.

Ebeke *C. and Armand Fouejieu (2015), "Inflation Targeting and Exchange Rate Regimes in Emerging Markets" WP15228, IMF,* the International Monetary Fund, Washington D.C., https://www.imf.org/external/pubs/cat/longres.aspx?sk=43370.0.

Fleming, Michael J., and Neel Krishnan, 2009, "The Microstructure of the TIPS Market", FRB of New York Staff Report, No. 414, https://www.newyorkfed.org/medialibrary/media/research/epr/12v18n1/1203flem.pdf.

Gurkaynak, Refet S., Brian Sack, and Jonathan H.Wright, 2010, "The TIPS Yield Curve and Inflation Compensation", American Economic Journal: Macroeconomics 2(1), 70.92, https://www.aeaweb.org/articles?id=10.1257/mac.2.1.70.

HM Treasury note (1981), "Indexed Gilts", Economic Progress Report, May 1981, The HM Treasury, London, www.dmo.gov.uk/documentview.aspx?docname=gilts/public/technical/epr1981.pdf&page.

Missale, *Alessandro, (1997). "Managing Public Debt: the Optimal Taxation Approach", Journal of Economic Surveys, Vol.11, No.3.*

Noyer C. (2004), "The role of inflation - indexed bonds in the process of setting monetary policy: a central banker's perspective", speech at the Morgan Stanley seminar on indexed bonds, Paris, 9 June 2004, www.bis.org/review/r040618a.pdf.

OECD (2016a), *OECD Pensions Outlook 2016*, OECD Publishing, Paris, http://dx.doi.org/10.1787/pens_outlook-2016-en.

OECD (2016b), *OECD Sovereign Borrowing Outlook 2016,* OECD Publishing, Paris; http://dx.doi.org/10.1787/sov_b_outlk-2016-en.

OECD (2014), "*OECD Sovereign Borrowing Outlook 2014",* OECD Publishing, Paris; http://dx.doi.org/10.1787/sov_b_outlk-2014-en.

Shiller R. (2003), "*The Invention of Inflation - Indexed Bonds in Early America*", NBER Working Paper No. 10183, December 2003, www.nber.org/papers/w10183.

OECD Sovereign Borrowing Outlook 2017

ANNEX A

OECD 2016 Survey on Primary Markets Developments

Overview of issuing procedures in the OECD

	Auctions		Auction type		Tap issues		Syndication
	Long-term	Short-term	Single-price	Multiple-price	Long-term	Short-term	
Australia	X	X		X			X
Austria	X			X	X	X	X
Belgium	X	X		X	X	X	X
Canada	X	X	X	X			X
Chile	X		X		X		
Czech Republic	X	X	X	X	X		X
Denmark	X	X	X		X	X	X
Finland	X		X		X		X
France	X	X		X	X	X	X
Germany	X	X		X	X		
Greece		X	X				
Hungary	X	X		X	X	X	X
Iceland	X	X	X				X
Ireland	X	X	X	Possible	X	X	X
Israel	X	X		X	X	X	
Italy	X	X	X	X	X	X	X
Japan	X	X	X	X	X		
Korea	X	X	X	X			X
Latvia	X	X	X	X	X	X	X
Luxembourg							X
Mexico	X	X	X	X	X	X	X
Netherlands	X	X	X	X	X	X	
New Zealand	X	X		X			X
Norway	X	X	X	X			
Poland	X	X	X	X			X

	Auctions		Auction type		Tap issues		Syndication
	Long-term	Short-term	Single-price	Multiple-price	Long-term	Short-term	
Portugal	T-Bonds	T-Bills	T-Bonds	T-Bills	T-Bonds*	T-Bills*	T-Bonds
Slovak Republic	X	X	X	X	X	X	X
Slovenia		X	X		X		X
Spain	X	X		X	X	X	X
Sweden	X	X		X	X	X	X
Switzerland	X	X	X		X*		
Turkey	X	X		X			
United Kingdom	X	X	X	X			X
United States	X	X	X		X	X	
Total	**31**	**30**	**22**	**25**	**23**	**16**	**24**

Country notes

Australia	Syndication is used on a selective basis. It is typically undertaken when there is a higher than normal level of risk associated with the issue of a new bond line (for example when issuing a bond line that extends the yield curve) or when there is a desire to issue a large volume of bonds in order to immediately establish a large liquid bond line.
Austria	In general, syndications are used for new issues only. Existing bonds are regularly tapped via scheduled auctions. Over the past years, Austria has successfully conducted parallel auctions (tap of two bonds at one auction).
Belgium	Auctions are done through the "Bloomberg Auction system (BAS system)" on our 2 standard products, the Treasury Certificates in the short term and the Linear Bonds in the long term. Issuance through our Commercial Paper (CP) and schuldschein programmes are done on tap. Under the Euro Medium Term Note (EMTN) programme, syndications and on tap issuance are possible
Canada	Canada issues the vast majority of its domestic debt through auction format. It auctions debt in sectors ranging from short-term treasury bills (i.e. cash management bills) to 30-year bonds. The only exception is the 50-year bond. In 2014, Canada has issued 50-year bonds through a syndication format. All nominal bond and treasury bill auctions are multiple price, whereas real return bonds (inflation-indexed bonds) are issued through a single price auction format. Canada also issues nominal bonds on a switch basis. Canada issues foreign currency global bonds through a syndicate format, Medium Term Note (MTN) /Euro Medium Term Notes (EMTNs) on a reverse inquiry basis, and operates a Commercial Paper program in USD.
Chile	From 2017, it is expected no issue just by tapping existing bonds. For this, 8 bonds has been designated as benchmark bonds, and are characterised by a greater stock in comparison to the other bonds. In the future, new benchmarks could be added in the future, through the auctions of new instruments.
Czech Republic	Syndication is used for long term foreign currency debt issuance Single-price auction for T-bills, multiple-price for bonds and Tap sales, fixed price for buy-backs.
Denmark	DKK denominated bonds are issued using single-price auctions and tap. Foreign currency denominated bonds are issued using syndication (no foreign bonds have been issued in 2015-16).
France	We use auctions for long term bonds (nominal and inflation-linked bonds) and short term bills. These are multiple price auctions, whatever the type of bond/bill issued. We regularly tap bond issues, we can also tap bill issues although it is less common than for bonds. We use syndications for long term bonds only, whatever very long term nominal bonds or long term inflation-linked bonds.

Hungary	After Bond auctions there can be a non-competitive tender, which is a single-price (average auction price) issuance. Some T-bills and bonds are sold via tap issuance or via subscriptions for retail investors. Syndication is used only for the issuance of foreign exchange debt.
Iceland	Single price format used for T-bills and T-bonds. Syndication is used for the issuance of external debt.
Italy	The Italian Treasury makes use of two kinds of auction: - a competitive (multi-price) auction on a yield basis, for T-bills; - a marginal price (single-price) auction - where the auction price and the quantity issued are determined discretionally by the Treasury within a preannounced interval - for zero-coupon, nominal fixed and floating rate, and inflation indexed bonds. The Treasury normally makes use of syndication: - in case of issuance of new types of bonds (for instance, Buoni del Tesoro Poliennali (BTP)€i in 2003 and variable coupon Treasury certificates (CCTeu) in 2010) or benchmarks in new segments of the nominal and European inflation curves (e.g.: 7-year BTP, 5-year BTP€I with a new coupon cycle, 20-year BTP); - in case of issuance of new bonds (both nominal and indexed to the European inflation) for maturities above 10 years. As for the BTP Italia (linked to the Italian inflation), the Treasury makes use of a specific method of issuance, which allows for collecting purchase orders through the retail screen-based market for government bonds, the MOT platform of Borsa Italiana. The coupon rate is to be determined at the end of the placement period based on market conditions, whereas the issue price is fixed at par. The placement period is divided into a First Phase and a Second Phase. The First Phase of the placement period is reserved to retail investors, while during the Second Phase all investors (including banks and other institutional investors) are allowed to participate.
Japan	We issue short-term (1-year discount) bonds, medium-term (2- and 5-year) bonds, long-term (10-year) bonds and super-long-term (20-, 30- and 40-year) bonds. All medium-term and super long-term bonds are issued with fixed rates only, while both fixed-rate and inflation-indexed bonds are issued for 10-year Japanese government bonds (JGBs). We implement yield-competitive, single-price auctions for 40-year bonds, price-competitive, single-price auctions for inflation-indexed bonds, and price-competitive, multiple-price auctions for the rest. For liquidity enhancement auctions, we implement yield-spread-competitive, multiple-price auctions.
Korea	Auction method: differential price auction (hybrid of single-price auction and multi-price auction) Syndication : On special occasion
Latvia	All domestic securities, be they short- or long-term, are issued through auctions. There are two types of auctions – competitive and non-competitive. Competitive auction takes place earlier and the price is determined at this auction. Later in the same day non-competitive, fixed price auction takes place at the single price, determined at the competitive auction. Tap issues of bonds are regularly used to build up liquid programmes outstanding. Short term bills have been taped (less regular) in order to increase liquidity. Syndications are used for international bond issuances. Note: Auctions in domestic market – under local law. International syndicate issuances – under English law.
Mexico	Since 2000, the Federal Government's securities auction program includes weekly issuance of various types of securities (treasury bills, fixed rate bonds, inflation-linked bonds and floating rate notes). The maturity profile for these securities ranges from 28 days up to 30 years and are placed through either multiple or single price auctions. Tap Issues or reopening policy is a characteristic of the Federal Government's issuing procedure, it is used for reopening outstanding issues of all types of securities in order to increase their size and thus promote liquidity in the secondary market. Since 2010, syndication method is used for the placement of new securities across the yield curve of both Fixed Rate and Inflation Linked Bonds.
Netherlands	For the new issuance of longer dated bonds (5 years and longer), the Dutch State Treasury Agency (DSTA) uses a Dutch Direct Auction (DDA) system. The DDA system is implemented as a rule-based single price auction (book building) in which the DSTA is the book runner. End investors have the ability to participate directly in this auction. Tap auctions (multiple price) are used for launching shorter dated bonds (3-years) and for re-openings of all Dutch State Loans (DSLs). For Dutch Treasury Certificates (DTC's), with maturities up to a year, the allocation takes place in accordance with the Dutch Auction method (book-building and single price).

New Zealand	We use syndications to establish new bond lines. Regular bond tenders by auction for normal bond programme.
Norway	Single-price auction: Issuing auctions in bonds and bills. Multiple-price auction: Buy-back auctions in bonds.
Poland	Single-price auction is used in T-bills and T-bonds sale auction, T-bonds switching auction and supplementary auctions. Multiple price model is used in buy-back auctions. There is a possibility of placing non-competitive bids on T-bond and T-bills sales and T-bond switching auctions There is a possibility of T-bonds' cash purchase after switching auction. Syndication is used for issuance of external debt.
Portugal	*Tap issues correspond to reopening the series via auctions in both T-Bonds and T-Bills; Sometimes T-Bonds can be tapped via syndication or other operations as exchange offers.
Slovak Republic	We always use single price auction for T-bills, but we mostly use multiple price auction for all other bonds (including zero coupon bonds with maturity longer than 1 year). However, we opened a new bond line via auction this year (instead of syndication) and we used single price auction for this opening of new bond line. We want to continue with this and use single price for this specific auctions.
Slovenia	Single price auctions are used for short term securities (T-bills). 18 months T-bills have been issued within T-bills programme since 2013. Due to strategic considerations no auctions of government bonds have been executed since beginning of 2007. Syndication remains the exclusive issuance method for the government bonds. However, the auctions system and auction rules for the government bond auctions are in place, but are currently under revision. The Ministry is planning to reintroduce the government bond auctions in the single price auction format next year.
Spain	Auction type is "modified Dutch": hybrid of simple- and multiple-price. bids above the average price are allocated at the average price, whereas bids between the average price and the cut-off price are allocated at the price offered by the investor.
Sweden	Bonds in foreign currency are issued via syndication whereas government securities in SEK are issued in auctions. Only occasionally syndication has been used for government and inflation-linked bonds.
Switzerland	In 2016, 50% of the bonds and 100% of the bills were auctioned at negative yields. * Between auction dates the Federal Treasury sells so called "own tranches" from time to time to support market liquidity and extraordinary market demand. Own tranches are issued bonds which are not sold at the initial auction. They are still owned by the Confederation and can be sold on demand (the whole issuance process is completed except the sale to the investor). Every time we auction a bond, we reserve own tranches of up to 300 million CHF of the issued bond (in addition to auctioned volume) if required. We consider the selling of own tranches as tap issues. In contrast, the reopening of already issued bonds (implemented by auction) is procedurally and legally comparable with auctioning of new bonds. To support market liquidity, we aim to have only one outstanding bond per year but with a volume of around 5 bn CHF when due. Because of our limited financial needs and market demand we are not able to auction the entire volume at once. Hence, we have to spread it across time and reopen existing bonds several times over their entire lifetime. In 2016 we haven't sold any own tranches yet.
Turkey	In local market lease certificates (sukuk) are issued via direct sales.
United Kingdom	Auctions are the primary method of issuance for gilts across the maturity curve. Index-linked gilts are issued using a single-price format while conventional gilts and T-bills are issued via multiple-price auctions. In the 2016-17 financial year, gilt tenders were introduced as a form of auctioning gilts outside the usual auction calendar in response to market feedback. Gilt tenders replace mini-tenders and sales via taps. A programme of syndications was introduced in the 2009-10 financial year and has been used every year since then.
United States	The U.S. Treasury taps its bill issues (each 12-month is tapped as a 6-, 3-, and 1-month), as well as its long-dated nominal coupon issues (10- and 30-year). It also taps each inflation-linked bond (Treasury Inflation-Protected Securities - TIPS) issue (the 5-, 10-, and 30-year).

1. Ireland's response is from the 2015 Survey of the OECD Working Party on Public Debt Management.
2. Estonia is not included in this survey because the Government of Estonia has not issued any securities since June 2002.

Source: Responses to the 2016 survey on primary markets developments by the OECD Working Party on Public Debt Management.

Overview of recent changes in issuing procedures and techniques in OECD countries

Australia	Buyback tenders - In May 2016 AOFM outlined a plan to provide holders of short-dated Treasury Bonds the opportunity to convert their holdings into holdings of other nominated Treasury Bonds. The mechanism for this is through holding a buyback tender for a short dated bond (<3 Years) followed by a tender for the issue of the same volume of another longer Treasury Bond. http://aofm.gov.au/operational-notice/treasury-bond-buyback-tenders/
Belgium	Our issuance strategy continues to be the combination of predictability and flexibility in order to respond adequately to changing market environments As from 2009, as a result of the financial crisis, the issuance strategy was adapted to offer more flexibility in combination with predictability and transparency. As such, the number of auctions increased from 6 to 11, switching from bi-monthly to monthly auctions. More points of issuance offer more flexibility as to the size per auction and maturities offered. If sufficient market demand is identified, off-the-runs can be reopened at the regular auctions. The choice of lines is thus fully in line with market demand. Obligations Linéaires Ordinaires (OLO) issuance is supplemented by alternative financing instruments: hedged foreign currency issuance and/or structured products issued under the EMTN program, possibly including inflation-linked notes, or other funding instruments, in particular Schuldscheine. The objective pursued when issuing alternative financing instruments is both cost effectiveness and investor diversification.
Canada	Canada's current debt distribution framework has been in place since the late 1990s. Since that time there have been very minor changes to the terms governing the auction framework. However, there have been no notable changes to the issuing procedures. The MTN program was re-introduced in 2012. The EMTN program was re-introduced in 2013.
Chile	2015: - Standardisation of settlement to international standards. - Allocation of bonds in just one auction for the total amount, instead the previous mechanism of allocating one bonds in several auctions for fewer amounts. 2016: - Liability Management programme in local market, in order to maintain 8 benchmark bonds -for both inflation-linked and nominal curves. These benchmarks have a higher outstanding amount in comparison with others.
Czech Republic	The situation is almost similar to last years: Flexible auction calendars (monthly), triple-bond auctions (this is new) with volume range, regular meetings with Primary Dealer (PD), indicative Q volumes of issuance, T+2 settlement of the auction. Opportunistic approach of MoF to the primary market.
Denmark	In 2015, an important step was to reintroduce switch operations. This gave the investors an opportunity to relocate large positions without paying large bid-ask spreads, since switch operation take place close to the mid-price in the secondary markets. Demand was high at the switch operations in 2015, and both investors and primary dealers welcomed the facility. As a consequence in 2016 it was decided to hold regular switch operations. Starting January 2016 two regular monthly switch operations have been conducted. Calendar dates are announced three months in advance in line with other bond and bill auctions. Papers are announced no later than one trading day before the switch takes place.
Italy	No substantial change has been introduced in the issuing procedures in recent years, except for a number of adjustments concerning the BTP Italia.
Japan	Since July 2013, the reopening rule has been generally applied to 20-year bonds to integrate new bonds into four issues per year. As to 10-year bonds, the reopening rule has been applied unless the spread between the market yield on the auction date and the coupon rate of the new issue is wider than a certain level. We have been widening this spread in recent years, and for 10-year bonds issued since fiscal year 2015 (FY2015), the reopening rule is applied to integrate new bonds into four issues per year unless the spread is wider than 30 basis points.
Latvia	The issuing procedures in general have been in place since implementation of a government securities market in 1990-ties. However, a significant change was made in 2013, when a Primary Dealership was implemented. This has provided for some important changes, e.g., stability in demand at primary market auctions, increased activity and transparency on the secondary market, better match between demand and issuance in terms of tenors and amounts.

Mexico	More than 15 years ago, the Ministry of Finance started announcing publicly its quarterly auction program. This has become an important tool for the Ministry of Finance to position itself in the market as a regular and predictable issuer. The most recent change in issuing procedures was made in July 2011 regarding syndicated mechanism, it changed from a book building to an auction scheme.
New Zealand	In 2015, last change was to be specific about which bond would be tendered when quarterly bond tender scheduled is released. We aim to be consistent and transparent in our operations.
Portugal	Treasury Bonds – auction mechanism: Our medium and long-term bond auction method was changed from multiple-price to single-price in 2014, after 3 years of not conducting any T-Bond auction, consequence of the sovereign debt crisis. In 2014 and after consulting our Primary Dealers and some other Debt Management Offices (DMOs), the pros and cons of each method were assessed, and we decided for the single-price auction system, as it was deemed as the 1st step in the normalisation of market access via auctions. The main arguments in support of this decision were: avoid paying above the market price ("winner's curse"), higher transparency since every order is allotted at the same price; and finally, it incentivises participation coming from investors that may be less informed than qualified investors. Treasury Bonds – dual tranche syndicated deals and auctions: In 2015, dual tranche syndicated deals and auctions were introduced, in order to give more alternatives to investors (satisfy multiple clusters of demand), and also give flexibility to the issuer (combination of benchmarks with off-the-run bonds). Treasury Bills: In the TBill auctions we used to issue 2 lines per auction (a reopening/tap and a new line) in order to give liquidity to existing Bills and issue a new line. In 2015, was introduced a method of issuance in which we continue to auction 2 lines, but depending on whether the month is odd or even we issue a new 12 months bill and reopen the 6 months line or we reopen both the 11 month and 3 months Bills. This way, we do a bills auction every month but bills only mature every 2 months, causing them to be larger and consequently more liquid.
Slovak Republic	We haven't changed the methods, however we introduced opening of new bond line via auction, where we used single price auction instead of multiple price that is used otherwise. See more details in previous question.
Slovenia	In addition to public issues of new benchmarks, syndicated taps of existing government bonds and syndicated private placements of government bonds were used in the last 3 years, whereas this type of debt distribution was not used before. The number of co-leads of a new benchmark bond issuance was substantially reduced. Now we have 2-3 co-leads which receive up to 10% of the bonds and economics of the new benchmark issue. Before, this was split among all the rest of the Primary Dealers that were not awarded the mandate of Joint Lead Managers which resulted in up to 10 co-leads each receiving up to 1% of the new issue.
Sweden	During the past year the Debt Office has issued two maturities instead of just one in many of the bond auctions. By splitting the auctions the Debt Office hopes to promote liquidity in the bond market.
Switzerland	No procedural changes, but the introduction of a new version of the electronic repo trading platform (on which our securities are auctioned).
Turkey	In previous years auction bids (data) are gathered by Central Bank and then evaluated manually. Now Turkish Treasury build an in-ho use application called Treasury Auction Management System. With this new system all auction data compiled in seconds and also analytical reports are prepared. Since 2012, in local market lease certificates (sukuk) are issued via direct sales.
United Kingdom	In the 2016-17 financial year, the United Kingdom (UK) government introduced a package of measures to permit greater flexibility to respond to changing market conditions and evolving investor preferences. Changes related to issuance procedure and techniques include the introduction of gilt tenders and an increase in the portion of issuance unallocated to any maturity or gilt type. Gilt tenders are used alongside the auction programme, although they can be scheduled with less notice than auctions. Gilt tenders may be for any maturity and type of gilt and will generally be smaller than auctions of comparable gilts; they may also be issued for market management purposes. The size of the portion of issuance initially unallocated to any specific maturity or type of gilt was increased to £8.0 billion (from £4.0 billion) in 2016-17. The primary intention of this is to accommodate sales by gilt tenders, as well as potentially increasing the syndication programme. It can also be used towards increasing the auction programme. The unallocated portion of issuance is intended to permit more responsiveness to changing market and demand conditions during the year.

Introduction of new types of funding instruments

	Yes	No	Inflation linked bonds	Variable rate notes (such as floating rate notes)	Longer dated securities	Other instruments? Please specify
Australia		X				
Austria		X				
Belgium	X		X		X	
Canada		X				
Chile		X				
Czech Republic	X					Zero coupon bonds
Denmark		X				
Finland		X				
France	X				X	
Germany	X		X			
Greece		X				
Hungary		X				
Iceland		X				
Israel		X				
Italy	X				X	
Japan		X				
Korea		X				
Latvia	X					In 2016 we introduced new instrument - 21day (3 week) T-bill, which was designed specifically to match the typical monthly budget execution cycle. 21-day T-bills are use within the liquidity management.
Luxembourg		X				
Mexico		X				
Netherlands		X				
New Zealand	X				X	
Norway		X				
Poland		X				
Portugal	X			X		
Slovak Republic		X				
Slovenia	X				X	
Spain		X				
Sweden		X				
Switzerland		X				
Turkey	X				X	
United Kingdom		X				
United States		X				
Total	**10**	**23**	**2**	**1**	**6**	**2**

Prospective issuance of new types of funding instruments

	Yes	No	Inflation linked bonds	Variable rate notes (such as floating rate notes)	Longer dated securities	Other instruments? Please specify
Australia	X				X	
Austria		X				
Belgium	X		On demand	On demand	On demand	
Canada		X				
Chile		X				
Czech Republic						
Denmark		X				
Finland		X				
France	X					The French Finances Minister has recently announced that France will issue a sovereign "green" bond in 2017.
Germany		X				
Greece		X				
Hungary		X				
Iceland		X				
Israel		X				
Italy	X*				X*	* Maturities longer than 30 years to be issued in a public format (Italy has already issued several ultra-long bonds through private placements) are under scrutiny but so far no decision has been taken
Japan		X				
Korea	X				X	
Latvia		X				
Luxembourg		X				
Mexico		X				
Netherlands		X				
New Zealand		X				
Norway		X				
Poland		X				
Portugal	X				X	
Slovak Republic	X				X	
Slovenia	X				X	
Spain		X				
Sweden		X				
Switzerland		X				
Turkey	X		X			
United Kingdom		X				
United States		X				
Total	**9**	**23**	**2**	**1**	**7**	**1**

Have you experienced structural changes in the composition of your investor base in recent years? Also, could you identify changing trends in your investor base? Which best describes trend?

▲higher demand ▼lower demand ⇆ no changes

	Domestic investor demand				Foreign investor demand			
	Banks	Central Banks	Institutional investors	Others	Banks	Central Banks	Institutional investors	Others
Australia	▲	⇆	▲	⇆	⇆	⇆	▲	⇆
Austria	▲	▲	⇆	▼	⇆	▼	▲	▼
Belgium	▼	⇆	▼	⇆	▲	▲	▲	⇆
Canada	⇆	▼	▲	⇆	⇆	▲	▲	⇆
Chile	⇆	⇆	⇆	⇆	⇆	⇆	⇆	⇆
Czech Republic	⇆				▲			
Denmark	▲	⇆	▼	⇆				
Finland	⇆	▲	▼	⇆	▲	▲	⇆	⇆
France	⇆	▲	⇆	⇆	⇆	▲	▲	⇆
Germany	▼	▲	▼	▼	▼	▲	▼	▼
Greece	▲	⇆	▲	▼	▼	▼	▼	▼
Hungary	▲	⇆	▼	▲				
Israel	⇆	⇆	⇆		⇆	⇆	⇆	
Italy	▼	▲	⇆	▼				
Japan	▼	▲	▼	▼				
Korea	▲	▲	▲	▲	▼	▲	▲	▲
Latvia	▲	▲	▼	▼	⇆	▲	▲	⇆
Mexico	▼		▼	▲	▼	▲	▲	
Netherlands	⇆		▼		⇆	varies by maturity	▼	▲
New Zealand	▲	⇆	▲	⇆	⇆	▲	▲	▲
Norway	▲		▼	▼	▲	▲	▲	⇆
Poland	▲	⇆	⇆	▲	▲	▲	▼	▲
Portugal	▼	▲	▼	▲	⇆	▲	▼	▼
Slovak Republic	▼	▲	▲	⇆	▲	▲	▲	⇆
Slovenia	▼		▲	▲	▲	▼	▲	▼
Spain	▼	▲	⇆	▼	▼	▲	⇆	
Sweden						▼		
Switzerland	⇆	⇆	varies by security	varies by security	(▲) but unclear on which type of investor	(▲)	(▲)	⇆
Turkey	▼	⇆	▲	⇆	▼	⇆	▼	▼
United Kingdom	▲	▲	⇆	⇆	⇆	▲	▲	⇆
United States	⇆	▲	▲	▼				
Total ▲	11	13	9	6	8	16	14	4
Total ▼	10	1	11	9	6	4	6	6
Total ⇆	**8**	**10**	**7**	**10**	**10**	**3**	**3**	**10**

Institutional Investors: (Pension, insurance and Sovereign Wealth Funds), Others: Retail investors etc

Could you rank the driving forces for changes in your investor base? For each driving force, please score (0-5) which best describes its impact

	Monetary policy actions	New regulations	Technological changes	Credit rating developments	Others
	no impact	⓪ ① ②	❸ ❹ ❺	highest impact	
Australia	❹	❸	①	②	❹
Austria	❺	❸	①	①	❸
Belgium	❺	❹	②	①	
Canada	❸	❸	②	❹	❸
Chile	②	❸	❺	❹	
Czech Republic	❺	⓪	⓪	⓪	
Denmark	❹	❹	⓪	⓪	
Finland	❹	❸	⓪	①	
France	❹	❸	①	⓪	
Germany	❺	①	①	❸	
Greece	⓪	⓪	⓪	❺	
Hungary	❺	❸	⓪	①	❺
Iceland		⓪	❸	❹	❺
Israel	⓪	❸	⓪	⓪	
Italy	❺	❸	❸	❸	
Japan	❺	❸	⓪	①	❸
Korea	②	❹	②	❸	
Latvia	❺	②	⓪	❺	❺
Mexico	❺	❸	⓪	❹	
Netherlands	❺	❹	⓪	⓪	
New Zealand	❹	❸	⓪	②	❸
Norway	②	❹	⓪	⓪	
Poland	❹	②	⓪	❸	❺
Portugal	❺	❹	②	❺	
Slovak Republic	❺	❸	①	❸	❹
Slovenia	❹	❸	⓪	②	
Spain	❺	❸	⓪	❸	
Sweden	❺				
Switzerland	❹	②	⓪	⓪	②
Turkey	❺	❸	①	❺	❺
United Kingdom	❺	❸	①	⓪	❹
United States	❹	❹	❸	⓪	

Others - Country specific detail

	Others	
Australia	❹	Liquidity of Sovereign Securities, Comparative return vis a vis other Sovereigns, Liquidity & comparative value of the AUD.
Austria	❸	negative interest rates
Canada	❸	Comparative monetary policy (i.e. other sovereigns)
Hungary	❺	Demand from retail investors
Iceland	❺	High interest rate compare to other countries, economic growth, lower internal and external debt
Japan	❸	Foreign investors have continued their net purchases of short to medium-term JGBs with falls in dollar-based yen fund raising costs.
Latvia	❺	participation in international organisations (Eurozone, OECD etc.)
New Zealand	❸	issuance strategy, longer dated bonds, Inflation-Indexed Bonds (IIB) reintroduction
Poland	❺	- introducing in February 2016 taxation on assets of some financial institutions, including banks and exemption of local treasury securities from the tax base.
Slovak Republic	❹	negative yields environment
Switzerland	②	Safe haven for foreign investors amid uncertain economic conditions in EU
Turkey	❺	Capital flows to emerging markets
United Kingdom	❹	Size of sterling market as a share of global bond indices Reserve currency status of sterling.

What are the implications of structural changes in your investor base for your primary market operations including auction mechanisms, instrument choices (i.e. linkers vs fixed coupon bonds, short vs long dated bonds) and borrowing costs

Australia	The implications of ongoing structural changes are more likely to see investor demand for Australian Government Securities, remain steady with growth in some sectors,. Demand is likely to continue from non-resident investors albeit at a slowing rate. However some specific, overseas regions and investor sectors should see demand growth while others will remain steady and even one or two sectors seeing diminished demand .Non-resident investors are only smaller participants in the Australian Government linkers market, due to the lack of global inflation and lower liquidity Domestic investors as a proportion of overall investors are likely to grow. Domestic banks, being affected by the global regulatory conditions, are likely to be more dominant than institutional fund managers. Investors have been affected by the AOFM's lengthening bias with many moving out along the curve, chasing increased duration and higher returns. Those with shorter duration benchmarks however are still able to comfortably invest with the AOFM's continued support and issuance into the short end. Structural changes are unlikely to greatly change the AOFMs modus operandi of auction issuance. The AOFM will still use the auction/ tender process predominantly with the judicious use of syndications while maintaining a lengthening bias . Although still a regular issuer of Australian Government inflation-linked bonds , due to the absence of offshore flows, only small new domestic flows and the increased regulatory effects of banks holding linkers on their trading books, the proportion of linker issuance versus nominal has declined. The AUD linker market at the moment is predominantly a domestic investor market. The lengthening bias of the AOFM and the subsequent ongoing extension of the yield curve was driven predominantly by internal considerations . This has occurred over the last 2-3 years. It was expected that this would also attract new investors and increase the diversity of the investor base. We do have some evidence of this, mainly from some offshore markets. Increased interest in this part of the curve from investors continues to support our issuance here. Borrowing costs for the AOFM have fallen over recent years . This can be attributed to a number of factors. However it would be generally accepted that the ongoing increases in the number of investors that entered the Australian Government Securities (AGS) market over recent years, and the growing volumes of AGS they own (either due to active management or passively via index lengthening changes),that this demand would have been one of several reasons , driving borrowing costs lower.
Austria	More investor demand for long-dated issuance due to negative interest rates in combination of Quantitative Easing (QE) purchases - Public Sector Purchase Programme (PSPP)
Belgium	The low yield environment is driving investors towards ever longer maturities and is driving borrowing costs substantially lower. This trend coincides with the Belgian Debt Agency (BDA's) strategy to lengthen the average life of the portfolio. At this moment, after having executed the 50 year transaction, the average life of the portfolio is 8.7 years.
Canada	Although it is difficult to show concrete evidence, it is likely that the increase in demand – especially from institutional investors and other customers – has helped reduce Canada's borrowing costs. Float refers to the general concept of how much of a given security is available for active trading in the market; a general estimate of float is based on several assumptions. It is believed that the increase in foreign investor demand has decreased the float of certain debt securities in recent years, thus reducing liquidity. To partially remedy this issue and increase liquidity in secondary markets, the Bank of Canada has decided that it would reduce its share at the auction from 20% to 15%. The Department of Finance has also structured its debt issuance to build larger benchmark sizes in order to mitigate liquidity concerns (it should be noted that the larger issuances are also due in part to a larger borrowing requirement). Furthermore, we are currently analysing the structure of our investor base of part of a review of our existing debt distribution framework.

Chile	- In general, an implication of the investor base should necessarily imply the increase of foreign investor, because the current participation is low. In this regard, they are more interested in nominal versus inflation-linked bonds, which is the contrary that what happens with Pension Fund, the main local investor. - In addition, an increase of competence due to the entrance of new participants would reduce borrowing costs.
Czech Republic	None.
Denmark	Due to a low issuance need new issuance is focussed on a few bond series (mainly the 2- and 10-year segments). This further supports liquidity in the market. In addition, insurance and pension funds that are traditional buyers of the long end of the curve (e.g. in the 30-year segment), have less demand for the very long dated bonds. This is in part a consequence of pension funds shifting customers away from schemes containing yield guarantees. Hence, slightly fewer long-dated bonds are being issued.
Finland	Some duration lengthening, i.e. longer bonds, but not driven by perceived change in investor base, more affected by funding needs and level of rates (i.e. monetary policy)
France	Due to the European Central Bank (ECB) PSPP which buys all bonds on our curve, we try to tap more regularly off-the-run bonds in order to maintain a good liquidity all along the curve. The strong appetite of investor for longer term bonds has also led us to lengthen the average maturity of our issuance (average maturity of medium and long term issuance at 8.9 years in 2014 and 9.1 years in 2015) by issuing higher volume at our long term auctions compared to our medium term auctions.
Germany	auction mechanisms: none instrument choices: none borrowing costs: none
Greece	Due to the fact that Hellenic Republic is under a fiscal adjustment program since 2010 there has been a change in investors' base, i.e. Less foreign more domestic investors.
Hungary	The increasing share of domestic banks' purchases is due to the measures taken by the Central Bank (CB) to drive banks' liquidity from the CB onto the government securities market. This has been successful and resulted in high demand by banks even at lower yields. The DMO has also been able to influence (i.e. decrease) the primary market yields by offering lower amounts, thanks to the good budgetary liquidity position. The CB previously supported banks' purchases of longer term bonds by an up to 10-year interest rate swap (IRS) facility, which was phased out by the middle of this year, but as it was a gradual process, the PDs said that it did not affect the market, and there is still relatively good demand for longer dated bonds. (Some short- to middle-term international uncertainties – Brexit, prospective Fed rate hike etc. – may even be in favour of longer bonds, as the 3-year bond yield and demand can be more volatile due to these events or market expectations.) Retail investors' demand can be maintained or increased by attractive yields, so in this investor segment the DMO faces higher borrowing costs, but at the same time the retail investor sector is more stable than the institutional investors/banks, as they have a very high rate of reinvestment. So in this case higher costs are the price of lower risks. Non-resident holdings have decreased in the past 1-year period, but their demand for wholesale instruments has been taken up by banks, so this structural change did not have any negative effect on domestic yields.
Iceland	No effects on the auction mechanisms. Higher demand from foreign investors for medium and long-term fixed coupon bonds has lowered the borrowing costs.
Israel	There might be changes in the strategy and the issuance policy to benefit the demand. It might influence.
Italy	In the current low yield environment, investors are trying to increase the return of their portfolios by moving along the yield curve toward longer maturities. Given the advantage of this trend for the issuer from an interest rate risk and a refinancing risk perspective, the issuance strategy since 2015 has been gradually adjusted by putting more weight on the issuance of instruments with a maturity longer than 10 years and by reducing that of bonds with a maturity equal or shorter than 5 years. However, the potential higher cost of the rebalancing in favour of instruments with longer maturity has been more than compensated by the reduction of the bond yields, leading to a decrease in the total borrowing costs

Japan	It is hard to articulate generally the influence of the structural changes in the JGB investors base on the primary market operations. However, we formulate JGB Issuance Plans and implement the reopening rule and auction methods, etc. in accordance with the latest market needs.
Korea	There have been no significant structural changes in investor base recently.
Latvia	There are several factors that influence our decision and activities in primary market. For example, the current low rate environment has made certain changes in our supply and investor base: a) in domestic market we currently focus on either very short instruments for liquidity management (21day Tbill and money market instruments) or medium term bond programmes (up to 5 years). Currently we have active 3y and 5y domestic bond programmes. That results in the situation when investors in short term securities are banks, but as for 3y and 5y bond programmes yields become closer to 0 or even negative, interest from institutional investors diminish for those tenors. Facing these changes we currently may borrow domestically with negative rates in short end, and for the first time (in 14th September, 2016) we even set at primary auction a negative average weighted yield also for bonds. b) Therefore for longer term borrowing with use more liquid benchmark offerings, and issuer in the international markets. We have just taped markets in May 2016 with our longest Eurobond issue (20 years). Because of ECB QE effect, we observe stable interest for tenors up to 10 y are coming from banks and are aware that in secondary market there is increased interest for bonds from ECB. The majority of our international bonds is bought by fund managers, but interest from particular type of institutional investor varies depending on the tenor. For the first time (in 2015) our international bonds were allocated to high quality international financial institutions (new investors that did not participate in primary placement before). Currently as Euro zone member country and a new OECD member, we have less interest from Emerging Market (EM) investors and more from rate market investors. Taking into account that in our international bond issuance we offer at least a minimum benchmark size due to the limited overall funding need, we benefit from this liquidity in terms of lower cost of borrowing (in comparison with domestic market where bond programmes are less liquid and certain liquidity premium exists).
Luxembourg	Not applicable
Mexico	Mexico has benefited from the increase in foreign holdings in terms of the liquidity that this change has provided, which can be reflected in the narrowing of the bid-ask spreads, higher market depth and immediacy, as well as a wider investors' base. All these factors have allowed the Federal Government to use debt denominated in local currency to cover the majority of its deficit, as well as increasing the weighted average life of its debt portfolio, which results in lowering the refinancing risk.
Netherlands	No implications on auction mechanisms or instrument choices. We do not see a noticeable effect on our borrowing cost despite a changing investor base. In general, demand – as measured by bid-to-cover ratios – remains healthy. More specifically, the changes in investor base have led to an increased allocation to the category Others in the 5-year maturity in 2016 compared to 2014, but more to real money investors in the 10-year maturity over the same period.
New Zealand	Greater diversification of investor type and geographic location given lengthening of our portfolio and reintroduction of IIB means greater support for auctions and syndications than might have been otherwise the case.
Norway	We are not planning any material changes in our primary market operations.
Poland	In recent years, two important legislative changes affecting the structure of investors buying domestic Treasury securities have been implemented - pension system reform (2014) and the introduction of a bank levy (2016). 1. The pension system reform and the cancellation of T-bonds held by open pension funds (OFE) had no significant effect on the primary market operations. The level of the net borrowing requirements of the State budget decreased by funds transferred so far to the OFE. The cancellation of the bonds held by the OFE caused a statistical increase in the shares of other groups of Treasury securities holders. The ban on OFE investment in Treasury securities and an absence of pension funds in the primary market did not influenced significantly the structure of instruments sold in the primary market.

2. The introduction of a taxation on bank and insurance companies assets and exemption of local treasury securities from the tax base resulted in an increase in banks' demand for these instruments. The share of banking sector in the domestic Treasury Securities (TS) increased by more than 6 percentage points in the first half of 2016. The increase in banks' demand for Treasury securities had no significant effect on the structure of the instruments sold in the primary market.

Portugal

After the Financial assistance program Portugal returned successfully to medium- and long-term (MLT) debt markets. Still, market conditions are significantly different from the pre-crisis era. And while some of the factors that explain these differences are particular to Portugal, not least the fact that it still has a sub-Investment Grade status in the three major credit rating agencies, many are common to other sovereign debt markets, where a number of flash crash events have been attributed to relatively low liquidity, possibly related with regulatory changes and bond purchases by Central Banks.

The investor base changed significantly during the Programme. The data shows that before the crisis, the syndicated deal's allocation was very well balanced across euro area countries with a strong distribution among pension funds and insurance companies. In the first issuances after entering the Programme, there was a strong take up from United Kingdom (UK) and United States (US) investors, namely from hedge funds, which played an important role in the early stages of the return to market access. In the most recent syndications, while there is a clear shift towards a distribution more identical to the one observed pre-crisis, there is still a strong take up from UK and domestic investors (offsetting a lower distribution towards euro area pension funds and insurance companies, namely from France), which is probably still related with the sub-Investment Grade rating.

The changes in the investor base have led us to conduct more regular auctions of MLT bonds and to offer more than one line per auction. Also, driven by demand we have been able to extend duration and are currently more active in issuing in the 10y+ time bucket than before the financial crisis. Despite the extension of duration, the borrowing costs continued to come down, except for 2016, when yields picked up, because of, among other factors, market disappointment regarding the delay in Portugal's recovery of investment grade (IG) status by the main Credit Rating Agencies (CRAs).

Slovak Republic

We always ask our group of PDs before each auction about the market situation and demand, before the decision what we will offer in the next auction. As the Central Bank (ECB) is (was) very active the feedback we got from PD was they want bonds, which are attractive for the Central Bank => banks therefore prefer longer bonds (available for PSPP of ECB) and also in the environment of negative yields we see demand for tenors with higher yields. However even the longer maturities doesn´t affect the borrowing cost in negative way (yet) as long term yields are more under short-term bonds yields sold in the past.

As we realize the current model of PD is under pressure we introduced an irregular auction with remuneration fee (for all PDs) to reward also PD, which cannot get a Syndicate deal – because it´s yearly performance is not sufficient to get the Syndication.

Slovenia

We have not observed any impact of shifts in the investor base for government bonds on the primary market operations. In fact, the structural changes in the investor base mentioned in sections above were in opinion driven by the offering of longer dated government benchmarks (20y, 30y government bond) in 2015 and 2016.

Spain

Balance-sheet restrictions increase investor's bargaining power in the dynamics of auctions and syndications.

Sweden

We haven't planned any changes. We just try to accept the realities of life.

Switzerland

The average bond term has increased from 7.3 years in 2010 to 9.7 years in 2015, issued maturity increased from 12 years (2010) to above 20 years (2015). Ongoing or increased demand by institutional investors for longer-term bonds supported our longer-term issuance-strategy.

No other implications on auction mechanisms or instrument choices. Therefore, the main shift towards foreign investors had no substantial implications on our primary market operations, as these investors satisfied their demands primarily on secondary markets or in a regular way via auctions (in the case of bills).

Amidst increasing economic uncertainty, Switzerland is still regarded as safe haven for investors and the situation on currency markets (i.e. fx forwards, swaps and cross-currency swaps) peg foreign demand for shorter termed securities. However, borrowing costs declined primarily due to low interest rates in general.

Turkey

The changes in investor base have an important impact on the primary market operations in Turkey. For instance, the share of public funds in the total domestic debt stock increased in the last decade. It is assessed that public institutions' decision of holding government bonds in their portfolio until the maturity date (buy & hold) affects the transaction volume and liquidity of government bonds in secondary market.

The liquidity of a security mainly depends on the amount of the security issued and the distribution of its

	investors. Thus, the higher the security's total amount in the market and the better balanced the distribution of its investors; the more the security's volume of transaction in the secondary market. In this respect, in order to diversify investor base (buy-and-hold vs trader) and to encourage secondary market trading, we increase total amount of securities by re-openings in the primary market. We have started to increase the issuance amount of benchmark securities with 5 and 10 year maturity in the primary market. In order to contribute to secondary market liquidity and to decrease the roll-over risk on their maturity dates, regular buy-back auctions for off-the run benchmark securities have been implemented since March 2016.
United Kingdom	In determining the split of gilt issuance, the government considers its analysis of the relative cost-effectiveness of the different gilt types and maturities, its risk preferences including for the portfolio as well as the issuance programme (for example, managing and mitigating its near term exposure to refinancing risk, the role of particular maturities in facilitating the hedging of a wide range of gilt market exposures through the futures market etc.), and feedback that it gathers on demand for gilts. In recent years there has been a significant increase in demand for shorter maturity conventional gilts from overseas investors (including central banks and reserve managers) and from domestic monetary financial institutions (in particular for regulatory purposes); there has also been strong demand from domestic pension funds for long-dated conventional and index-linked gilts as part of ongoing programmes of liability-driven hedging. Consequently, demand for gilts has been well diversified across the maturity spectrum and by instrument type (conventional and index-linked). Taking these considerations into account, the government's intention in 2016-17 has been to deliver a well-diversified gilt issuance programme across types and maturities of gilts. Whilst not directly related to the changing investor base, market conditions have been reported in general to have deteriorated and concerns regarding liquidity and volatility in the gilt market have been expressed. Given the potentially challenging market backdrop, the government introduced in 2016-17 a package of measures to support gilt distribution, including holding smaller auctions, increasing the non-competitive allowance for primary dealers, modifying gilt issuance methods (gilt tenders), increasing the initially unallocated portion of gilt issuance and the proportion of gilts that can be bought post auction.
United States	In the last year, the Federal Reserve has become a significant investor in Treasuries at auction; these purchases (as auction 'add-ons') are reinvestments from the Federal Reserve's maturing Treasury portfolio. For every dollar the Federal Reserve chooses not to reinvest, Treasury must raise an additional dollar of funding from the public. Thus, the Federal Reserve's reinvestment policy going forward will have a significant effect on Treasury's funding needs over the next few years, in particular. Additionally, in May 2015, Treasury noted that "demand for Treasury bills is high and expected to grow even more significant." One factor for this increase in demand is money market mutual fund reform that was implemented this October. As a result of this expectation for increased demand, Treasury announced its intent to increase the supply of Treasury bills outstanding. Since this announcement, Treasury has indeed increased supply by more than $200 billion.

ANNEX B

2016 Survey on Liquidity in Government Bond Secondary Markets

What percentage of your bonds are held domestically vs offshore? Please explain possible implications for the liquidity of your bonds

Australia	Around 60% of our bonds are held offshore (see http://aofm.gov.au/statistics/non-resident-holdings/). The offshore holding appears to have little real implications for liquidity due to a relatively diverse group of generally active non-resident investors. Diversity is well spread geographically and between sectors and is comprised of several different investor groups including central banks and sovereign wealth funds, institutional fund managers, a growing number of pension funds and hedge funds. The domestic space particularly the banks and their balance sheets are active investors and intermediaries as well.
Austria	If Eurozone is seen as the domestic market the share of domestically held bonds would be 80% whereas if Austria is seen as the domestic market the share of domestically held bonds would be 28% (as of end-March 2016).
Belgium	41% domestically vs. 59% abroad (of which 32% in the euro-zone, i.e. in the issuer's and investors' domestic currency). This internationalization shows the diversification of the investor base in Belgian bonds which we see as a very positive element. We do not see this internationalization having negative impacts on the liquidity of our bonds
Canada	As of May 2016, 31% of domestic Government of Canada bonds were held by non-residents. Global bonds are sold to offshore investors. Data on non-resident holdings of Government of Canada (GoC) bonds for June 2016 has not yet been released. A large proportion of non-residents who purchase domestic Government of Canada bonds are buy and hold investors, who transact relatively infrequently in the Canadian secondary market. Consequently, the float that is available for trading in the secondary market may not always be as large as market participants would prefer. This may lead to a potential reduction in liquidity in the Government of Canada bond market.
Chile	Approx. 3% of the bonds are held offshore. It is estimated that it has a great impact on liquidity, since the main local holder are pension funds, which are acting as buy and holders. These pension funds state that such behaviour is due to the lack of counterparties to do transactions for greater amounts, like foreign funds.
Czech Republic	Foreign investors hold approximately 23% of Czech Government Bonds (incl. savings bonds and excl. Treasury Bills).
Denmark	The June 2016 foreign ownership share was 40%. Apart from a temporary increase in 2015, the foreign ownership share has been stable for several years. Our view is that having a broad and diversified investor base (whether foreign or domestic) is important. It adds to liquidity in the secondary markets and diversity in our market access through primary markets.
Finland	Estimated around 15% domestic, 85% outside of Finland. Large part held in the Euro area, which can be considered as home market. This is a positive factor to the liquidity of the bonds.
France	As of the end of 2016Q1, 38.7% of our bonds are held domestically, and 61.3% are held offshore. The relatively high share of our bonds held offshore is a sign of a highly diversified investor base (we estimate that half of this share is held in euro area countries, and the other half in non-euro countries),

	which is positive for the liquidity of our bond market.
Germany	≈ 15% domestically, ≈ 85% offshore
Greece	Not applicable.
Hungary	28% of domestic currency bonds (including retail bonds) and 84% of Foreign Exchange (FX) denominated bonds is held by non-residents. At the same time 70-80% of Primary Dealers' (PDs) secondary market trading of domestic bonds in 2016 has been with non-residents. FX Bonds: international issuances are mostly held by non-residents, domestic retail EUR bonds are almost totally held by resident investors. Liquidity from foreign investors can come in bursts: macroeconomic indicators, FX rate movements, rating decisions, global market sentiments can induce sudden buying or selling momentum. Foreign investors deal usually in bigger volumes than domestic ones, therefore their trades, activities significantly influence the market.
Iceland	Bonds held domestically: 76% Bonds held offshore: 24% We do not have accurate information on the liquidity of the issues held offshore, but it is much less liquid then the bonds held domestically.
Ireland	43% of bonds are held domestically, including all of the Floating Rate Notes (FRNs) which are with the Central Bank of Ireland. Excluding these FRNs, 31% of bonds are held domestically.
Israel	5.2% of the domestic tradable debt is held offshore. 94.8% of the domestic tradable debt is held domestically. As the vast majority of our bonds are held domestically, we do not perceive a liquidity issue with the percentage of offshore holdings.
Italy	Considering the total stock of government securities, the percentages are around 63% held domestically vs 37% held offshore. Since the peak of the euro sovereign debt crisis in 2011-12, foreign investors have been gradually increasing their holdings in Italian government securities in absolute terms and with respect to the total outstanding stock. This is a positive trend for liquidity, given that a more diversified distribution among investors (by location and by type) tends to increase the liquidity of the secondary market as there are more trading strategies and behaviours in place.
Japan	Foreign investors hold just above 10% of Japanese government bonds (JGBs), It is difficult for us to answer clearly because the quantity in each trading would be influenced largely by market circumstances, investor type and their behaviour.
Korea	Domestically held bonds account for 86.4% while offshore accounts for 13.6%
Latvia	Almost all domestic bond issues (LV International Securities Identification Number (ISIN) codes) are held domestically, whereas all international issues (XS and US ISIN codes) are held with International Central Securities Depository (ICSD) and data shows that lion share of international bonds outstanding are held by non-residents (20% residents). The liquidity of international bonds is higher due to bigger volumes outstanding and much broader investor base, using ICSD's.
Luxembourg	Not available.
Mexico	As of June 2016, foreign investors held 59.5% of the Fixed Rate Bonds and 33.7% of total domestic debt, respectively (see page 6). Mexico has benefited from the increase in foreign holdings in terms of the liquidity that this has provided, which can be reflected in the narrowing of the bid-ask spreads, higher market depth and immediacy, as well as a wider investors' base. All these factors have allowed the Federal Government to use debt denominated in local currency to cover the majority of its deficit, as well as increasing the weighted average life of its debt portfolio, which results in lowering the refinancing risk.
Netherlands	We do not have information regarding our bond ownership
New Zealand	33.8% domestically, 67.2% offshore. New Zealand Government Bonds (NZGBs) have been held offshore in a reasonably tight range of 60% - 70% since 2010. Over this time, liquidity has improved (both on an absolute and relative basis) as the amount of bonds outstanding and investor relations activity have risen. Both the offshore and domestic investor bases feature a diverse range of investors so no obvious implications from the split.

Norway	59% total bonds outstanding (including government's own holdings) was held by foreign investors at the end of Q2 2016. Excluding government's own holdings foreigners held 69% at the end of Q2 2016. Anecdotal evidence indicates that a fairly large share of foreign investors is "buy and hold", which could have a negative impact on liquidity.
Poland	As of June 2016, foreign investors held 52.9% of Polish sovereign bonds, while domestic investors held 47.1%. Relatively high percentage of sovereign bonds held by foreign investors means that liquidity of bonds is dependent to a large extent on investment decisions and activity of non-residents. Stronger short-term foreign capital inflows as a result of turmoil on international financial markets may temporary influence liquidity of the Treasury Securities (TS) secondary market.
Portugal	As of May 31st, based on public information available on European Central Bank (ECB) and Bank of Portugal, the percentage of bonds from the Portuguese Government Bond (PGB) curve that is held by domestics is 39%, by foreigners is 38% and the ECB owns 23%. In the past, before the crisis, the percentage of Bonds held by foreigners were close to 80%, however it is difficult to take any conclusions based solely on that factor, because a lot of factors have changed since then in our market: credit rating, investor base characteristics, etc.
Slovak Republic	46% domestic vs. 54% foreign (by domicile)
Slovenia	As per end of June 2016 87% of bonds were held by Non-residents. Non-residents are also bond holders whose accounts are managed via fiduciary accounts of ICSDs in local CSD, Slovenia's Central Securities Clearing Corporation (called KDD d.d.), upon assumption that the holders who have the bonds deposited with ICSD are not residents of Slovenia.
Spain	As at 30th June 2016: Non-stripped Bonos and Obligaciones: 48,89% of the registered holdings is held by non-residents; 51,11% is held domestically. Registered holdings include securities held as collateral in bilateral repo operations. Principal-Only strips: 20,63% of the registered holdings held by non-residents; 79,37% held domestically. Interest-Only strips: 20,28% of the registered holdings held by non-residents; 79,72% held domestically.
Switzerland	According to banking statistics based on surveys of the Swiss National Bank, approximately 25% of our bonds are held by foreign investors (as of May 2016; at end of 2015: 30%). Cross currency basis swap driven government bond purchases by foreign investors might have temporary reduced domestic market liquidity.
Turkey	18.5% of the Domestic Debt is held by non-residents vs 81.5% is held domestically. All domestic bonds are held in domestic custodies. Foreign investors prefers longer term bonds, therefore the trading volumes of bonds with longer maturity are greater than the bonds with short maturity.
United Kingdom	As at 31 March 2016, 27.0% of United Kingdom (UK) government bonds (gilts) were held by investors who are based abroad. Over the last ten years, this investment by overseas investors has increased significantly, particularly since the Global Financial Crisis. The investor base for gilts is relatively well diversified across a range of investor types, both domestically and overseas. We believe that this diversification helps to create a healthy and liquid gilt market.
United States	Approximately 53% is held domestically (Source: Treasury International Capital System). U.S. Treasuries are a deep and liquid global market.

Have you observed/experienced changes in liquidity conditions of your domestic sovereign bonds -in terms of bid-ask spread, trading volumes etc.- in recent years? If so, please elaborate on the main reasons (e.g. changes in investor base, investor sentiment, credit ratings; market infrastructure developments, issuance strategies; electronic trading; impact of new regulations; Brexit; central bank policies etc.)

	Changes	Reasons
Australia	While annual turnover growth in Australian Government Securities (AGS) appears to have stabilized a couple of years ago at around AUD 1 trillion a year, liquidity conditions in AGS appear to have deteriorated slightly. Turnover ratios have continued to decline slowly but steadily since the Global financial crisis (GFC) years. Anecdotal evidence would suggest bid/offers remain reasonably tight in marketable sizes however there appears to have been a slight widening in larger quoted volumes (> 100m) and for bonds longer than 12 years maturity. The market reaction to our issuance can also be seen as a gauge for observing the liquidity of the market. The fact that the Australian Office of Financial Management (AOFM) is able to issue large volumes via tender (1billion) and syndication (up to 7 billion) with very limited effect on the market yields suggests that these volumes are able to be absorbed fairly well. Liquidity in Australian linkers however is at quite different level and has become increasingly impaired at times. Investors in the market appear to be able to transact but do so more via a broking approach (IE. working orders) rather than receiving active quotes.	Liquidity in the AGS market appears to have been impacted predominantly by issues such the rationalization and concentration of AGS market makers, the impact of new regulations and investor sentiment. Over the past few years although the number of market makers (MM) has only fallen slightly, the number of active price makers has become more concentrated. The ability of banks to warehouse stock and their allowable holding periods have also been affected. Credit charges applied to securities which are deemed less liquid have certainly widened bid/ offer spreads. Although this is applicable more to Non AGS securities it is increasingly being felt for the Treasury Indexed Bonds (TIBs) markets which have fewer MMs and are considerably less liquid than the Treasury Bond (TBs). Although investors remain positive about liquidity generally in the TB market, there are areas of the yield curve that are less liquid, of which investors are more cautious. This is predominantly the ultra-long end (15+ years). Investors inform us although they realize this is a new area of curve development for the AOFM, the volume on issue in particular lines, fewer participants in the is part of the curve, less liquid hedging instruments and the current low interest rate environment and future direction of interest rates adds to their more cautious participation here.
Austria	No big changes. In 2015, we have seen a small decline in secondary market turnover in RAGBs (Republic of Austria Government Bonds) vs. 2014. However annual turnover is still in-line/above the levels seen between 2008-2011. In terms of turnover ratio (secondary market turnover as a ratio of outstanding volume) we have seen a small decline in 2015 vs. 2014 of around -8%. However the ratio is still above 180% and higher than it was between 2008-2011. Bid-ask spreads are relatively stable but have increased somewhat in H1 2016 vs. FY 2015. However, they are still in-line with 2013 levels. E.g., for the 10-year benchmark bonds the average bid-ask spread (on price basis) is as follows: 2013 16 ct 2014 12,5 ct 2015 14 ct 2016YTD* 16 ct * until July 19, 2016	In our view, secondary market turnover in Eurozone government bonds (including RAGBs) is currently influenced by: • lower investor diversity due to an increase of passive trading strategies • QE (quantitative easing) programme -Public Sector Purchase Programme (PSPP) of the Eurosystem • lower ability of primary dealers for market making activity (partly due to regulatory reasons)

	Changes	Reasons
Belgium	A number of indicators is being tracked on a regular basis. No worsening in liquidity conditions can be observed in bid-ask spreads, repo conditions or orderbook data. The number of secondary market trades in Obligations Linéaires Ordinaires (OLOs) decreased over the past years, particularly in the largest trade sizes. As a consequence, average ticket sizes are also down. The drop in overall traded volumes on the secondary market over the past 2 years has been quite significant. Over a longer period, we note a 50% reduction in comparison with pre-crisis volumes. Interdealer volumes also showed a temporary substantial reduction during the spring of 2015 crisis. However, the proportion of volumes traded by our Primary Dealers with other dealers on one side and with customers on the other has not significantly changed, indicating that proportionally, they still provide the same sort of liquidity provision service to final investors.	We believe that the main driver towards the lower secondary market trading volumes lies in the wider economic context, central bank policies depressing yield levels and investor reaction to this environment. In this extremely low yield environment where all spreads are being compressed too, diverging trading ideas are hard to find and hence trading volumes are likely to be depressed. It should also be noted that part of the volumes are driven by the presence of the continuous buyer: the ECB. Even though the Primary Dealers are still providing sufficient liquidity to the market –at least under normal market conditions- one should not deny that the regulatory context is de-incentivizing some banks in market making bonds to final investors. In this context we should also not underestimate the effect of the changes observed in the final investor spectrum i.e. the ever growing importance and relative size of fund managers, requiring size and immediacy.
Canada	We have observed a decline in domestic sovereign bond market liquidity over the last several years, however, liquidity conditions have begun to stabilize over the last twelve months. The bid-offer spread is a highly responsive measure of liquidity conditions in the market, which reflects changing market dynamics and market volatility. Overall, the spread has been narrowing since the 2008 financial crisis. However, during the past two years, we have observed slightly wider spreads across the curve. These wider spreads are a likely reflection of the increased levels of regulation found on banks' balance sheets, post-financial crisis. Recent monthly average bid-ask spreads (cents): 2-year bond – 0.01 3-year bond – 0.03 5-year bond – 0.03 10-year bond – 0.05 30-year bond – 0.11 Government of Canada Bond Trading: (2015, average monthly volumes): 0-3 year sector: $49B 3-10 year sector: $72B 10+ year sector: $18B Between 2014 and 2015, the average monthly trading volumes for Government of Canada securities slightly declined.	A number of factors have been driving the lower levels of liquidity in the domestic sovereign bond market: • Dealers are seeing reduced profitability in their trading business for domestic sovereign bonds • The low interest rate environment combined with balance sheet constraints, have limited dealers ability to take on risk • Smaller inventories and smaller trade sizes have become more prevalent in the market; meanwhile, dealers continue to make adjustments to reduce staffing levels in their government fixed-income group. Foreign central bank purchases of large quantities of Canadian sovereign bonds, has caused some bond issues to be on 'special'. At the same time, supply-constraints have led to some repo market tightness. Recent higher demand coming into Canada for AAA-rated duration has caused some supply-demand imbalance in the longer-term sectors of the yield curve.
Chile	As a result of a liability management program, which has resulted in 8 bonds with higher stocks, these bonds have shown higher liquidity in comparison to others.	It is due to a higher stock

	Changes	Reasons
Czech Republic	In general, there is low liquidity in the domestic market. Market participations observe changes in liquidity in Government Bonds (GBs) up to 3Y. Gradual increase of excess reserves of domestic banking sector as a result of Czech National Bank (CBN) foreign exchange interventions is the main cause of increasing demand for domestic bonds. Especially foreign investors look for alternative investments (yield, tenor, etc.). On the other hand, liquidity is lower on GB market over 5Y. Despite new preferred electronic platform supported by MoF (Ministry of Finance) MTS (electronic trading platform) Czech Republic, total number of trades and total volume of traded securities decreased. Bid/Ask spread showed on platform is just slightly wider, quoted just in requested amount most of the time. Also the issuance activity of MoF is smaller.	The main reasons are: • generally central bank policies with zero or negative rates and related change in investment sentiment with changes of preferred asset classes • Czech National Bank foreign exchange interventions • increase of market and investment regulation • changes in MoF issuance strategy (low issuance activity connected with more opportunistic behaviour- more flexibility and less regularity)
Denmark	Generally, markets have become less liquid. Bid-ask spread are slightly more elevated and average daily trading volumes smaller. In addition, fewer large trades occur, which may indicate that investors increasingly seek best execution by breaking up trades into smaller ticket sizes. Investors also argue that trading larger positions has become more costly and difficult and that more attention has to be put into execution. Trading a position generally takes longer.	This is a very big question. Some relevant reasons are new regulation and the low level of interest rates. New regulation to strengthen the resilience of banks to shocks is making it more costly for banks to take positions in government bonds. This is adversely affecting the capacity of banks to hold inventory and hence act as liquidity providers in the government bond market. In addition, the very low level of interest rates has made government bond trading less attractive. Because of this, some investors have sought alternative and higher yielding options.
Finland	The average ticket size is slightly smaller. The total number of transactions monthly is relatively stable; however some minor intra-year variation so that the numbers diminish towards year-end. Bid-ask spreads did stabilize after 2010, were stable 2012-2015, but some volatility has been observed in 2016.	Liquidity impact based on new regulations, investor sentiment in low yield environment, credit rating, central bank policy (ECB PSPP).
France	Bid-ask spread have remained broadly stable in recent years, with a slightly higher volatility on particular market segments (very long term, inflation-linked bonds) since the beginning of the ECB PSPP and during episodes of market stress. With regard to secondary market trading volumes as reported by our primary dealer reporting (data unaudited, which excludes by design transactions not involving a primary dealer, and also the volumes sold by primary dealers to the Eurosystem for the PSPP), they are broadly stable in absolute terms but have been gradually and slightly decreasing as a percentage of outstanding. We also observe in some parts of our curves (typically inflation, off-the-run) a slight decrease in the average ticket size. Overall the liquidity of our curves behaves well in comparison to those of our peers, thanks in part to some elements of flexibility which are part of our issuance strategy (market-driven approach).	The slight decrease in volumes traded is a consequence of low interest rates and the ECB PSPP. Also, our primary dealers report that new regulations are diminishing their capacity of warehousing bonds, which decreases the liquidity of the market.

	Changes	Reasons
Germany	Yes, trading volumes have gone down slightly and for certain maturities the bid-ask spreads have widened.	We think two factors have driven that development: (i) the buying programme of the ECB and (ii) the regulatory environment which has influenced intermediaries` capacity for warehousing and market making respectively.
Greece	We observed wider bid-ask spreads and lower trading volumes	- Bailout fiscal adjustment program since 2010 - No access in capital markets - Low level credit rating CCC
Hungary	In 2008-09 and in 2012-13 there were longer periods of low liquidity, wide spreads. In between and after, liquidity conditions normalized. The maximum bid-ask spreads of the mandatory price quotation have been stable, but have gradually decreased since 2009. There was a small tightening in 2013 as well as in August 2016. Currently the maximum bid-ask spread is 20 bps (in terms of yield) for benchmark lines and 25 bps for non-benchmark lines. On the Over-the-counter (OTC) market primary dealers and other market participants (including end-investors) usually quote even tighter spreads among each other (typically 5-10 bps). According to the statistics secondary market turnover declined significantly in the second half of 2015, but we would like to see data from longer periods to draw conclusions.	• The global credit crisis in 2008-09. • The gradual downgrading of Hungary's credit rating from 2006 until reaching the below-investment-grade category in the end of 2011. • European debt crisis around 2011-13. Between 2008-2011 the rules of the obligatory quoting of HUF government securities by PDs allowed smaller volumes and wider spreads than before and after. In Hungary, central bank policies had a different effect compared to most of the other Central Banks (CBs) that started QE programs: instead of asset purchases by the CB, the National Bank of Hungary's new measures supported banks' purchases of domestic government securities and this effectively increased the liquidity of the government securities market.
Iceland	Not remarkable. However the trend of the trading volume is on downward path since 2011 mainly due to reduction in refinancing need of the Treasury that transmit to the secondary market	
Ireland	Liquidity conditions have improved considerably for Irish sovereign bonds since exiting the European Union (EU)/ International Monetary Fund (IMF) Programme of financial assistance at end-2013 and a return to regular scheduled market issuance. Bid-ask spreads have tightened, particularly on the most liquid bonds. Trading volumes for 2016 are marginally lower than 2015, but still high by historical standards.	The investor base for Irish sovereign bonds has broadened as a result of improving investor sentiment towards the Irish economy along with Credit Rating Agency ratings upgrades and European Central Bank bond purchasing activity. Regular market access has increased turnover, and allowed dealers to improve bid-offer spreads. The National Treasury Management Agency (NTMA) has also assisted with liquidity by providing repos and switches for Primary Dealers when required.
Israel	We didn't experienced any change in liquidity conditions, excluding times in which global markets (equities and fixed income) were characterized with high volatility (due to various reasons: United States (US) interest rates, China, un-clarity in Europe etc.). In those time periods we could detect a drop in liquidity. We also experienced a decrease in trading volumes since the middle of 2015, in compared to the years beforehand.	There were no infrastructure developments or regulatory changes in the local market in the last two years. The drop in liquidity may be explained mainly with the uncertainty and volatile in the global markets, as so the decrease in volumes, which may also be explained with low yields environment.

	Changes	Reasons
Italy	After the peak of the euro sovereign debt crisis in 2011-12 the liquidity conditions of our sovereign bond market have significantly improved even if we did not get back to situation before the start of the international financial crisis (pre 2007). In recent years, from 2014 onwards, however, we have observed some new deterioration in the liquidity conditions of our domestic sovereign bonds. This trend has been significant on bonds with a maturity above 10 years even if in recent months some partial retracement of it has also been observed. There are a number of elements that support this finding: - wider bid-offer spreads on the long-end of our curve (beyond 10 years); - reduced daily traded volumes (as a percentage of the outstanding amounts) on Buoni del Tesoro Poliennali (BTPs), from an average of 1.3% in 2014 to 0.7% in 2016; - reduced depth of trading volumes and market response. On days characterized by some general market turbulence – i.e. not specifically related to the Italian domestic government bond market - we tend to observe some sudden widening of bid-ask spreads in all segments of the government curve, associated to reduced trading on electronic platforms, that tends to be more pronounced on long dated bonds; - increased price impact of large trades; - increased intraday price volatility.	The recent trend of the liquidity of our sovereign bond market, that seems to be shared by most of our peer countries in Europe, may have been influenced by regulation-driven changes in the behaviour of dealers and market makers in quoting and trading sovereign bonds. Indeed the new European regulatory framework on financial intermediaries and markets seems to have changed quite significantly the economics of market making activity with strong repercussions on the underlying liquidity of bonds. Due to new capital requirements, for instance, the cost related to bond risk warehousing has risen under different perspectives, reducing de facto their capacity to quote and then trade at tight levels. This trend has brought in some cases dealers to change their business model or, in some other cases, to put in place strategies aimed at increasing the profitability of market making that in most of the cases have resulted in some reduction of the liquidity of bonds on the secondary market. This phenomenon is taking place at the same time when an ongoing change in the nature of market participants is also unfolding, which is bringing additional potential imbalances. Indeed in these last years we have been witnessing a process of reduction in the number of international and global fund managers and a parallel increase in the asset size under their control. These investors tend now to address dealers for much larger volume transactions on average, something that has to be matched with the above mentioned decreasing capability of market makers to provide that service and to act as shock absorbers in case of volatility. These general trends may help explain the evolution of liquidity conditions in the last couple of years.
Japan	Bid-ask spread and trading volumes do not present consistent patterns, and it is difficult for us to answer clearly in terms of these indices. However, some JGB market participants voiced concerns on the decline in the liquidity in the JGB secondary market in the context of the Bank of Japan's (BOJ's) monetary policy from April 2013.	It is difficult for us to answer clearly because the quantity in each trading would be influenced largely by market circumstances, investor type and their behaviour.
Korea	Spread in 10-year KTB benchmark(bp) : '12: 2.1, '13: 2.7, '14: 1.9, '15: 2.0, '16.6: 1.6 Trading volumes in 10-year KTB benchmark(USD bil) : '12: 2.1, '13: 2.9, '14: 2.4, '15: 2.0, '16.6: 1.9 There has not been a big change in recent times.	While preferences for safe assets have become stronger amid global uncertainties (ex. Brexit), the recent upgrade in Korea's credit rating, expectations of monetary easing by BOK, Korea's sound fiscal position, and etc. have led to increase in demand for KTBs.
Latvia	We have observed tightening of bid-ask spreads during the last year. Traded volumes have not changed considerably and neither have trade counterparties. Some new investors from other EU countries have been observed, however with limited amounts only. In general liquidity conditions have not changed, except the tightening of spreads mentioned above.	The implementation of primary dealer system has improved the situation – secondary market is more transparent, competition in primary auctions has increased, investors from new EU regions have appeared. However, there is still very low liquidity in secondary market. The tightening of spreads is caused mainly by central bank's (ECB and Bank of Latvia) policy of quantitative easing and Public Sector Purchase Programme (PSPP).

	Changes	Reasons
Luxembourg	No.	
Mexico	No, generally speaking, steadiness in both bid-ask spreads and trading volumes has been supported by the solid performance of Market Makers in the secondary market of government securities and the efforts of the Mexican financial authorities to widen its already broad investor base. Nevertheless, since 2013 there are signs of declining depth and immediacy in the sovereign debt market, as characterized by falling transaction sizes.	Not applicable
Netherlands	For the 10-year benchmark bonds, bid/ask spreads are stable. But for the long-term maturities, we have observed higher volatility in terms of occasional wide bid-ask spread recent years. We observe a slight decrease in secondary market volume. Interdealer turnover has decreased stronger than customer volume. Average ticket sizes have been stable over the past few years.	Anticipation of QE (Q1-2015) and absorption by QE (FromQ2-2015), negative yield environment could be the possible reasons for decline of relative turnover Less issuance due to low funding need. (Monthly turnover volatility can to a large extend be explained by gross new issuance per month.)
New Zealand	A small, but noticeable, impact on liquidity in recent years. Some indicators below: • The size of the market has tripled since pre-GFC, allowing greater number of maturities, reintroduction of inflation-indexed bonds, larger programmes and an extension of the yield curve – all of these developments have led to increased turnover. • Turnover as a percentage of bonds outstanding has remained reasonably steady over this time, but lifted slightly over the past years. • Bid-ask spreads are at the low-end of the 10-year range at ~4bp across all products • Average trade size is slightly higher now than pre-GFC.	We have noticed a change in investor behaviour when executing orders to work with intermediaries rather than asking for multiple prices. Seemingly, this is in recognition of intermediaries' ability to manage flow. In addition, we are seeing successful intermediaries enhancing their ability to broker, rather than warehouse, flow.
Norway	Total trading volumes have increased in the last four years (since 2012). The turnover ratio (turnover relative to outstanding volume of bonds) has been fairly stable.	
Poland	Since 2011 the liquidity of the secondary market for domestic T-bonds (calculated as a ratio of an average value of transactions to average amount outstanding) remained in quite stable range. The notable exception appeared in 2014 when the measure increased to 190.6% from 172.5% in 2013 which was connected to the pension system reform - reduction of Treasury securities outstanding (over PLN 130bn of T-bonds previously held by open pension funds was cancelled) with a slight decrease in the value of transactions at the same time. Since 2009 the value of transactions on the repo market (including both repo and buy/sell/back transactions) was continuously increasing. An average monthly transaction amounted to PLN 260bn in 2009, when in 2014 it was above 2.5 times higher (PLN 674.2bn). In 2015 the value of	

	Changes	Reasons
	transactions dropped by approx. 6% to PLN 635.4bn. The liquidity on the outright market was smaller and since 2010 it was constantly decreasing. In 2015 the average monthly value of transactions on the outright market constituted ca. 30% of the appropriate value on the repo market and amounted to PLN 197.2bn. Due to the changes introduced to the criteria of evaluation of applicants to the PD role – especially introduction of quality quotation index (algorithm comprising spread, volume and quoting time for particular TSs, all referred to appropriate reference values) bid-ask spreads narrowed significantly. The applicants are enhanced to quote tight spreads which are translated into higher scores. In 4Q 2011 minimum spreads constituted on average 23% of the maximum bid/offer spreads allowed by electronic trading platform rules. Due to the market situation (investor sentiment, turmoil on financial markets connected with Greek crisis in 2015) the difference increased in the past years to 31% in 2015 and 32% in 2Q 2016.	
Portugal	Trading volumes (i.e. transactions in electronic platforms and data received from the Harmonised reporting format (HRF) reports) in the first semester of 2016 has decreased when compared to the year of 2015. Regarding the bid-ask spreads we have not experienced a widening of this measurement in the past few months. Given Portugal's specifics, we have seen bid-ask spreads decreasing since 2012, and they have now stabilized at pre-crisis levels.	We believe that the percentage of Bonds held by foreigners has been decreasing since PSPP implementation, the same for Bonds held by domestics, which might explain part of the decrease in liquidity of our Bonds. The increase in volatility that has characterized our market for the past year, in part due to the new market technicalities such as the importance of the PSPP presence in the market and new regulation imposed on Banks, which has diminished the capacity for PDs to act as a buffer in volatile periods, among other factors, has created some constraints in the willingness of our investor base in holding Portuguese Bonds. We believe that investors are now more careful about the timing of trading decisions and that has diminished liquidity.
Slovak Republic	Liquidity of our secondary market is still poor with wide bid-ask spreads. During the crisis years (2011-2012) it was even worse, as all banks wanted to sell all bonds and there was no buyer at the market. We estimate the liquidity is now at the pre-crisis levels.	We have changed our issuance strategy since 2011 in favour of foreign investors. Since the year we issued bonds denominated in CZK, CHF, USD, JPY, NOK to diversify our investor base. It was visible the foreign issuances also contributed to increase of demand in domestic bond auctions. In some years we increased the share of foreign investors to 70% - it decreased now to 55% as some issuances were redeemed. Quantitative easing of ECB is present and it strongly influenced our yields (decrease) and also demand in our auctions, as ECB was buying more than we regularly sold via bond auctions. At the moment we don't have suitable tool for the monitoring of the secondary market – we consider to implement from 2017 MTS together with the Bloomberg E-bond platform, which could enhance the liquidity.

	Changes	Reasons
Slovenia	In most distressed year in recent Slovenia history, that is 2013, we observed significantly reduced liquidity as a consequence of widened bid-ask spread, illustrated below. Since 2014 bid-ask spread has been tightening and liquidity has been significantly improved. Correspondingly to bid-ask, we can observe lower trading volumes in 2013. In past two years trading volumes increased.	In our view, the biggest impact on liquidity is due to new regulatory requirements, namely the Capital Requirements Directive IV / Capital Requirements Regulation (CRD IV/CRR) requirements associated with market making, but also other regulation adopted in this area. Pre- and post-trade transparency requirements under The Markets in Financial Instruments Regulation (MiFIR) are also likely to affect these markets. It appears that overall, regulatory requirements are having a cost on all markets and market participants including primary and, secondary sovereign debt markets as well as repo markets, with the attendant risk of possible rising cost to government funding. We have not detected any other relevant changes in the categories listed in your question (changes in investor base, investor sentiment, etc.).
Spain	Although spreads have remained stable over the past year, trading volumes are showing a declining trend.	Volatility, low interest rates and the cost of regulation (with the subsequent balance sheet constraints) are the most commonly cited reasons for the declining turnover.
Switzerland	According to market participants liquidity has diminished throughout the last years, particularly in long running bonds. Although we didn't profoundly analyse liquidity conditions (in contrast to market makers), from our point of view trading volumes seem to remain rather constant, while bid-ask spreads have slightly increased in recent years.	As outlined above, increasing shares of foreign investors may reduce market liquidity. Furthermore regulations such as Basel III (e.g. Liquidity Coverage Ratio - LCR) or Swiss Solvency Test (SST) and reduced risk appetite of bank's trading desk are supposed to have had negative impacts on liquidity.
Turkey	In Borsa Istanbul, average daily trading volume of Government Domestic Debt Securities in the Debt Securities Market was TRY 1.3 billion in 2014 and TRY 1 billion in 2015. Thanks to measures imposed, it increased to TRY 1.5 billion in first half of 2016.	The reasons of decline in secondary market liquidity in 2014 and 2015 would be classified as global factors, such as volatility and uncertainties arise from monetary policies of central banks, and country specific factors for Turkey, such as (i) increased share of public funds and (buy-and-hold investors) in total domestic debt, (ii) decrease in supply of government bonds due to recent decline in borrowing requirement. The regular buyback auctions introduced in March, 2016 positively affected the secondary market liquidity. Also, our credit rating remained at investment grade. In order to diversify investor base (buy-and-hold vs trader) and to encourage secondary market trading, we increase total amount of securities by re-openings. We have changed the primary dealership obligations by decreasing the maximum spread between bid and offer rates of benchmark securities, the maximum spread between bid and offer quotations were 50 Kurus. However, in the new Primary Dealership contract of year 2016, the maximum spread between bid and offer rates differentiated according to maturities of benchmark securities.

	Changes	Reasons
United Kingdom	Data from an electronic platform suggest that bid-ask spreads for some of the UK's most liquid benchmarks (e.g. 10-year and 30-year gilts) have largely remained stable in recent years and, therefore, have not been indicative of reduced liquidity. Secondary market trading volumes in conventional gilts (as reported by primary dealers) have declined slightly in the past two years, but nonetheless have remained at relatively high levels. Index-linked gilts' turnover has followed an upward trajectory for the most part over the last 5 years, a trend that is still being observed currently. However, liquidity conditions in the gilt market are reported to have worsened over the last twelve months or so. Primary dealers are experiencing cutbacks in balance sheet capacity and risk appetite, which is also reported to have had a negative impact on the secondary market in gilts, and has led to a greater propensity to hedge immediately.	Regulatory impact on the banks' balance sheets (in particular as a result of the leverage ratio), the Bank of England's expansion of the asset purchase scheme for gilts and innovations in financial technologies (such as in the field of electronic trading) are among the factors that have been reported to have impacted gilt market liquidity. In particular, and with regards to the impact of new regulations, it has been reported that primary dealers in the gilt market are under increasing pressure in terms of balance sheet constraints and in their role as intermediaries between issuer and investors. With exception of the immediate aftermath, we have not yet noticed any changes in the long-term liquidity of the gilt market directly attributable to the result of the 23 June EU referendum. However, we are yet to assess the full impact and we are closely monitoring ongoing developments.
United States	No, current liquidity conditions are consistent with historical levels. See: "A Deeper Look at Liquidity Conditions in the Treasury Market" by James Clark and Gabriel Mann (https://www.treasury.gov/connect/blog/Pages/A-Deeper-Look-at-Liquidity-Conditions-in-the-Treasury-Market.aspx)	Not applicable.

Have you observed changes in liquidity conditions of your foreign bonds (if any) in recent years? Please explain.

Australia	Not applicable. We only issue in Australian dollars.
Austria	Foreign currency bonds continue to trade at similar or slightly wider bid/ask spreads compared to domestic currency bonds but indicated and traded volumes are lower.
Belgium	Liquidity in our foreign currency issues under Euro Medium Term Note (EMTN) documentation, has always been relatively limited. We have no indications of changes.
Canada	Canada issues foreign global bonds denominated in both USD and in Euros. Regarding foreign bonds issued in USD, these are typically issued to buy and hold investors, and hence are not actively traded instruments. When investors want to sell, they are often able to find dealers who are willing to make markets for these bonds. Foreign USD bonds are typically issued through a syndication process. To be considered for the syndicate, dealers must meet eligibility criteria including the provision of market-making services for these Foreign USD bonds. There has not been a large change in the past year in terms of liquidity for these instruments. Over the last few years, bid-ask spreads have generally widened, and dealers are less willing to warehouse excess inventory due to balance sheet constraints. In the case of Euro denominated issuances, it has become more challenging to find pockets of liquidity during the past few years. Increasingly, dealers have begun to price defensively on bonds that don't fit in with their asset portfolio mixes or target holdings. There has also been an increase in crowded trades and herding behaviour as dealer positions have become more similar. Oftentimes, the market tends to trade in the same direction, as the underlying factors driving dealer behaviour reflect similar macroeconomic and technical factors. Euro and USD medium-term notes are also issued through a private placement process. There have not been any observed changes in the liquidity of these instruments.
Chile	No.
Czech Republic	No. The foreign bond market is very small; and more over the last foreign issuance was carried out in year 2012.
Denmark	No. We have not been active in foreign funding in recent years.
Finland	Not really, outstanding foreign denominated bonds are smaller than euro benchmarks and therefore liquid secondary market doesn't exist.
France	The French state does not issue foreign currency bonds.
Germany	-
Greece	Due to Private Sector Involvement (PSI) outstanding amounts of foreign bonds have been significantly reduced.
Hungary	No, these bonds are rather illiquid.
Iceland	No.
Ireland	Not applicable.
Israel	In general we have seen a pickup in the liquidity in our secondary bonds this year, especially after our sovereign issuance in March. In general we see approx. USD 50M in liquidity per month, but in march we saw nearly double that in the one month alone. This might be due to the fact that we didn't issue in the USD market in 3 years, and with the issuance it might have spurred more interest in our bonds.
Italy	We have not been placing foreign bonds through public offerings since more than five years, therefore liquidity in this sector is minimal and limited to the occasional execution of small tickets. In recent years we have been more active through private placements, for which by definition there is no real secondary market.

Japan	Not applicable.
Korea	No changes observed.
Latvia	After ECB introduced PSPP, we have observed international bond (denominated in EUR) credit spread tightening and limited responsiveness to market tendencies as the main indicators which signalled liquidity drop in the market. Also available information about ticket sizes in Bloomberg and received irregular trading volume data from market participants indicates general liquidity decrease. With regard to international bonds denominated in USD by liability management transaction – buyback tender offer ensured sufficient liquidity for existing USD bondholders and ultimately total outstanding amount was reduced. Two lines of three existing were influenced by the issuer and refinanced by a new EUR line. The market liquidity was decreased by 37% in total for both lines in foreign currency and increased by the same amount for domestic currency – EUR.
Luxembourg	Not applicable.
Mexico	Yes. Based on constant discussions held with market participants, including institutional investors, traders and others, over the last years there has been an increasing demand for Mexico's international bonds that has had a positive impact on trading and liquidity. Besides the strong macro fundamentals compared to our peers, one of the reasons that outstands when discussing this increase in demand is that most of Mexico's international bonds are eligible for Emerging Market (EM) and Latam debt indices (based on size, tenor, rating, etc.), which have also been growing and expanding over the last years.
Netherlands	No.
New Zealand	Not applicable.
Norway	Not relevant.
Poland	Not measured.
Portugal	We have only one foreign bond that is actively traded in the market, and we haven't experienced any relevant change in the liquidity of this bond.
Slovak Republic	No changes observed, as our foreign bonds are mainly kept by real money investors.
Slovenia	We haven't observed any relevant changes in liquidity conditions in foreign (US$) since 2012, most likely due coupon levels as well as investor structure which is rather coined as 'hold to maturity'. However, in May 2016 Republic of Slovenia executed US$ bonds buyback transaction for the part of its US$ debt portfolio. This is how Republic contributed to enhancement of liquidity for the US$ bonds with cash prices above 110% and at the same time profit in positive net present value economics and duration extension.
Spain	No remarkable trend observed. Foreign bonds account for 0,31% of our debt portfolio.
Switzerland	No foreign currency bonds.
Turkey	The secondary market liquidity of our foreign bonds is not something we can directly keep track of. However, our regular communication with the investors and the investment banks suggests that the liquidity conditions have continued to remain healthy in recent years. As a frequent issuer, we have a well-diversified and liquid curve for our foreign bonds and we haven't seen a significant deviation in bid-ask spreads either.
United Kingdom	Sample size too small. Given the very small size and the currency of the sole foreign bond issue, the bond was not expected to be liquid.
United States	Not applicable. The U.S. Treasury does not issue foreign currency bonds.

Have you observed changes in liquidity conditions of bond derivate and repo markets in recent years? Please explain.

Australia	Liquidity in the Treasury Bond futures market remains robust. The three and 10-year Treasury Bond futures contracts are highly liquid: they are the ninth and eleventh most traded long term interest rate futures products in the world, respectively. Turnover in the 20-year contract (launched in September 2015) is considerably lower. Liquidity in the repo market deteriorated to some degree in recent years. Repo rates have increased relative to Overnight Indexed Swap (OIS) and repo funding is less easily available to some parties
Austria	-
Belgium	We have indications that volumes in the OLO repo market have dropped even more than the volumes on the secondary outright market since pre-crisis times. Even though the phenomenon is still limited we start seeing some bonds becoming special, whereas this was absolutely not the case before.
Canada	Liquidity varies across term types. When comparing different term to maturities, liquidity has often been the highest in the 10-year sector. Furthermore, in the 10-year sector, bond futures at times have been more liquid than the cash market. Liquidity in the futures market for the 2–year and 5-year sectors has improved, although trading volumes are lower than those observed in the 10-year sector. Overall, Repo markets have been functioning well with good levels of liquidity. However, there has been some evidence of repo tightness as a result of lower interest rates across the globe and increased regulatory pressure on dealers' balance sheets. In the past, we had observed regular repo market tightness in certain benchmark and non-benchmark Government of Canada bonds with 3 to 10 years remaining to maturity. A recent change in investor demand resulted in the release of certain domestic sovereign bonds into the market. The release of this inventory helped to alleviate some of the tightness in the repo market particularly in the 5-year and 10-year sectors of the curve.
Chile	No. In special, the repo market is not well developed, so is difficult to observe important changes in liquidity.
Czech Republic	There is no bond derivatives market in Czech Republic. Repo market is relatively limited due to significant excess of liquidity in Czech banking system, mostly motivated and concentrated to cover short trading position than to use it as money market instrument. Decrease of activity is in line with change of liquidity on bond market.
Denmark	We are not active in the repo markets (we have our own securities lending facility, but that is slightly different). We have only recently begun trading interest rate swaps again. Our observations are hence limited.
Finland	We have observed that the liquidity in bond repo markets has decreased in recent years, however the State Treasury is not actively participating in the repo market.
France	Repo market volume as reported by our primary dealers has remained stable (these reported volumes are unaudited and only track transactions under French legislation). Future market volume on the main future instrument (long-term Obligations Assimilables du Trésor (OAT)) has slightly increased, in absolute terms as well as relative to the volume traded on the German Bund future.
Germany	The statement given above for the security market applies as well for the repo market. For the swap market one has to differentiate – for single sided collateral agreements liquidity has gone done significantly whereas for centrally cleared swaps we don't see a negative shift.
Greece	Post PSI era- No liquid Greek Government Securities that could allow the existence of a bond derivative and repo market.
Hungary	Bond derivatives are practically non-traded in Hungary. Repo activity with ÁKK (Hungarian Debt Management Agency) has increased in recent years, ÁKK supported this by higher trading limits and counterparty limits.

Iceland	No. There has not been an active derivative or repo market for bonds.
Ireland	Repo market liquidity has improved in recent years in response to Ireland's return to regular scheduled market issuance.
Israel	In the recent years, the liquidity conditions of bond derivate were pretty good with large trading volume (after consistent incline till 2012 in volume). In the last 6 months we experience a decline in liquidity - mainly because of the historical low yield domestic and worldwide. The repo market in Israel is yet to be developed.
Italy	In the case of the Italian repo market with sovereign bonds as collateral, we do not observe significant changes in liquidity conditions. The repo market has continued to play a fundamental role in contributing to the orderly execution of market-making activity in the cash market. Even though the repo market has been - and will be - impacted by the introduction of several pieces of European legislation on the supervision of intermediaries and the functioning of financial markets, activity has remained buoyant also by market makers.
Japan	It is difficult for us to answer clearly because the quantity in each trading would be influenced largely by market circumstance, investor type and their behaviour, but the trading volume of 10-Year JGB futures decreased after the introduction of Quantitative and Qualitative Monetary Easing in April 2013. The volume of repurchase transactions has recently increased compared with that in 2012 and 2013.
Korea	No changes observed
Latvia	The secondary market is rather illiquid regardless of its setup and currently there is no active derivate or repo market in Latvia. This is first and foremost due to the limited liquidity in the outstanding amount of the securities.
Luxembourg	Not applicable.
Mexico	No, liquidity conditions regarding bond derivative market have remained stagnant for the past years since demand for this type of derivatives is still low. On the other hand, liquidity in the repo market has been picking up since the 2008 financial crisis, in terms of total volume.
Netherlands	Volumes in the repo market have declined.
New Zealand	Futures market in New Zealand (NZ) has not been a key part of the market for decades. Recently, a working group of key market players (including New Zealand Debt Management Office (NZDMO)) has met in order to identify challenges and opportunities within this market. Turnover in the repo market has improved in line with outstanding and is at the lower end of the range as a proportion of bonds on issue.
Norway	Repo trading in government bonds has increased in the last four years (Oslo Børs/Oslo Stock Exchange).
Poland	Bond derivative market is of a very poor liquidity. Turnover on bond futures market (based on data from WSE – Warsaw Stock Exchange) in 2015 amounted to PLN 65.3 mn what constituted 0.0003% of turnover on secondary bond market (in first half of 2016 it was PLN 6.5 mn and 0.0001% respectively). After financial crisis of 2009 the value of transactions on sovereign bond repo market (including repo and buy/sell/back transactions) was continuously increasing. In 2015 the average monthly value of transactions dropped slightly by 6%.
Portugal	Since the regaining of market access, we have observed a growing liquidity in the repo market. Nonetheless our market is still small, having a great room to improve in the future.
Slovak Republic	Not available, as Slovak REPO market is not well functioning. Still some legislation obstacles together with depositary problems with Delivery Versus Payment (DVP).
Slovenia	Republic of Slovenia has not pursued any of such instruments in recent years.

Spain	Significant decrease in repo turnover of Bonos & Obligaciones between 214 and 2015. 2016 year to date is showing a decrease as well.
Switzerland	We do have a bond future market (CONF Futures), however due to the lack of involvement in this market we aren't aware of changes in liquidity conditions. In general turnover on repo markets dropped after 2008 as a consequence of liquidity oversupply. With the introduction of negative interest rates by the Swiss National Bank (SNB) in 2015 turnover rose again, as participants are now trading their exemption thresholds on SNB sight deposit accounts. The share of repo transactions which were collateralized with bonds of the Swiss Confederation did not change significantly. This although the introduction of new regulations such as Basel III (i.e. LCR) or SST and enhanced trading of collateral (instead of liquidity) via repo market.
Turkey	As data provided by Borsa Istanbul, it can be seen that total average daily trade volume of all kinds of REPO markets under Borsa İstanbul was TRY 18.3 million in 2014 and increased to TRY 29.6 million in 2015. With the further increase, this indicator rose to TRY 42.8 million in the first half of 2016. We have no data on the liquidity conditions of bond derivative markets.
United Kingdom	Evidence (anecdotal and from the Debt Management Office's (DMO's) cash management unit) suggests that liquidity in the repo market has deteriorated markedly in recent years, particularly over the last year and in term trading. The total gilt repo amount outstanding has declined and average trade sizes in this market have fallen. The range of participants in the market has declined as banks have become more unwilling to take on positions. This has, in turn, resulted in wider bid/offer spreads. Liquidity conditions are reported to be much worse at longer maturities and the cost of term repo has increased over time, although volumes and liquidity in overnight markets have held up/increased as traded flows gravitate towards shorter maturities. The UK DMO is not a significant participant in derivatives markets; however, market counterparties have noted decreasing liquidity and increasing volatility in these markets.
United States	No, the U.S. Treasury repo market continues to function well. See: "Examining Changes in the Treasury Repo Market after the Financial Crisis" by James Clark and Tom Katzenbach (https://www.treasury.gov/connect/blog/Pages/Examining-Changes-in-the-Treasury-Repo-Market-after-the-Financial-Crisis.aspx)

Do you regularly attempt to measure liquidity? How? Which metrics do you use?

Australia

One of our key performance indicators is the turnover ratio: Annual turnover in the secondary market of Treasury Bonds and Treasury Indexed Bonds as a proportion of the average volume of stock on issue.

Another metric is the amount of usage of our securities lending facility (discussed under question 11).

We are going to conduct regular surveys of market makers about their trading activities, but this is yet to commence.

Austria

Liquidity is measured and monitored on a daily basis. Real-time and near-real-time data is used for this assessment. Most prominent metrics are: bid/offer spread; bid/offer sizes; quotation time; turnover. Data from a variety of different platforms is used and aggregated within a scoring system.

Belgium

Yes, we monitor secondary market volumes and bid-ask spreads on a daily basis. Furthermore, we follow a number of metrics on a monthly basis. These are indicators that we have tried to standardize at European level in a workgroup of the European Sovereign Debt Markets (ESDM).

These metrics track:

- Secondary market volumes
- Daily average volumes and distribution of these volumes
- Activity of different investor types
- Bid-Ask Spreads
- Average ticket sizes and numbers of tickets
- Information on the volumes and spreads in the orderbooks on electronic trading platforms

Canada

We have been developing a well-functioning markets liquidity dashboard to track and review liquidity metrics. The dashboard is updated on a monthly basis.

We use multiple secondary market data sources (including micro-trade data), to update and maintain the liquidity dashboard each month. Liquidity metrics are tracked and maintained for the cash market, repo market, futures and spreads market.

For the cash market the following four key metrics are tracked:

- GoC bond bid-ask spread and price impact
- GoC price dispersion
- Trading volume of GoC bonds
- Median trade size of GoC bonds

For the repo market the following four key metrics are tracked:

- Weighted average O/N repo rate for GoC bonds
- Daily number of GoC bond ISINs on special
- Settlement fail volumes in GoC bonds
- Daily Bank of Canada securities lending volume

For the futures and spreads market the following three key metrics are tracked:

- Overall provincials spread and price impact
- Overall corporates spread and price impact
- Trading volume and open interest of GoC bond futures

On a regular basis, we hold consultations with dealers and other market participants in order to assess the liquidity conditions observed in the market.

Chile

Liquidity is measured on an ad hoc basis. It has been especially monitored during the last year, due to the implementation of a liability management program.

The metric used is the percentage of rotation of papers of the Stock (transactions in US$mm/Stock in US$mm).

Czech Republic	This is exclusively agenda of MoF. Czech National Bank only monitors trading volumes, bid/ask spreads and swap spreads, in order to monitor financial markets performance.
Denmark	Yes. We continuously monitor bid-ask spreads and trading volumes on the inter-dealer market (MTS), and monitor trading volumes on a variety of trading platforms, incl. OTC trading based on reports from Nasdaq OMX and the Financial Supervisory Authority (FSA). On a regular basis and using data encompassing all Danish government bond trades we estimate price tightness (using Roll's measure of the effective bid-ask spread), the price impact of transactions (Amihud) and look at indicators for price resilience, e.g. by comparing trading volumes and the number of trades. In addition, but less frequently, we evaluate the variation the applied current liquidity measures (e.g. price tightness and depth).
Finland	Bid-ask spreads in interdealer market making platforms, volumes in secondary market trading.
France	We monitor liquidity on a regular basis, using various metrics related mainly to volumes traded on the secondary market. We also use bid-ask spreads on interdealer electronic platforms. We also assess liquidity qualitatively using the feedback of our primary dealers and our investor base.
Germany	We have a good sense for the liquidity in our own market because we are an active participant in the repo and in the cash market. We look at the development of bid-as spreads on a quarterly basis in order to measure liquidity.
Greece	Bid –offer spreads Volumes in secondary markets
Hungary	Weekly and monthly trading volumes via HRF reporting from PDs. Daily bid-ask spreads via primary dealers' obligatory quoting.
Iceland	We use bond turnover (trading volume divided by outstanding debt) with information received from the stock exchange.
Ireland	Liquidity is measured in terms of daily monitoring of turnover, bid-ask spreads and through discussion with Primary Dealers of Irish sovereign bonds. Further assessments of liquidity include monthly compliance analysis of Primary Dealers in terms of their daily price quoting activity. Ireland is also involved with an EU Sovereign Debt Markets (ESDM) working group, which analyses various liquidity metrics on a quarterly basis.
Israel	No (but currently being examined and should be implemented by the end of the year). Mainly we observe the bid-ask spreads and monitor the trading volumes.
Italy	Yes, we do. Given the extreme difficulty of the identification of a single metric able to capture all the different aspects of liquidity, we tend to use several of them as follows: 1. bid-offer spreads on different points of our nominal and inflation curves; 2. daily and monthly volumes traded on MTS and on all other electronic platforms; 3. monthly volumes traded outside electronic markets; 4. daily and monthly depth (defined as the overall volumes for any price quoted, that is, how much a market maker could buy or sell at any given moment) on MTS; 5. average trading ticket size on electronic markets and outside; 6. slope (aimed at gauging the price impact of an hypothetic large size contract exchanged on the interdealer electronic market, that a market participant must accept in order for the trade to actually take place at any given moment); 7. statistics on the geographical distribution and types of investors involved on trading activity; 8. analysis of the specialness of the bonds in the repo market. Occasionally we may use additional metrics to analyse specific aspects of liquidity.
Japan	Yes we do. We watch bid-ask spread, trading volumes, historical price volatility, daily price range to turnover ratio and results of surveys of bond markets by the BOJ as a reference.

Korea	We receive necessary data from the Exchanges when needed, and also obtain data we need from data systems (Yonhap Infomax, Bloomberg terminal, etc).
Latvia	The liquidity in domestic market can be evaluated based on reporting provided by primary dealers in EU-wide harmonized reporting format (HRF). Bid-ask spreads and offered amounts can be derived from Bloomberg quoted for the respective securities, provided by primary dealers. With regard to bonds issued on international markets, the liquidity is not measured on regular basis by specific metrics, the analysis is more based on received indicative information and market data on Bloomberg.
Luxembourg	No.
Mexico	Yes, sovereign debt liquidity is a major concern to both the Ministry of Finance and the Central Bank. Therefore, such liquidity is constantly measured by trading volume or turnover ratios and bid-ask spreads.
Netherlands	Yes. We use bid-ask spread, changes in secondary volumes, and average block-size.
New Zealand	Liquidity is among the most important variables NZDMO monitor and there are a number of partial metrics we use to monitor liquidity, including those mentioned above. More qualitatively, we find regular discussions with market players helps us establish whether liquidity is improving or deteriorating from year to year.
Norway	Yes - Bid-ask spreads - Turnover and turnover ratio
Poland	These are: • ratio of an average value of transactions to average amount outstanding (monthly, daily), • quality quotation index (spread, volume, quoting time; daily), • bid-ask spread of the benchmark bonds (daily), • daily reports on market depth (market snapshot available every second of 5 best bid-ask prices and their volumes), • weekly Treasury Securities Dealers (TSD) Liquidity questionnaires on the T-bonds (where we ask for opinion of TS Dealers and applicants on a maximum amount of a single sale transaction possible to be executed that will not impact the bond price and, on the other hand, impact of a given significant amount of transaction to the price), • additionally: daily reports on secondary market trading on the electronic market (traded volumes, transactions).
Portugal	We keep records of the volumes traded in the electronic platforms and the data from the HRF reports. We also monitor bid-ask spreads.
Slovak Republic	At the moment we receive monthly only report from our PDs – HRF (harmonized report for EU) and use the same tool (access based tool invented by the Belgian Agency) as other members of the Eurozone.
Slovenia	For the purpose of measuring liquidity we observe bid-ask spreads (implying indication level of transaction costs and viability of execution itself) and trading volumes of our bonds on MTS Slovenia and on other secondary market on an inter-daily and daily basis.
Spain	- Bid/offer spreads - Turnover
Switzerland	Currently there's no regular and profound analysis on liquidity conditions. We only evaluate daily turnover in our bonds on a monthly basis and receive quarterly on- and off-market evaluations (turnover, pricing) from Swiss exchange (SIX).

Turkey	We monitor daily trading volumes of the Debt Instruments Market under Borsa Istanbul. Moreover, we inspect monthly trading volumes of the Debt Securities Market under Borsa Istanbul and Over-the Counter Markets. For measuring daily trading volumes in Debt Securities Market, we use trading platform of Borsa Istanbul. For monthly volume figures, we get the monthly transaction data for both Debt Securities Market and Over-the Counter Markets from Borsa Istanbul. We make analysis and comparisons for each type of markets and prepare secondary market report for internal purposes. On the other hand, we evaluate the bid-ask spreads of benchmark securities. We also observe the liquidity providers; net sellers, net buyers and the investors made highest transactions in volume in trading bonds. Lastly, we monitor the secondary market obligation for the Primary Dealers to give quotations daily.
United Kingdom	In assessing liquidity, the UK DMO monitors market data (such as bid-offer spreads and transaction volumes) as well as weekly turnover data as reported by primary dealers. The UK DMO also takes into account qualitative indicators, such as feedback received from primary dealers, investors and other market participants.
United States	Yes. Metrics considered include: average daily trading volumes, bid/ask spread, average trade size, price impact of trades, market depth, etc. See: "A Deeper Look at Liquidity Conditions in the Treasury Market" by James Clark and Gabriel Mann (https://www.treasury.gov/connect/blog/Pages/A-Deeper-Look-at-Liquidity-Conditions-in-the-Treasury-Market.aspx)

What measures (if any) do you have in place to motivate dealers to provide liquidity? Please explain which measures are the most effective according to your experience.

Australia	We do not have any such measures in place.
Austria	According the General Primary Dealer Agreement, primary dealers have to take care of the market for all RAGB during trading hours. The bid/offer spread needs to be reasonable and bid/offer sizes shall allow for bigger tickets, too. The secondary market performance of primary dealers is monitored and part of the overall primary dealer performance ranking.
Belgium	Providing liquidity through market making is one of the criteria in the global evaluation of the primary dealers, next to successful bidding at the auction, distribution of bonds with investors and some qualitative items. Moreover a direct incentive for the traders with regard to market making is provided in the form of special non-competitive subscriptions at the auctions. A ranking is made with regard to the quoting performance and volumes traded on the selected e-platforms. The 5 best primary dealers are entitled to the special non-competitive subscriptions at the weighted average price of the auction one week after the competitive part of the auction.
Canada	The dealer model used in Canada creates incentives for dealers to provide liquidity to the market. To participate as a dealer in the Government of Canada primary market, entities must meet specific criteria: • Dealers must maintain certain levels of domestic fixed-income trading activity • Dealers must demonstrate adequate levels of participation at auctions Once an entity has obtained dealer status, it benefits by having direct access to the primary market. Other benefits may include: increased visibility and recognition, along with the potential to attract more clients for its business. Furthermore, in the past few years, the Government of Canada has given its top four primary dealers (based on trading behaviour), the opportunity to syndicate its 50-year bond issuance. This syndication opportunity is one type of incentivized action that the Government may take to motivate the dealers to continue their efforts in providing liquidity to the market. Government securities distributor's (GSD) dealers are encouraged to provide liquidity. Bidding limits for Government of Canada bond and treasury bill auctions are calculated based on the government securities distributor's (GSD) trading activity in primary and secondary markets. GSD may be designated with a primary dealer (PD) status when its calculated bidding limit reaches a threshold level of 10% based on its primary and secondary market share, and buyback activity. GSD must also provide evidence of sufficient resources and the desire to participate actively in the market-making activity of Government of Canada securities to the satisfaction of the Department of Finance and the Bank of Canada in order to achieve their PD status. The Government of Canada employs an open and collaborative approach for its debt management function. Actions such as engaging in market consultations and also incorporating dealer feedback into the decision-making process have been effective. This approach has helped to ensure well-functioning markets and favourable conditions for market liquidity in both the primary and secondary Government of Canada securities markets. Being transparent in the communication strategy with dealers has also been effective in terms of motivating dealers to provide liquidity to the market. Two examples of our transparency in communication with financial market participants are: • Publication of the quarterly bond schedule prior to the start of each quarter in advance of auctions • Publishing details for each operation in a call for tender a week prior to the auction
Chile	There are no market makers in this country, but it is a possibility that is being analysed. In addition, there is an agenda to include local bonds in international indices. This agenda includes the mentioned liability management program and a modification to tax collection of interest payment, which will allow the installation of Euroclear in Chile (the bill that implements these changes was already sent to the Congress and is pending approval). The final objective is to attract new participants in local markets, in special foreign investors, to increase liquidity of local securities.
Czech Republic	PDs Agreement sets number of obligations, privileges and evaluation rules of PDs with the aim to build transparent, liquid and deep market for Czech GBs. Quarterly evaluation results (ranking) of PDs are published. More information: www.mfcr.cz/en/themes/state-debt/primary-dealers/basic-information

Denmark	11 dealers have signed up to be primary dealers in Danish government bonds. At the moment we do not have any measures to reward dealers, since we no longer issue bonds via syndications. Part of the agreement, however, is a requirement for primary dealers to quote prices within a defined range and minimum volumes in the inter-dealer market, MTS. We set the terms, i.e. the compliance criteria, and may change them, if deemed necessary. To comply, primary dealers currently have to quote bid-ask spreads that are no wider than 1.25 times the average quoted spread for the whole primary dealer group. In addition, we may verbally intervene. This includes direct feedback to dealers on their current market performance and pointing to areas, where we expect improvements. We are currently assessing whether to introduce a primary dealer payment model, where primary dealers may receive a fee depending on their performance.
Finland	Weekly follow-up of the bid-ask spreads in the interdealer market platforms. Monthly secondary market customer volumes follow-up.
France	Liquidity providing is part of primary dealers obligations as per our primary dealer charter. Each primary dealer has to reach a minimum market share on the secondary market and provide executable price quotes for French bonds on interdealer electronic trading platforms with a maximum bid-offer spread. The respect of these obligations is monitored on a regular basis and is taken into account to compute the annual primary dealer ranking.
Germany	There are no specific measures or benefits in place.
Greece	Not applicable.
Hungary	• PDs are required to buy at auctions a minimum amount of Bonds and 1-year T-Bills in every calendar half-year period. • They are also required to quote two-way prices with minimum amounts and maximum spreads set. Failing to meet these requirements results in sanctions. • Best price quotation data is published together with a benchmark fixing. • ÁKK supports PDs' price quotation by a stand-by repo facility, where PDs can ask ÁKK for government securities. • In 2012 MTS Hungary was introduced and PDs' price quotation was moved to this platform. Some other functionalities of this platform can be attractive to PDs. Mid-price crossing function was introduced in August 2016 in order to generate higher trading volume on the MTS Hungary platform. • Every year the best PDs in certain categories (auction participation, secondary market share, repos with ÁKK etc.) are awarded and the first 3 in each category is published.
Iceland	The Treasury pays primary dealers a commission that is calculated as a share of all primary dealers' trade on the stock exchange. The total amount at all primary dealers' disposal is decided by the Treasury on annually basis.
Ireland	Dealers are mainly motivated to participate in the Primary Dealer system to gain access to auctions and syndications of Irish Government Bonds. Primary Dealers are required to make two-way prices in at least €5 million nominal for a minimum of five hours daily. Regular monitoring of compliance and spreads is further motivation for dealers to provide liquidity. Repos are provided on a continuous basis to Primary Dealers, while switches are provided when necessary. Both are provided on a reverse-enquiry basis.
Israel	Primary dealer are required to participate on a regular basis on both the primary market auction and the secondary market (MTS). In return they are entitled to a few benefits: 1. The Ministry of Finance earmarks at least 66% of all auctions for the primary dealers. 2. Access to the government bonds lending facility. 3. Eligibility for either 10% or 20% in the Non Competitive (Green-shoe) Auction after each auction, based on each banks weekly ranking. This ranking is based on the primary dealer's performance in the secondary market (in accordance with the Rules of Primary Dealers Ranking) In addition primary dealers may participate in hedging transactions as counterparties to the MOF, as well be nominated for participating in global issuances as underwriters. From our experience the lending facility is a very requested benefit, but it varies for each participant.

Italy	Our Evaluation Criteria of Specialists in Government Bonds provide a detailed and systematic set of parameters to measure the contribution of each market maker to trading and quoting activity, both in the cash and in the repo markets. These parameters are subject to review in the medium term, according to market conditions and public debt management objectives. Such changes are introduced when the evolution of market conditions makes some parameters less effective in motivating market makers to bring enough liquidity in the market or when the DMO updates its debt management goals (for example by changing emphasis on issuance activity from some products to others), which may require a consistent re-orientation of market makers' efforts. The Evaluation Criteria of the last decade (and even more) can be found on the Italian Treasury's Public Debt website (www.publicdebt.it).
Japan	We conduct "Auctions for Enhanced-Liquidity" to maintain and enhance the liquidity in the JGB market by additionally issuing off-the-run bonds. We also offer "Non-Price Competitive Auctions I & II" for primary dealers, which allow them to purchase the bonds auctioned at the weighted average accepted price (in a multiple-price auction) or the accepted price (in a single-price auction), up to a specified amount (Non-Price Competitive Auctions I are offered at the same time as the price competitive auction, whereas Non-Price Competitive Auctions II are carried out after the competitive auction is finished).
Korea	Primary dealers have the exclusive right to participate in the primary market and receive incentives such as non-competitive purchase options. Also, based on their performance, their designation as PDs can be suspended or cancelled if the score is below the criteria.
Latvia	The agreements between Treasury and Primary dealers require dealers to ensure the liquidity of the government debt securities market by promoting secondary trading on NASDAQ Riga (regulated market) and Bloomberg systems and by providing two-way quotes for benchmark securities. The performance of primary dealers is reviewed on regular basis. The Treasury has a right to terminate primary dealership agreement, should the particular dealer failed to meet its obligations under that agreement. Primary dealers have exclusivity in consultation process with the Treasury for the upcoming auction calendar.
Luxembourg	None
Mexico	The Ministry of Finance hasn't planned a strategy to motivate dealers directly in order to foster liquidity.
Netherlands	We have a quotation obligation for all our Primary dealers. A Primary dealer must fulfil the quotation obligations: quote within 1 standard deviation of average b/a-spread in a peer based system for 6 hours a day and for 90% of all days within one month. Another requirement is that Primary dealers have to provide monthly reports on their activities on the secondary market. And finally Primary dealers are ranked on the basis of their performance.
New Zealand	NZDMO distribute a range of opportunities (e.g., appointment to syndication panel, hosting of investor relations activities) to intermediaries based on an assessment of their performance – a key component of this assessment is the ability and track-record of providing liquidity.
Norway	- Primary dealers have exclusive right to bid at auctions for the issuance or reopenings of government bonds. - exclusive access to the repo facility.
Poland	The change introduced in October 2011 referring to quality quotation index stimulated the liquidity on the TS market. Although the measure comprises the prices from the electronic market which is small, but simultaneously it is important as it constitutes the reference for calculations for other entities to evaluate their portfolios (real-time prices available to all market participants). Appointment of PDs is based on scoring, which comprises in 40% of quality quotation index.
Portugal	We allocate 30% of the PD evaluation to liquidity related criteria: 15% to quoting criteria (divided into 3 categories) and 15% to turnover with end-investors (from HRF reports). Quoting Total points = 15% (divided into quoting obligation (mandatory), additional amount and time quoted (non-mandatory), and volatility adjusted quoting obligation (non-mandatory)) -Quoting obligations = 5% On the quoting criteria we ask PDs to quote our PGB curve for a minimum of 5 hours, with 5 million each side and with a bid-ask spread that cannot be larger than the average of the bid-asks spreads of

	all PDs times 1.5. -Additional amount and time quoted = 5% We give additional points to PDs that quote with extra amount and extra time on top of the mandatory by the first criteria. -Volatility adjusted quoting obligation = 5% We multiply the daily score in the quoting obligation of each PD by a volatility factor, giving extra points to the PDs that quote on volatile days. (We observed that in our quoting obligations criteria all the PDs were quoting on calm days but only a few quoted on very volatile days, and those were not be sufficiently rewarded by us. By having fewer PDs quoting on volatile days you can even have higher volatility, because there are no PDs market making on that day. So we introduced this measure to motivate dealers to quote on volatile days as well.
Slovak Republic	We consider the reported turnover of each PD in selection for Syndicate issue – it is more part of qualitative criterion, as the reported turnover cannot be double-checked.
Slovenia	Performance index, which includes measuring of the secondary market activity of the Primary Dealers for the domestic currency bonds. Performance index is one of the most important factors when awarding a mandate among the Primary Dealers to lead a syndicated bond issue of the Republic. In accordance with the Primary dealer agreement the Primary Dealers are obliged to contribute to the liquidity of the domestic currency government bond market by market making on the designated electronic trading platform (currently MTS Slovenia) in accordance with its Rules as well as by their other intra-dealer and customer trading. They are expected to allocate and maintain sufficient resources in terms of human resources, financial situation and organization of its trading and sales forces to support an orderly, efficient and liquid secondary market of government bonds.
Spain	The Spanish Treasury provides an incentive scheme implemented in a legal tool (2012 Primary Dealers Resolution). Primary Dealers are rewarded both for their performance in primary and secondary markets. Participation in syndications carried out by the Kingdom of Spain and access to the noncomp of Spanish Government Bonds (SPGB) and Letras auctions (up to 24% depending on the PD performance) are the principal rewards to a notable performance.
Switzerland	We have no instruments or incentives to motivate dealers.
Turkey	We have a secondary market obligation for the Primary Dealers to enhance liquidity of secondary market for government securities. This clause states that each primary dealer has to quote bid and offer prices on every day for six securities they choose from the nine benchmark securities specified by Treasury in Debt Securities Market. There is also a restriction on the spread between bid and offer quotations for different maturity levels to prevent the misuse of this clause. As we monitor the secondary market, we observe that the securities chosen by the primary dealers for quotation are more liquid than others. Overall, this measure seems quite effective.
United Kingdom	The DMO requires primary dealers to make, on demand and in all conditions, continuous and effective two-way prices to their customers and monitors the secondary market turnover share of each primary dealer providing feedback to the dealer on performance. The DMO has limited specific tools to motivate dealers to provide liquidity – rather it is the overall primary dealer franchise arrangements, as well as the issuance programme and associated market infrastructure that facilitate the willingness and ability of dealers to provide liquidity. The DMO does not mandate bid offer spreads or minimum bid or offer sizes, but has set a number of obligations and expectations with regards to participation in the gilt market (described in paragraph 12). Privileges available to Primary Dealers include exclusive eligibility to submit competitive bids directly to the DMO, preferred counterparty status, participation in consultation meetings and, for Primary Dealers in the wholesale market, eligibility for selection as a syndication Lead Manager (with accompanying fees). In general though, client demand for a service in UK Government bonds, plus the reputational and marketing benefits to PD banks, is sufficient motivation.
United States	Our fiscal agent, the Federal Reserve Bank of New York, designates primary dealers and evaluates their participation in Treasury's primary and secondary markets. As a condition of being a primary dealer, promoting the liquidity of the Treasury market is a clear expectation.

Do you undertake any other measures in order to enhance liquidity? (e.g. buy backs of illiquid lines, benchmark issuance, a set auction schedule, a strips program) Please elaborate your experience with these measures.

Australia	We issue into a small number of relatively large benchmark bond lines. We offer a securities lending facility – a lender of last resort facility which supports liquidity by providing market makers with the confidence to take short positions in our bonds, improving their capacity to continuously make two way prices and reducing the risk of settlement failures. We are planning to conduct buyback tenders for short-dated bond lines, which tend to be less liquid.
Austria	Existing issues are regularly tapped via monthly auctions. A strip program is in place and can be used by investors. Benchmark issuance occurs on a regular basis, with a set auction calendar. Buybacks occasionally take place on a case-by-case basis.
Belgium	We use syndications to issue new OLO lines in order to provide sufficient size as from the start and in order to efficiently distribute the new issue so as to favour liquidity. OLO lines are tapped following a predictable auction calendar, further increasing the outstanding sizes of the different OLO lines. The choice of the lines auctioned is in line with market demand, again further creating optimal liquidity conditions. There is a continuous Buy-back program for bonds when their remaining life to maturity is less than 12 months. The Treasury can decide to change this period with prior advice to its primary dealers. The buy-back program is essentially geared at enhancing cash management around redemption dates. But is also improves liquidity of almost maturing lines and provides an incentive to the traders to switch out of OLOs into Treasury Certificates. All fixed coupon OLO's are strippable. Since some years all strips are fungible (interest and capital). This new feature has also increased the attractiveness of the OLO lines. The Treasury introduced an EMTN and Schuldscheine program in order to be able to issue tailored bonds. This led to further diversification in the OLO bondholders.
Canada	The Government of Canada strives to maintain a debt management program that is based on the pillars of transparency, regularity, liquidity, and prudence. This approach allows for borrowing that is also supportive of a liquid and well-functioning Government of Canada securities market. Government securities distributors and customers are subject to minimum bidding requirements (MBR) and maximum bidding limits, which fosters a level of diversification of participants at Government of Canada securities auctions. Establishing auction rules helps prevent auction participants and other market participants from engaging in predatory behaviour in markets for Government of Canada securities. As the Government of Canada strives to be a transparent, regular, and predictable issuer, its actions demonstrate its intent. One example of this is the posting of a quarterly bond auction schedule prior to the start of each quarter. The auction schedule informs the market of upcoming issuances, which are spread out across the year to allow for an even and predicable flow of supply. Dealers' recommendations are also sought before the Bank of Canada publishes a call for tender. The call for tender specifies the upcoming auction details in the week leading up to the auction. Being a transparent and predicable issuer helps the Government of Canada to reassure investors that the bonds they wish to purchase will be available, and it also allows investors to plan out their investment strategy. A combination of these measures helps to boost investor confidence which contributes towards enhancing market liquidity. Benchmark target range sizes are planned and announced at the beginning of each fiscal year as part of the Debt Management Strategy. Recently, the debt issuance strategy has called for building larger benchmark bonds in response to a much higher borrowing requirement of the Government and a demand for larger benchmark sizes by market participants. Larger benchmark sizes help in contributing to more liquid markets. Bond buyback operations "on a switch basis": These operations involve the exchange, on a duration-neutral basis, of less liquid bonds for building benchmark bonds and have the benefit to reduce participants' market risk at repurchase operations. These operations help build larger supply in benchmark bonds and provide more liquidity to the market. These switches have been typically conducted for longer-term bonds, such as 30-year issuances. Securities Lending Program: The Bank of Canada supports the liquidity of Government of Canada securities by providing a secondary and temporary source of securities to the market through the Securities Lending Program. Under this program, securities are made available to the market when the securities are trading below a pre-set threshold (in terms of spread below the target rate) in the repurchase market. Bond buyback operations "on a cash basis": These operations are conducted shortly after a bond auction (20 minutes) and involve the exchange of less liquid or off-the-run bonds for cash. These

	operations help to enhance market liquidity in the primary market for Government of Canada securities by purchasing bonds with a remaining term to maturity of 12 months to 25 years. However, these operations have not been used recently. Cash Management Bond Buybacks (CMBBs): CMBBs operations are typically conducted on a weekly basis. The CMBB program is designed to reduce the amount of bonds outstanding as they approach maturity. This is intended to smooth out the demand for cash balances throughout the year and reduce large demands for cash as a result of any unusually large maturities and coupon payment dates. These operations help reduce variations in the issuance of treasury bills over the year and act to support market liquidity. Use of fungibility and/or reopening of off-the-run bonds: This helps the Government build and maintain large individual bond sizes, which is believed to promote liquid bonds. A recent example of the use of this issuance feature is the Government of Canada structuring of its 3-year bond issuance to be fully fungible with the off-the-run 5-year bond. This enables the 5-year to become a very large benchmark as it rolls into the 3-year term to maturity sector.
Chile	As mentioned, a buyback program was implemented during the first half of 2016, in order to strengthen 4 selected benchmarks for each nominal and inflation linked curve. In addition, the financing operations, which are independent from this buyback program, consisted in reopening of these maturities. It has been observed a marginal increase of the liquidity for the selected benchmarks, but the implementation of the program is very recent to have a final conclusion.
Czech Republic	Buy-backs, Tap-sales, Triple primary auctions, Switch auctions, Flexible auction schedule and strips, Lending facilities, Reverse repo operations.
Denmark	Yes, all of the above except a strips programme. In addition, we conduct bimonthly switch operations. Buy-backs: We conduct monthly buy-back auctions in off-the-run series. In addition, we can buy back bonds directly in the secondary markets. Our experience is that market participants increasingly want the DMO to take an active role in secondary markets. Benchmark issuance: Due to a limited issuance need and to support liquidity, we have focused issuance on fewer series (primarily in the 2- and 10-year segments). Our experience is that this is welcomed by the market. Investor focus on liquidity is increasing and building bond series faster to larger volumes makes the bond easier to trade. This again attracts further investor interest and hence trading and liquidity. Switch operations: In 2015, an important step was to reintroduce switch operations. This gave the investors an opportunity to relocate large positions without paying large bid-ask spreads, since switch operation take place close to the mid-price in the secondary markets. Demand was high, and both investors and primary dealers welcomed the facility. Starting January 2016 two regular monthly switch operations have been conducted. Calendar dates are announced three months in advance in line with other bond and bill auctions. Papers are announced no later than one trading day before the switch takes place. Switch operations also make it easier to quickly build large on-the-run bond series, cf. the comment above. Auction schedule: We have a three month calendar, where the dates for auctions and switch operations are announced. Papers are announced three days prior to auctions. Investors generally appreciate this type of openness and predictability.
Finland	The State Treasury reopened the lender-of-last-resort type of bond repo facility for the primary dealers in February 2016. The facility has not been used by the market makers to this date.
France	We have a discretionary buyback program on the short end of our curve. It allows easing liquidity conditions on that segment even if it is not its primary objective. We also have a strip program, but it is not clear to us that it significantly improves the liquidity of our curve at this juncture. Also, we have a set auction schedule with regular benchmark issuance and also tapping of off-the-run bonds. Generally speaking, we implicitly commit to tap each bond we issue so as to reach an amount outstanding which guarantees the bond liquidity on the secondary market.
Germany	Germany's debt management is characterized by the following measures, among others: - a planned funding volume of around USD 230 bn in 2016 (high issuance volume); - a well-established and credible issuance policy, e.g. annual and quarterly issuance calendars (transparency, reliability); - the option to retain a portion of securities for secondary market operations at each auction which will be sold successively in the secondary market afterwards (market support); - additional investment opportunities by a strip program of 10y and 30y Bunds; and - a fully established nominal and real yield curve.

Greece	Not applicable.
Hungary	• Buy-backs (both via reverse auctions and switch auctions) of illiquid lines. • Benchmark issuance, with reopening of the same series at several auctions to build up series of USD 3+ billion equivalent. • Set auction schedule for a whole calendar year. • Switch auctions help enhance the liquidity of the destination bonds, which are usually already off-the-run bonds. All the above measures and activities have been successful.
Iceland	Government Debt Management (GDM) both have benchmark issuance and auction schedule and we buy back illiquid lines which mainly have less than 6 months to maturity.
Ireland	The NTMA provides a quarterly issuance schedule and an annual target range for its funding requirement in the coming year. Regular auctions of benchmark bonds assist with liquidity. Repos and switches are occasionally provided to Primary Dealers on a reverse-enquiry basis. Such transactions can supplement liquidity at times when market turnover is low due to seasonal or issuance-related lulls.
Israel	1. Primary Dealership program. 2. A monthly set auctions schedule. 3. Benchmark issuances. 4. Switch auctions in which mostly off-the run bonds are issued. 5. Buyback auctions to acquire bonds nearing maturity. 6. Offering a government bonds lending facility, for all bonds above ILS 2 B and maturity greater than 15 months. 7. In the process of developing a repo market and a strips program.
Italy	We undertake all appropriate measures, including those mentioned in the question as an example. The most important one is the adherence to a regular, transparent and predictable issuance policy, in close coordination with the Primary Dealers and, more in general, with all market participants, including investors. Of special importance are also the following measures: - issuing on-the-run bonds regularly until they reach a benchmark size; - reopening illiquid (off-the-run) bonds at ordinary auctions or via exchange auctions when the lack of floating paper make them difficult to trade; - buying back cheap bonds that may create distortions along the curve - and therefore damage the liquidity of surrounding bonds - via reverse auctions or exchange auctions; - improving the efficiency of the strip market with ad hoc regulatory and organizational improvements.
Japan	We implement reopening rules, yearly announcement of JGB Issuance Plan, announcement of auction date in advance (about three months), and a buy-back program. Also, we have reduced the maximum amount of bidding by each auction participant to one-half of the planned issuance amount since April 2015 (bidding up to the full amount of the planned issuance was permitted before then). l As to the reopening rules, the government will, in fiscal year 2016 (FY2016), reopen 10-year issues to integrate them into four issues per year unless interest rates fluctuate wildly . The reopening rule will also be used in principle to integrate 20- and 30-year issues into four issues each per year, and the 40-year issues will be integrated into one issue per year. l The maximum amount of bidding by each auction participant has been reduced to one-half of the planned issuance amount (from the full amount), while the minimum bidding responsibility of JGB Market Special Participants has been raised to 4% or more of the planned issuance amount (from 3% or more), since April 2015. l Details of the Buy-back operations will be determined by taking market conditions into consideration, based on a discussion with market participants. In FY 2016, we bought back inflation-indexed JGBs by 20 billion yen each in April, June and August 2016 in order to solve supply-demand imbalance and improve liquidity in the secondary market (the schedule for the buy-backs from October has not been decided.).
Korea	We undertake various measures to enhance liquidity including buy-backs, conversion offer, strips, benchmark issuance, annual or monthly announcement of issuance plan.

Latvia	Buy backs are used in case of international bonds. Domestic benchmark bonds are issued regularly, mostly as tap issues of existing lines. Auction schedule for every consecutive quarter is agreed with primary dealers in advance. By providing regular tap issues we ensure larger bonds outstanding thus we facilitate liquidity in secondary market.
Luxembourg	We just try to issue at least benchmark size of 1 billion EUR in order to have a minimum of liquidity. No other actions in order to enhance liquidity.
Mexico	Yes, the Ministry of Finance undertakes several measures and strategies to promote the correct functioning of the markets and to foster liquidity in its sovereign debt securities, among those: • Exchange transactions. The Federal Government executes exchange transactions in order to foster liquidity in targeted or illiquid lines, improve the price discovery process, implement liability management strategies to smooth out the Federal Government's maturity profile and to fix distortions observed across its sovereign debt curve. • Buybacks. These strategies have been used to buyback debt outstanding in the market, particularly when some issues become illiquid. They are also used for reducing the impact of financial crisis on market liquidity, such as the 2008 period. • Benchmark issuance. The Federal Government makes use of the syndication method and the reopening policy to develop liquidity in either new tenors of the curve or existing ones. • Auction Calendar. The Federal Government announces its auction program every quarter, which includes amounts, frequency, tenors and type of securities to be auctioned during the quarter. The auction calendar is consistent with the Annual Borrowing Plan and the Economic Program approved by the congress. • Strips of securities. In 2004, the rules for stripping both Fixed rate bonds and Inflation Linked Bonds were created. The Federal Government has included the auctions of this type of instruments in its quarterly auction calendar since 2012. These strategies have allowed the Ministry of Finance to create a highly liquid market with participation of both local and foreign investors, and to position itself in the market as a regular and predictable issuer.
Netherlands	Yes. We have regular benchmark issuances (5, 10, and 30 year). We publish forthcoming yearly auction calendar at the end the year as well as quarterly calendar at the beginning of each quarter. Dutch State Treasury Agency (DSTA) offers a repo facility .
New Zealand	NZDMO has undertaken buy-backs of the two most recent maturing nominal bonds – the April 2015 and December 2017 maturities. Motivating factors for these buy-backs include reducing refinance risk and managing cash flows around large maturities, assisting market-makers by being able to relieve them of unwanted positions in size, ensuring a more gradual increase in the various NZ government bond indices.
Norway	- Buy-backs of bonds near maturity. - An auction calendar with auction dates is published yearly. Bond and volume is published two business days before the auction. - New 10-year bond issued every year. - Investor relations, road-shows. - Transparency/information: Annual strategy, reports (quarterly and annual).
Poland	Key measure to ensure an adequate liquidity of domestic Treasury securities market is to build of a large issues of fixed rate benchmark bonds in the segment of 2, 5 and 10 years. Given bond is sold at several subsequent auctions (cash and switch) until it reaches a debt level of approximately PLN 25-30bn. A similar mechanism can be applied in case of Treasury bills (if it is issued). Another measure is to adjust issue policy including outright, switch and buy back auctions, to market conditions including the demand in different segments of Treasury securities market.
Portugal	We try to provide liquidity to our bonds and for that we keep a close relationship with our Dealers in order to understand which bonds are "squeezed" or "heavy" and based on that we might act on the market, either by issuing those bonds or buying them back (although we usually buyback bonds as part of our liability management strategy and as a consequence buybacks are primarily concentrated in the short-end of our curve). We understand the importance of the most liquid points by nature, the on-the-run benchmarks, and we tend to issue those bonds more often than off-the-run benchmarks.

Slovak Republic	We increased our benchmark sizes from EUR 1.3 billion to EUR 3.0 billion and reduced existing bond lines. We publish auction dates calendar for the whole year, asking our PDs 3 weeks before each multiple auction which bonds line they prefer to be auctioned. This year we introduced new type of auction – remunerate auction for new bond line opening – it was comparable with Syndication (demand and accepted bids). We are ready to do OTC buy-backs of bonds maturing this and next year – each PD knows we are ready to buy it at market price.
Slovenia	The envisaged primary instrument for funding of the central government budget financing needs is borrowing by way of issuance of benchmark government bonds and T-bills. In addition to issuance of benchmark bonds the intention of the Treasury is also to tap the existing lines of bonds in order to increase the overall outstanding amount and consequently the liquidity of these bonds. A reintroduction of bond auctions is planned in 2016, which will be executed via taps of existing bonds which should provide additional liquidity. An indicative calendar for bond auctions will be published at the beginning of the year specifying the possible dates of auctions. Before the auction (3 business days) the exact bonds and the indicative amounts will be published.
Spain	We stick to a benchmark issue policy that ensures a longer span of liquidity for bonds and our auction schedule is announced yearly. In essence, our debt management policy has adopted liquidity as one of the main intermediate objectives. Further to some the specific questions posed, in order to improve liquidity of certain "off the run" coupon bonds, the Treasury has the option of convening special auctions. The combination of regular and special auctions thus provides the Treasury with more flexibility to manage its issuance, helping to reduce secondary market volatility around auctions. Regarding buy backs and switches, we have used them in the past and we deem them useful tools when they are needed.
Switzerland	In order to support secondary market trading in Confederation bonds insofar as possible, outstanding bonds are regularly reopened. In the important maturity range of one to 13 years, the Confederation aims for a minimum total outstanding volume per bond of approximately 2 billion, which can then be further increased up to the time of maturity. In order to limit the refinancing risk and smooth out the maturity profile, the bond volume at maturity should be in the region of around 5 billion. By selling so-called "own tranches" directly to investors on demand and at market prices, the Treasury may bridge temporary illiquidity in certain bond lines.
Turkey	We introduce regular buyback auctions for primary dealers since March 18, 2016. Through these regular buyback auctions, we buy maximum amount TRY 100 million in net figures for each 5 Year and 10 Year Fixed Coupon Bonds that became off the run recently. Therefore, with regular buyback auctions we provide continuous selling opportunity for the primary dealers. Also, we increase the supply for on-the run 5 year and 10 year fixed coupon bonds according to the bonds we buy back through auctions. Thanks to regular buyback auctions we increase liquidity of the market in two ways; we can increase further the supply of the on the run bonds and provide selling opportunity for primary dealers which leads more transactions for the bonds subject to these auctions.
United Kingdom	In order to promote liquidity in the gilt market, the DMO aims to maintain regular issuance in the key benchmark maturities (in particular, 5-, 10- and 30-year) and by building individual bonds to a benchmark size. The gilt issuance schedule is announced on a quarterly basis and at least one month in advance of the first auction in the quarter. It is complemented by a supplementary programme of syndications, which are flagged in advance, and gilt tenders. In the 2016-17 financial year the UK DMO also introduced a package of measures that are intended to support smooth delivery of the financing programme and to alleviate emerging pressures on debt intermediation via our primary dealers. The package of measures allow the DMO to be more flexible in responding to changing market and evolving demand conditions, for example, through more flexibility over the maturities of bonds issued and the methods used to issue them. An intention in so doing is to support smooth market functioning whilst remaining consistent with the predictable and transparent approach to debt management.
United States	The U.S. Treasury does not presently conduct buybacks of illiquid lines, but does have benchmark issuance, a set auction schedule, and a strips program.

Have you imposed –new- requirements on market-makers in their provision of liquidity in recent years?

Australia	No.
Austria	No.
Belgium	Currently market makers have quoting obligations on 12 bonds, which are chosen in dialogue with the market makers. Those 12 bonds should be quoted for at least 5 hours a day, with a minimum quantity of at least 5 or 10 million (depending upon the maturity) and with a maximum bid/offer spread which cannot be wider than the average bid/offer spread quoted by all PDs plus a margin of 25%. The market makers consciously observe these rules, not only for the 12 chosen bonds but also for all other bonds which are free of quoting obligations. Quoting obligations can be fulfilled on one of the 3 selected electronic trading platforms: MTS Belgium, BrokerTec or BGC Brokers eSpeed. The Treasury is monitoring the PDs on a daily basis, providing the dealers with reports on their performance. As mentioned, this performance is part of a global evaluation.
Canada	None observed.
Chile	There are no market makers in Chile.
Czech Republic	None.
Denmark	No, but. cf. the answer to q10 and q11.
Finland	We have introduced a maturity weighting in ranking the primary dealers' secondary market customer trade volumes.
France	No.
Germany	We do not impose any requirements on market-makers. The only requirements are imposed by the trading venue.
Greece	Not applicable.
Hungary	The latest changes affected price quotation rules and repo limits in August 2016: tighter spread for non-benchmark securities and higher repo limits, together with the start of MTS Hungary's new mid-price crossing functionality.
Iceland	No.
Ireland	No.
Israel	No new requirements were implemented in recent years. The quoting obligations (spreads and quantity) are being revised every once and a while according to the primary dealers' rules.
Italy	In the last couple of years we have updated our requirements with a specific focus on the contribution to liquidity conditions on long dated bonds. Beyond that, no major material changes have been recently imposed on our market makers (Primary Dealers).
Japan	We have not imposed –new- requirements in their provision of liquidity in recent years. We continue to require that primary dealers offer adequate liquidity for the market.
Korea	Regular supply of Separate Trading of Registered Interest and Principal of Securities (STRIPS) (beginning Sept 2015)
Latvia	There have not been changes to the requirements for the primary dealers after the implementation of Primary dealership system in February, 2013. When establishing the PD system, discussions on requirement to provide continuously two-way quotes in the secondary market for benchmark securities and participation in actions were most challenging. Therefore commitment for participation is soft – on a best effort basis to provide competitive bids that correspond to prevailing market conditions; and two-way quotes in Bloomberg system is subject to the primary dealer having the relevant paper on the trading book.
Luxembourg	No.

Mexico	No, in this regard the primary dealer's rules haven't been modified.
Netherlands	No.
New Zealand	Not recently, although we have begun work looking into this.
Norway	No.
Poland	The latest changes were introduced in October 2011 (the rules were simplified by reducing the number of criteria to be assessed and quality quotation index was introduced). Their aim was to improve the targeted features of liquidity (by quality quotation index – in which spread, volume and quoting time – all count). The results have been monitored on a daily basis. And we have an option of fine-tuning those measures (adjustment of the weights between spread and volume), which can be done smoothly, if necessary. Since then our strategic approach remains unchanged (continuation of issuing large series of benchmark bonds in the domestic market, adapting the issuance policy to market circumstances etc.).
Portugal	Please see answer to question - What measures (if any) do you have in place to motivate dealers to provide liquidity?
Slovak Republic	Not yet. We still discuss whether we will oblige the PDs for firm quoting in MTS or not, as the whole PD model is at the moment under pressure.
Slovenia	No.
Spain	Not lately.
Switzerland	No.
Turkey	As stated in the answer in an earlier question, we have changed the primary dealership obligations by decreasing the maximum spread between bid and offer rates of benchmark securities, the maximum spread between bid and offer quotations were 50 Kurus. However, in the new Primary Dealership contract of year 2016, the maximum spread between bid and offer rates differentiated according to maturities of benchmark securities.
United Kingdom	Starting from the 2016-17 financial year, the DMO has encouraged an expectation that primary dealers should aim to bid (whether or not successfully) for a minimum of 5% of each auction averaged over a rolling 6-month period, in order to encourage primary dealers to participate more fully in the price formation process. This is in addition to the existing obligation that primary dealers should aim to achieve a minimum auction allocation of 2.0% and a 2.0% market share in the secondary market, both measured on a 6-month rolling average basis.
United States	No.

OECD Sovereign Borrowing Outlook 2017

ANNEX C

2016 Survey on Auction Mechanisms

Section A: Multiple vs Single Price Auctions

Q1 What is the auction method for different types of bonds/bills?

	All types		Fixed-rate		Floating-rate		Inflation-indexed		Discount/Bills	
	Single -price	Multiple -price	Single -price	Multiple -price	Single -price	Multiple -price	Single -price	Multiple -price	Single -price	Multiple -price
Australia		X		X				X		X
Austria		X		X		X				
Belgium		X		X						X
Canada	X	X		X			X			X
Chile	X		X				X			
Czech Republic	X	X		X		X			X	
Denmark	X		X				X		X	
Finland	X		X							
France		X		X				X		X
Germany		X		X				X		X
Hungary		X		X		X				X
Iceland	X		X				X		X	
Ireland	X		X						X	
Israel		X		X		X		X		X
Italy	X	X	X		X		X		X	X
Japan	X	X	X	X			X			X
Korea										
Latvia	X	X	X	X					X	X
Luxembourg										
Mexico	X	X	X			X	X			X
Netherlands	X	X	X	X					X	
New Zealand		X		X				X		X
Norway	X		X						X	
Poland	X		X		X		X		X	
Portugal	X	X	X							X
Slovak Republic	X	X	X	X		X			X	
Slovenia	X	X		X					X	
Spain		X		X				X		X
Sweden		X		X				X		X
Switzerland	X		X						X	
Turkey		X		X		X		X		X
United Kingdom	X	X		X			X			X
United States	X		X		X		X		X	
Total	**20**	**22**	**16**	**19**	**3**	**7**	**10**	**8**	**13**	**17**

Notes: The United Kingdom Debt Management Office (UKDMO) may also hold gilt tenders, with index-linked gilt tenders normally held using a single-price format and conventional gilt tenders using either a multiple price or single price format. The UKDMO's gilt auction programme in any year may be supplemented between auctions by official sales of gilts of any type or maturity via gilt tenders. Gilt tenders will typically be for existing gilts and for a lower size (in cash terms) than gilt auctions of equivalent maturity and may be used for market management purposes. While conventional gilt tenders are normally held using a multiple-price format the UKDMO also has the option to use the single-price format. Korea uses differential price auction method in fixed-rate bond auctions. Differential price auction aligns bid rates below the highest winning rate into different groups, and the highest rate of each group is used as a winning rate. Estonia has not introduced auctions and has no auction process in place.

Q2 Reasons for the choice of the auction method (pros and cons)?

Australia	Treasury Bonds (TB's) – Treasury Bonds (nominal) are tendered at multiple-price auctions. Treasury Indexed Bonds (TIB's) – Up until 2013 the Treasury Indexed Bond market was less liquid than the nominal bond market and as such single-price auctions were considered the appropriate auction mechanism. TIBs have been tendered at multiple-price auctions since July 2013. T-Notes (TN's) – Treasury Notes (discount short term securities) are tendered at multiple-price auctions. Whilst some markets have issues with price discovery Australia has a highly liquid secondary market for bonds with transparent pricing. multiple-price auctions allow investors to bid at their required yield whether for themselves or investors.
Austria	Overall no auctions for Inflation-linked and bills. Austria employs a multiple-price auction method with allotments at the individual bid prices (American auction) for fixed-rate and floating-rate bonds. The auction method has been employed since February 1991. The only change in method has been from a multiple yield auction to a multiple-price auction in 2001, as price bids are most common in European auctions.
Belgium	Our dealerships are set up as a partnership with our dealers. We impose a number of strict requirements on our dealers in terms of market making and market shares in the auctions and on the secondary market, but at the same time allow them earn fee-business with us in function of their performance. We try to incentivize a large part of our dealers in this manner. As a medium sized country and market we believe such a setup allows us to optimize the cost of our recurrent funding programs in long term fixed rate bonds (Obligations Linéaires Ordinaires - OLOs) and short term bills (Treasury Certificates - TCs). Indeed, in this context we feel a multiple-price auction allows: • a fairer expression of dealers' interest to purchase the bonds at the price they set, taking all elements into account. This will include the costs of winning market share in the auction, but also the benefits of o the non-competitive bidding that is granted to the most successful bidders in the auctions and to the most consistent market makers o improving the dealer's chances of being selected as joint lead manager in the syndications of our new long term bonds o improving the dealer's chances of being selected for other mandates for the Kingdom of Belgium • an optimized cost of funding for the Kingdom of Belgium through its liquid instruments' funding programs
Canada	Rationale underpinning the Government of Canada's choice of a multiple-price auction format for nominal bonds and treasury bills: • Research conducted by the Bank of Canada staff shows that participants in the Government of Canada securities auctions, which include Primary Dealers (PDs) and a small group of institutional investors, are relatively well-informed and that there do not appear to exist any major information access asymmetries between them. The multiple-price auction method allows the Government to raise cost-effective funding by rewarding auction winners with prices that correspond to their bids, while fostering a competitive auction process and price discovery. Rationale for the choice of a single-price auction format for inflation-indexed bonds: • The Government of Canada inflation-indexed bond market is a relatively illiquid market, where for the most part, securities are held to maturity. The pricing of Canada inflation-indexed bonds tends to be characterized by greater uncertainty in the secondary market compared to nominal bonds, and the price for these inflation-indexed securities tends to be especially volatile around the auction deadline. The single-price auction format incentivizes auction participants to bid aggressively at the auctions as no penalty is incurred as a result of a potentially aggressive bidding behaviour.

Chile	Both for inflation-linked and fixed rate are the same. Pros: through a single-price competitive auction -in particular, Dutch auction- is possible that each investors offer their best price. In addition, it is a well-known mechanism also used in corporate issuances, and until now has worked well, so for the moment there are no reasons to change. Cons: it is not the most common mechanism used in foreign markets, where the book-building is well known. Due to this, Dutch auction mechanism could be an impediment to attract foreign investors.
Czech Republic	single-price auction for T-bills is mainly driven by income taxation issues multiple-price auction for longer term bonds allow price discrimination.
Denmark	The choice of the single-price system is in some degree historical. We have historical only used auctions for opening of new bonds. Here the uncertainty about the price is in favour of single-price-auctions. We have analysed the two different systems and both empirical and theoretical show that the choice of auction mechanism depends on conditions on the individual government securities markets. This is emphasised by the fact that the two formats are used with more or less the same frequency by OECD countries. Together with these finding and the good experience we have with the single-price system, we made the decision of using single-price.
Finland	single-price pros: easy to execute, PD can ensure allocation by bidding above market, overbidding alleviates curve cheapening after announced supply; cons: overbidding, which PDs can find costly
France	The multiple-price system ensures the maximal commitment of primary dealers by incentivizing them to reveal their reserve price. More specifically, it avoids free rider behaviours where the primary dealer bids a large amount at an irrelevant price without consequence. It guarantees therefore a better functioning of our primary dealer system.
Germany	Bills / Nominal Bonds / Inflation-linked bonds: We think that because of the liquidity of our securities the price discovery process is transparent enough so that we can conduct auctions in the multiple-price style
Hungary	Since the introduction of the regular auctions in Hungary multiple-price method has been applied. The Hungarian Debt Management Agency (AKK) considers that this method can better support the price discovery, and the average price of a particular auction can be closer to the secondary market levels. Market participants are pleased with this auction format and have never requested any changes in this respect. Auction demand is traditionally rather volatile in Hungary reflecting foreign capital flows and changing investors' sentiment. Therefore the electronic auction platform used in Hungary actually supports only multiple-price method. (On the other hand, ÁKK offers the possibility for PDs to put in non-competitive bids at the average price of the auction. Non-competitive bids are available at the end of the competitive auction phase for a relatively small amount. Since 2009 ÁKK also provides the non-competitive tender phase a few hours after the bond auctions, where – subject to ÁKK's decision, based on the demand seen at the competitive phase – ÁKK may offer a maximum 40% top-up of the winning bids for those PDs who had winning competitive bids at the auction. In this top-up the PDs can buy the given bond at the average price of the auction.)
Iceland	Debt Management Office (DMO) in Iceland has used single-price auction method since 2008. The reason for using this method is based on results of number of public science studies throughout the years. Small size, low liquidity and high price volatility in the secondary market as well as few numbers of primary dealers was a big factor in this decision. Also single-price auction method decrease the fear of the winner´s curse and leads to more aggressive bidding strategies from the primary dealers and their customers. Reducing uncertainty due to the effects of the winner´s curse is especially important when the same investors are repeatedly attending the auctions. Finally DMO is not allowing non-competitive bids in the auctions making single-price method even more relevant. Cons: Difficult to estimate the actual gain of the single-price auctions versus multiple auctions method. It can also vary from time to time (sometime lose) depending on factors such as financing needs and debt ratio of the Treasury.

Ireland	To date our benchmark bonds and treasury bills have been neither floating rate nor inflation-linked. As such we have exclusively used single-price auctions for fixed-rate bonds and treasury bills.
Israel	The financing plan is installed from domestic market and external market for funding the government's activity and refinancing the government debt, and part of the strategic goals of the debt management unit. In order to meet these goals we use diversified funding sources (domestically and abroad), advanced liquidity tools and a reliance on the deep local market, diversifying the funding sources and creating benchmarks for issuances abroad of Israeli market and external market. The goal of using multiple price auction is to reduce funding costs by using the high demands in the domestic market, increase the demand level and the liquidity in the markets.
Italy	In general, we see the single-price auction as a format that may help reduce the problem of the "winner's curse". In a single-price auction, each participant can bid the maximum price at which it is willing to buy the bond; if the auction stops at a lower price, the dealer may still buy and reap the advantage of a better price. On the contrary, the multiple-price format may encourage participants to bid lower than their maximum price, in order to obtain the asset on more favourable terms and avoid being stuck on the "wrong" price. Therefore, we see single-price auctions as instruments that diminish risk and encourage dealers' participation, reduce the long-run yield differential between auctioned issues and secondary market prices, and promote liquid secondary markets. This mechanism should encourage stable markets, continuity of funding and lower yields in the longer run. However, we still adopt multiple-price auctions (precisely: competitive yield auctions) for domestic money market bills (Buoni Ordinari del Tesoro - BOT), because of the different investors' base and lower risk characteristics of these shorter instruments. BOT have less market risks, therefore participation by dealers is not significantly discouraged by bidders not knowing the exact valuation by other market participants. In this segment of the market, the multiple-price (yield) format may help achieve more precise valuations as well as lower yields.
Japan	We issue 2-year, 5-year, 10-year, 20-year and 30-year bonds and T-Bills by multiple-price method. Under the multiple-price method, auction participants can purchase the bonds at their own bidding price. Therefore, in our view, the auction result and the market after the auction tend to be stable. As to 40-year bonds, we started their issuance by single-price method because it was perceived as difficult for market participants to identify the adequate level of market yield. We still keep the single-price method because, as the liquidity of 40-year bond market remains low, it is still difficult to identify the adequate level of market yield. As to 10-year inflation-indexed bonds, we resumed their issuance in October 2013 with improved marketability after temporarily halting their issuance in August 2008. We implement the single-price method for 10-year inflation-indexed bonds because their liquidity and price transparency are poor, and the bidders' expectation of the auction result may widely differ from the cut-off price.
Korea	Auction method :Differential Price Auction Differential price auction method align bid rates below the highest winning rate into different groups, and the highest rate of each group is used as a winning rate. Bids are divided into different groups based on bid rates submitted by PDs to induce submission of reasonable rate bids. The highest winning rate of each group applies to all the bids in the same group to reduce PDs' burden in underwriting Korean Treasury Bonds (KTBs). Inflation-linked bonds are issued through non-competitive biddings, and single-price auction method is used when issued.
Latvia	The auction methods described above refer to domestic issuance only (under local law) and do not apply to retail instrument – savings bonds – which is distributed via a specific website directly to end investors – private individuals, or Post Offices. Furthermore, for international issuance (under foreign law) in the form of Eurobonds syndication is the most common distribution method. All these methods are used already since the very first issues, for more than 20 years already (except savings bonds, which were introduced in 2013). Being a relatively small issuer, we regard these methods as best suited for our financing needs and we believe unmodified Dutch auction method that is applied at multi-price auctions provides best outcome for finding fair price levels on the primary market.

Mexico	Currently, Mexican government securities are placed through multiple and single-price auctions. In both cases, these auctions are "closed" systems, i.e. the allocation price is only disclosed after the auction is closed. Only the Central Banks' Floating-rate notes auctions use an "interactive" system in which the marginal allocated price for the entire issuance is disclosed in real time, allowing bidders to improve their bids as long as the pre-established time for such purpose has not ran out. Multiple-price auctions allow for more efficient allocations from an issuer perspective. In this regard, Floating-rate notes (Bondes D) and T-Bills (Cetes) are placed via multiple-price auctions. However, longer term securities such as Fixed-rate (Bonos M) and Inflation-linked bonds (Udibonos) are allocated via single-price auctions method. single-price auctions intend to prevent price distortions and limit the impact to investor's portfolios. In the other hand, allocations at multiple-prices can have significant impact on market conditions, which could affect market participants. Therefore, we believe this practice contributes to improve market dynamics in those types of securities.
Netherlands	Auctions of fixed-rate bonds: Initial issuance: Dutch Direct Auction (DDA). The DDA is a single price auction designed by the Dutch State Treasury Agency (DSTA) and resembles a syndication. The DSTA runs a book during auction day. Before the auction a spread guidance (versus a reference bond, normally a German bond) is announced. While the book is opened investors can directly bid into the book through PDs (who function as brokers). Closure of the book is followed by a rule-based allocation. After allocation the price of the reference bond is spotted, after which the bond has received an initial price. Pros: DSTA is sole bookrunner (only one who sees the book), as bookrunner the DDA offers the DSTA a large amount of information on investors Cons: No obligation of underwriting (since there's no syndicate involved), DSTA is responsible for everything (IT systems, potential hedging and allocation) Tap auctions (Bonds) In the tap auctions the DSTA puts a price in the MTS (an electronic trading platform) systems. PDs can than hit the quote for an amount of their choosing. In principle, this is a multiple price auction, because the DSTA has the right to adjust the price during the auction. There is no book building process, unlike with the other 2 auction formats Pros: PDs can directly hedge their exposure, very small chance for failed auctions, the DSTA can always lower the price further Cons: DSTA is the risk taker if prices are not in line with demand Dutch Treasury Certificates (DTC) Auction – auctions for the Dutch Treasury Certificates (T-Bills) are done through a bookbuilding system within Bloomberg Auction System (BAS) Pros: Easy system (very low maintenance); price determined by the 16 dealers participating in the auction Cons: Little influence on the price of the DTC (DSTA is price taker)
New Zealand	Given size of the market, multiple-price auction encourages price tension It's cost effective for the issuer Consistent with auction methodology across the region
Norway	Norway uses single-price auctions for new issues and reopenings of both bonds and T-bills. This is partly for historical reasons, and the system is easy to manage. The Norwegian government debt market is fairly small with rather low liquidity and turnover. We have only four primary dealers. In this setting we have decided to continue using single-price auctions as we believe this system will reduce the fear of winner's curse. For buy-back auctions, however, we use multi-price auctions as we think this better reflects investors' preferences for selling back their holdings.
Poland	Single-price formula is used for each type of T-bonds and T-bills. The introduction of single-price formula results from: • developed countries debt markets' experiences, • the increase in demand quality (speculative demand reduction), • the increase in submitted bids quality (competitiveness of bids resulting from the reduction of the

"winner's curse" effect, and elimination of the "bid shading" phenomenon),

- expected higher budget revenues,
- limitation of securities price fluctuations in the secondary market,
- the results of quantitative research

Portugal	Medium and Long-Term Fixed Rate Bonds: When the Portugeuse Treasury and Debt Manamgement Agency (IGCP) reintroduced the medium and long-term bonds auctions in 2014, we opted for the single-price method (vs the multi-price method), as we assessed that it was the first step in the normalisation of market access via auctions. Our background analysis of the characteristics and pro and cons of the two auction methods convinced us that the single-price auction would smoothen this process and allow for a steady reintroduction of long-term debt auctions in our market. Currently we still maintain the single-price auction method, as we consider that, namely by mitigating the winner´s curse effect, it maximizes the participation rate at the auctions and therefore the expected outcome for the issuer. Tbills: The issuance of tbills was never discontinued, even during the crisis, and it always worked quite efficiently with multiple price method, so we saw no reason to change that.
Slovak Republic	We have never issued inflation linked bond. We always use single-price auction for T-bills, but we mostly use multiple-price auction for all other bonds (including zero coupon bonds with maturity longer than 1 year). However, we opened a new bond line via auction this year (instead of syndication) and we used single-price auction for this opening of new bond line. We want to continue with this and use single-price for this specific auctions. The reason why we use this mix of auction types is the best practice we observed during the last years. According to theory single-price auction should bring more aggressive bids – in fact we have no relevant empirical experience to confirm or not confirm this.
Slovenia	Multiple-price Auction for Fixed-rate (bonds): Till the year 2007 the Ministry of Finance held auctions for Bonds in the multiple-price auction (on the domestic market before entering the common Economic and Monetary Union (EMU) market) due to the following reasons: pros: + high number of auction participants (mostly buy and hold investors) and high-volume bids in the auction; + the issuer maximized revenue for a given demand curve since the issuer obtained the maximum price each participant is willing to pay cons: - might tend to shift the demand curve down for a given quantity as a result of "winners curse" After entering the EMU market, the bonds have been issued via syndications and not auctions. The Ministry is planning to reintroduce Bond auctions in the beginning of next year in the single-price auction format. Single-price for Discount/TBills: For TBills the Ministry of Finance holds single-price auctions. pros: + due to extremely low liquidity of the TBills market it is difficult to price the TBills at the auction which could emphasise the winner's curse. In order to mitigate this issue the single-price format is more appropriate; + increase the number of bidders, encourage broader participation of investors and strengthen the role of the primary market cons: - the issuer might not obtain the maximum price each participant is willing to pay although recent empirical studies show that the uniform-price format may be more advantageous in most markets in the long term in terms of revenue generated for the issuer.

Spain	Spanish multiple-price auctions are "Dutch modified auctions": bids above the average price are allocated at the average price, whereas bids between the average price and the cut-off price are allocated at the price offered by the investor. A simple-price auction foregoes substantial "investor surplus" (the difference between the average price and the highest price offered by the investor). In a multiple-price auction the "investor surplus" above the average price suffers from the "winner's curse", which could induce less aggressive bids in the future.
Sweden	We have always used multiple-price auctions for all SEK instruments, government bonds, inflation-linked bonds and T-bills, in our regular funding. It is a well-established format that both end investors and primary dealers are familiar with and prefer. We consider the multiple-price format to be the most cost-effective method. The pros for the issuer with multi-price is a longer tail and of course the advantage of price discrimination. We discuss the format with market participants from time to time. Sporadically the question about single-price for T-bills is raised to avoid the winner's curse. To achieve an aggressive bidding with a single-price method, the prerequisite is a high number of bidders. We believe that the T-bill market in Sweden is far too small for that technique.
Switzerland	The Swiss Treasury introduced the auction mechanism for selling Treasury bills in 1979 and for Treasury notes and bonds in 1980. For both types of securities the uniform-price format was chosen from the outset and this has never been changed since. The reasons for this decision were i) equality of treatment (since everybody pays the same price), ii) the proximity of the auction price to the (secondary) market price and iii) its relative (strategic) simplicity. Uniform-price auctions were deemed to be less complex and hence more appropriate for retail investors. Retail investors (or Swiss citizens) were always a target group of Federal Treasury (e.g. also the denomination of the T-bonds is only 1'000 CHF). By contrast, discriminatory-price auctions were believed to give rise to difficulties in bidding for less experienced participants.
Turkey	Due to the reason of the economic crisis in Turkey in February 2001, the Treasury changed the auction system from multiple-price to single-price in March 2001 and used single-price method until February 2004. The main reason of this changed was that in multiple-price auctions held during the crisis in 2001, the difference between the lowest and highest bids in the auctions was relatively high so that the return for investors differs, damaging the investment appetite. In this respect, implementing the single-price system during market turmoil positively affects investors' sentiment in such a way that investors do not face with "winners' curse" effect of multiple-price system in volatile market conditions. The pros of the single-price method is that the investors are not subject to "winners' curse" so that retail or corporate investors could attend to the auctions without any concern about the "winners' curse". From the issuer perspective, by eliminating this uncertainty ("winners' curse") and related risk premium, the single-price method decreases the cost of borrowing during market turmoil, especially when the borrowing requirement is high. After returning to normal market conditions, the Treasury started to use multiple-price system in 2004. The borrowing cost is expected to be lower in multiple-price system relative to single-price method when the price competition is high in the auction and borrowing requirement of the Treasury is relatively low. One of the disadvantage of the multiple-price system is that the investors shall bid more professionally to inhibit "winners' curse" effect, which reduces retail investors' appetite to direct access to auctions so that the share of retail investors in the auction has a decreasing trend. Moreover, the Treasury started to issue Consumer Price Index (CPI) Linked Government Bonds in 2007. From the investors perspective, the pricing method of the CPI Bonds seems as more complicated than fixed coupon bonds so that when starting to issue a new type of bond, single-price method may be more suitable. On the other hand, the primary dealers (PDs) have right to submit non-competitive bids and can attend to post- auction sales in Turkey. In multiple-price auction system, the average price in the auction is used for non-competitive bid sales and post auction sales. However, in single-price auction system the single-price, which is the cut off price (lowest price), is used for non-competitive bid sales and post auction sales. In this respect, by assuming that the bidding behaviour of the investors are same in both single-price and multiple-price systems, the cost of these (non-competitive and post auction) sales are relatively high in single-price auction system relative to multiple-price system.

United Kingdom	Conventional (fixed rate) gilts are viewed as having less execution risk than some other securities. There are often similar gilts already outstanding in the market to allow ease of pricing (or, if more of an existing gilt is being issued (a "tap"), there is price information on the existing parent bond); auction positions can be hedged using gilt futures; and the secondary market is relatively liquid. This suggests that bidders are not deterred from participating in the auction by not knowing the rest of the market's bids. Index-linked gilts. Positions in index-linked gilts cannot be hedged as easily as positions in conventional gilts. The secondary market for index-linked gilts is also not as liquid as for conventional gilts. Both of these factors increase the uncertainty associated with index-linked auctions and increase the risk of the "Winner's Curse" for successful bidders - that is the cost of bidding high when the rest of the market bids low. Single-price auctions therefore reduce this uncertainty for auction participants, thereby encouraging participation. In addition, there are fewer index-linked gilts than conventional gilts in issue, so pricing a new index-linked issue may be less straightforward than a new conventional owing to fewer reference points. The single-price format helps to mitigate the risks associated with this greater pricing complexity. Treasury bills. Treasury Bills are short-dated discount instruments (generally issued by auction in 1-, 3- and 6-month tenors), and, as such, bid prices and clearing prices tend to fluctuate much less than auctions for bonds. But, as the certainty of price/yield execution level is important to individual money market participants, the multiple price format allows bidders to tailor their bids to individual needs or limits. As a cash management instrument for the issuer, auction sizes may also vary according to needs.
United States	Currently, the U.S. treasury employs single-price auction method for all securities. Through empirical studies, the U.S. treasury has found single-price auction promotes aggressive bidding and reduces the overall costs of financing the Federal debt. Specific pros and cons of single-price auction found in our past studies and experience are following (Source – Uniform-Price Auctions: Evaluation of the Treasury Experience (October 1995);https://www.treasury.gov/resource-center/fin-mkts/Documents/final.pdf; Uniform Price Auctions: Update of the Treasury Experience (October 1998); https://www.treasury.gov/resource-center/fin-mkts/Documents/upas2.pdf) Pros: • Lower average spreads of auction yield to when-issued (WI) yield. • Possibly encourages more bidders to participate in competitive bidding and reduces the concentration of awards. Cons: • Higher volatility in auction yield. • There are less participants bidding in the range of price discovery.

Q3 If an auction method was changed in the past five years, could you explain the reasons for the changes?

Australia	Treasury Bonds – Auction mechanism unchanged in past 5 years (remains multiple price) Treasury Notes – Auction mechanism unchanged in past 5 years (remains multiple price) Treasury Indexed Bonds - Up until 2013 the Australian Office of Financial Management (AOFM) tenders for Treasury Indexed Bonds were conducted on a single price basis with allotments made at the highest yield accepted. From July 2013, tenders for the issue of Treasury Indexed Bonds were held on a multiple price basis with allotments made at the yields bid. This aligned the basis for setting process at Treasury Indexed Bond tenders with that used at tenders for the issue of Treasury Bonds and Treasury Notes. The change followed feedback and consultation with indexed bond market participants.
Austria	There was no change in the auction method in Austrian government bonds in the past five years.
Belgium	We changed the format of our bills auction when rates became negative for the first time; switching from a yield based system to a price based system and back again. Apart from this technical point, relatively speaking, we have made the requirements we impose on our dealers a bit less strict, as the number of our dealers has decreased, while the thresholds in terms of minimum market shares they need to reach have remained unchanged. To some extent, this is a reaction to the more challenging environment we believe dealers are facing under the form of higher regulatory requirements and constraints.
Canada	The Government of Canada has not changed its auction method in the last five years.
Chile	No changes in auction method have been implemented.
Czech Republic	No auction method change occurred over past five years
Denmark	No chance in our auction method within the last five years, but we have increased the number of auctions during the year. Between the auctions we have implemented a switch facility in order to support liquidity in the secondary market.
Finland	No change.
France	Auction methods have remained unchanged during the last 5 years.
Germany	We increased the number auf auctions and reduced the auction-size. Main Reason: Decreasing warehousing capacity of dealer-banks, due to banking-regulation.
Hungary	No change.
Iceland	No change.
Ireland	Not applicable.
Israel	There was no change in the auction method in the past 5 years.
Italy	We did not change auction methods in the last five years. However, the Buoni del Tesoro Poliennali (BTP) Italia (Italian inflation linker) was introduced in 2012 with a new method of issuance. It allows for collecting purchase orders through the regulated retail screen-based market for government bonds (the MOT platform of Borsa Italiana). The coupon rate is to be determined at the end of the placement period based on market conditions; the issue price is fixed at par. The placement period is divided into a First Phase and a Second Phase. During the First Phase that is reserved to retail investors the bond is issued "on tap" with no set quantity; during the Second Phase institutional investors are allowed to participate for a set amount with possible pro rata allocation. This new issuing method was designed also to address directly investors without impacting on PDs' balance sheets, due to concerns related to the observed changes in the regulatory requirements and market structure.

Japan	No change.
Korea	none
Latvia	With the aim to make our small domestic government securities market more liquid and transparent, we introduced a Primary dealer system back in 2013. And as of today we can say that because of existence of this system we see several improvements both for market participants, investors and for us as an issuer. Through the consultation process with PD's we have not received any proposals for a new auction method to be implemented.
Mexico	No recent changes have been made to the auction methods.
Netherlands	Not applicable.
New Zealand	No change.
Norway	No changes in the auction system for bills and bonds over the past five years. The number of auctions has been substantially increased since 2011.
Poland	Starting from January 2012 all T-bond and T-bill sale auctions have been carried out in uniform price formula. Starting from October 1st, 2013 uniform price formula was implemented on T-bond switching auctions. Introduction of the new formula resulted from the experiences of developed countries debt markets' experiences and outcome of scientific research on theory of efficient auctioning. Analysis of the auctions results, showed the following effects of the introduction of changes: • increase in quality of demand at sale auctions – change in bid-to-cover ratio combined with an increase in single bid value and reduction of the number of submitted bids on a single auction, • improved quality of the submitted bids – in case of the analysed auctions yields determined at auctions were lower than that observed in the secondary market, • reduction in the scale of securities price fluctuations in the secondary market after the auction outcome.
Portugal	Our medium and long-term bond auction method was changed from the multiple-price to single-price, in 2014 (as explained in answer to Q2), after 3 years of not performing any tbond auction, consequence of the sovereign debt crisis. When reintroducing long-term debt auctions, we noticed that countries more comparable to Portugal, peripheral countries, used the single-price auction system or had characteristics similar to the single-price auction system, which led us to study what type of system to use, as we had the multiple-price system in the past. After consulting our Primary Dealers and some DMO and having analysed the pros and cons of each method, we opted for the single-price auction system. The main arguments in support of this method were: avoid paying above the market price ("winner's curse"), higher transparency since every order is allotted at the same price; and finally it incentivises participation coming from investors that may be less informed than qualified investors.
Slovak Republic	We haven't changed the method, however we introduced opening of new bond line via auction, where we used single price auction instead of multiple price that is used otherwise. See more details in previous question.
Slovenia	Until the year 2007 the Ministry of Finance held auctions for Bonds in the multiple price auction (on the domestic market before entering the common EMU market). With the intention to reintroduce Bond auctions in the beginning of next year a shift to the single price auction format is envisaged. The reasons for introducing the single price auction are the following: • increase in demand and quality and competitiveness of bids due to the reduced "winner´s curse" effect • limitation of securities price fluctuations in the secondary market • recent empirical studies show that the uniform-price format may be more advantageous in most markets in the long term in terms of revenue generated for the issuer

Spain	Our auction method has not changed over the past years. Main news has been the inclusion of the European inflation-linked bonds in the auctions. The Spanish Treasury announces a separate volume range for this type of bonds. Weight of the primary market in our PD's evaluation has remained stable as well.
Switzerland	No changes.
Turkey	In the last five years, the Treasury did not change the auction method.
United Kingdom	Not applicable.
United States	The U.S. treasury auction method has not been changed in past five years.

Q4 (A) Are your auctions affected by overbidding phenomenon (orders received at prices highly above the secondary market levels and/or fair value and/or expected cut-off price)?

Australia	No – most bids are received in a narrow spread to the weighted average yield.
Austria	We see a slight overbidding when comparing the weighted average price of the allotments with secondary market levels.
Belgium	Yes (multi price method), both for our long term nominal fixed rate bonds (OLOs) as for our bills (TCs) we observe a phenomenon of over-bidding. The extent of this is hard to quantify, as the sizes traded are quite different from those in the secondary market and much depends on the time at which the secondary market reference is taken.
Canada	No evidence of overbidding in the Government of Canada auctions.
Chile	No.
Czech Republic	All auction prices are generally in line with market pricing
Denmark	This has not been an issue. This mainly reflects that we have no forced bidding and no compensation for primary dealers activity in the primary market.
Finland	Yes, for single price
France	Yes, we observe regular overbidding at our medium and long term auctions. It generally remains limited (less than 1 pb).
Germany	Depends on how one defines "highly". In the past we had observed a positive auction premium but usually only in the magnitude of a few ticks.
Hungary	This had happened sometimes during the time of heavy foreign capital inflow, when new demand exceeded primary issuance. Not during the last few years.
Iceland	Single price: Yes sometimes. The buyer do not face the same value in the primary and the secondary market if the amount is large enough. Due to low liquidity at the secondary market it can be difficult to buy large amount without affecting the price. Therefore the buyer sometimes tend to bid aggressively in the auction to get full allocation at a fixed price.
Ireland	No.
Israel	Multi-price: The auction are not affected by overbidding phenomenon.
Italy	Yes, but only occasionally (for both methods).
Japan	While overbidding is theoretically possible (not only with single-price auctions but also multiple-price auctions, in our view), we have not seen any concrete evidence that such a phenomenon actually occurs in the Japanese government bonds (JGB) market.
Korea	No.
Latvia	We have experienced some cases of overbidding phenomenon at multi-price auctions, when one of bidders places orders well below market rate levels and thus decreases average weighted price for a single-price auction. In such a case we have seen lower demand at single-price auction.
Mexico	Market Makers have to comply with bidding requirements during the auctions in terms of minimum amount requested for each security. As a consequence, Market Makers sometimes tend to submit bids above market levels in order to comply with requirements stated in the primary dealer's rules.
Netherlands	There is overbidding in all the 3 kinds of auctions the DSTA conducts.
New Zealand	Multiprice. Generally no, but on occasion there has been large bidding interest from single counterparty.

Norway	As we have a single-price system we usually experience some overbidding in the auctions, as the bidder/PD will ensure that he will be allocated some bonds, knowing that he will pay the same cut-off price as the other bidders. Normally the auctions clear at a premium to the secondary market
Poland	No.
Portugal	Multiple Price auctions: Not significantly, our tbill auction is performed under the multiple price method and bids are introduced in the auction close to the secondary market level. Single Price auctions: Yes, in our long-term debt auctions we witness that some bids are introduced significantly higher than the secondary market level. The PD that wants to make sure he will be allocated simply bids significantly higher than the market, making sure he will get the bonds, not bothering with the price of the bid, as he knows he will be allocated at the cut-off price, not paying more than any other PD.
Slovak Republic	Yes, but not significantly. We see approximately 5-10% of total bids being at substantially higher levels for both types of auctions.
Slovenia	TBills (Discount): Due to the low volume of TBills programme there is no active trading with TBills and consequently there is no price for TBills available on the secondary market which would allow us to compare the primary and secondary price of the security. However, when we compare the issuance price of TBills with peers of the Republic of Slovenia or with Republic of Slovenia bonds with the residual maturity being equal to the maturity of the TBills being issued, we do not detect any overbidding phenomenon (orders received at prices highly above the fair value). Bonds (Fixed): As mentioned, currently bonds are issued via syndication. However, we are planning to reintroduce Bond auctions in next year (complementary to syndicated method of issuance).
Spain	Yes (multi-price method)
Sweden	No.
Switzerland	Not really. The zero or negative rate environment in Switzerland started in January 2009. Due to a 100% price cap, 3M T-bills have been allocated at the ceiling price since then, even though in some auctions a higher allocation price would have been more in line with the market conditions. In this period we experienced an increasing amount of non-competitive bids (offers without price) without harming the functioning of the auction mechanism. In 2011, due to an increasingly expansionary monetary policy, short term rates slid below zero and Federal Treasury decided in August 2011 to accept also bids above par in T-bills auctions. Since then T-bills have been recording negative yields and the amount of non-competitive bids reduced to pre-crisis levels.
Turkey	No.
United Kingdom	Auction bidding theory suggests that Winner's Curse risk may be reduced in the single-price format, as participants might be expected to bid at a higher price relative to multi-price auctions, in the knowledge that they will pay the cut-off price, not the bid price. The UKDMO also has a Post Auction Option Facility through which successful bidders (primary dealers and investors) may purchase up to an additional 15% of the gilt allotted to them at the relevant auction between midday and 2pm on the day of the auction: in multiple-price format auctions purchases will be at the average accepted price and at the strike price in single-price format auctions. The amount of the option is linked to each dealer's auction allocation so the facility may act as a bidding incentive.
United States	Single-Price Method: Yes, we have a high Bid-to-Cover ratio for all securities and there have been some auctions with negative tail (tail=auction yield-WI yield).

Q4 (B) If yes, what measures have you implemented, or do you intend to implement in the near future, to avoid overbidding behaviour from auction participants?

Austria	As the overbidding is not significant, there are no measures planned in the near future.
Belgium	None (multi-price method), we do not receive feedback in this sense from our dealers and still feel that the over-bidding is a rational part of our dealers' behaviour in their overall relationship with the Kingdom of Belgium.
Finland	None so far
France	We haven't implemented measures to avoid overbidding behaviour as it is a consequence of (mainly) the right to participate to non-competitive auction and (secondary) of our multiple price auction system which conduces primary dealers to put a safety margin on their bids.
Germany	Currently even those small auction premiums have mainly diminished – without having taken a measure.
Hungary	We have not implemented any particular measures following the above-mentioned few cases, however in case of bond auctions there is a 50% purchasing limit for each auction participant (i.e. one particular primary dealer cannot buy more than 50 % of the accepted amount at the given auction).
Iceland	No, intention except trying to increase the liquidity of the secondary market for government bonds.
Italy	We use an Auction Aggressiveness Index Ratio as one of the criteria to evaluate our primary dealers, both for single-price and multi-price methods. This metric measures the combined effect of overbidding (i.e. placing orders with prices higher than market levels) and over-demanding (i.e. rationing the volumes available to other market participants), by rewarding the primary dealers with a regular behaviour at auctions and penalizing those which are overly aggressive and try to crowd out their competitors.
Japan	There are no measures that we have implemented or intend to implement.
Latvia	Overbidding is not a regular phenomenon and this has been discussed with PD group. After discussions certain technical changes in the auction process have been implemented to diminish this risk. For example, the Treasury does not announce the offered amount for the single price auction. In the same time there is maximum amount one PD may bid in the single price auction. After the Treasury decides about the amount to be sold, the principle of proportionality is applied to PDs who participated. Currently we do not have any specific further plans or measures to implement. This may change in the future, if overbidding would appear on a regular basis.
Mexico	The bids that are considered above market levels aren't taken into account for the Market makers' performance measurement in order to avoid overbidding practices.
Netherlands	In our DTC auction we do prevent one party to take more than 40% of the amount auctioned (per line).
New Zealand	Multiprice. No changes; not a regular occurrence.
Norway	We are not concerned about overbidding behaviour from our PDs and we have no plans to implement any measures. Even if some bids are highly above the secondary market price, our experience is that overbidding does not have a large influence on the behaviour in the secondary market.
Portugal	We introduced penalties on "overbidding behaviour". After each auction we analyse all the bids of the auction and through a statistical metric identify the orders considered "overbidding", this leads to the imposition of a penalty to the PD responsible for that order. The penalties are reflected in a loss of points in the PD annual evaluation, which than affects the choice of PDs to participate in syndicated deals. Periodically we announce the PDs that have been penalized due to "overbidding" in debt auctions.

Slovak Republic	As the situation is not significant, we haven't introduced any measures.
Spain	Ongoing discussions with our Primary Dealers. The Spanish Treasury does not currently penalise overbidding in auctions.
United Kingdom	No formal measures to avoid overbidding behaviour are planned or have been implemented, but the UKDMO did introduce a minimum Gilt-edged Market Makers (GEMM) bidding expectation (not a formal requirement) of 5% of the auction volume (over a rolling 6-month period) effective from the start of the financial year 2016-17. This measure was introduced because the UKDMO sees it as important to encourage wholesale GEMMs to participate effectively in the price formation process at auctions in the current challenging market conditions. This expectation applies to both conventional (fixed rate) gilts and index-linked gilts.
United States	We have not implemented any measures to avoid overbidding.

Q4 (C) Do you have concerns that excessive overbidding at auctions could compromise future funding auctions, even though it may represent a lower funding cost in the very short term? Please elaborate.

Australia	No.
Austria	Excessive overbidding is not the case in Austria. In general excessive overbidding can be a problem as it could lead to a reduction of the auction panel (smaller participants could withdraw from the auction panel, as they don't see a chance for allotments). The issuer could become dependent on a smaller number of participants, competition between participants could decrease.
Belgium	No (multi-price method), we expect over-bidding patterns to adjust should the overall equation no longer work for our dealers. It remains critical that our dealers take a holistic view of the relationship and profitability of their dealings with the Kingdom of Belgium, as this likely requires a form of subsidising of trading activities by some of the other debt capital market activities
Canada	At this point in time, the Government of Canada does not have any express concerns regarding excessive overbidding at auctions. However, overbidding could pose significant challenges to frameworks that allow non-PD participation at auctions, and in particular, in situations where PDs find themselves squeezed out of the auctions by non-PDs on a regular basis. Over time, this phenomenon could weaken the market position of the PDs and ultimately compromise the stability of the framework.
Chile	Not applicable.
Czech Republic	Not applicable.
Denmark	Not applicable.
Finland	No excessively – banks voice concerns but continue to participate and overbid
France	No, we don't have concerns as the overbidding phenomenon is limited overall and as the total net cost for primary dealers is low due to the non-competitive auction right.
Germany	Generally speaking yes, but as stated above not a worrisome issue for Germany
Hungary	We do not have such concerns. We have frequent auctions (weekly or bi-weekly) and we actively use the reopening of existing lines, which can make overbidding unreasonable for market participants.
Iceland	No, but we have concerns that it could affect the turnover volume at the secondary market.
Ireland	No.
Israel	We do not encounter any overbidding phenomenon, so we do not concern about it.
Italy	Given the size of the Italian public debt and yearly refinancing requirements, the new supervisory and financial markets rules, and the inclusion of a specific Auction Aggressiveness Index among the evaluation criteria for our PDs, the overbidding for Italian government bonds and bills is normally kept within physiological limits and it may be indicative of sound investors' demand.
Japan	While such concerns theoretically exist, we have not seen any concrete evidence that overbidding might adversely affect our bond issuance operations, for example in terms of prices and bid-to-cover ratio. In any case, it is difficult to provide a concrete assessment on the matter, since the prices are determined as a result of competitive auctions in which each market participant places bids based upon its own market outlook and calculations.
Korea	No.
Latvia	For the time being we do not have such concerns as this is not treated as excessive overbidding.
Luxembourg	

Mexico	No, this is a practice that has only been observed in certain auctions where liquidity conditions have been historically poor, such as holidays in the United States (US) or first auctions of the year. It is worth noticing that 62% of the long term sovereign securities are held by foreign investors.
Netherlands	Not per se. For the tap auctions the DSTA team makes an elaborate analysis and often concludes that up until the auction, prices of the bond cheapen. A part of what looks like overbidding vis-a-vis the secondary market is partly the compensation for the cheapening (as well as compensation for the non-comp option). The overbidding for auctions differs widely between different auctions and we don't see a specific trend in the overbidding.
New Zealand	Multiprice. Not usually concerned.
Norway	No.
Portugal	The fact that some end-investors place orders into a PD to come to an auction, and get filled at a level significantly higher than the secondary market level, due to overbidding, causes concerns to the issuer. When there is overbidding in the auction, the cut-off price will be significantly higher than the secondary market level, causing the end-investor to pay more for the bonds than what they would have to pay if they had bought it in the secondary market. If this behaviour is persistent over time, it will likely lower end-investor demand in each auction going forward (and discourage bids in future auctions).
Slovak Republic	No.
Slovenia	Although we do not experience excessive overbidding at our TBill auctions we are of the view that overbidding/overpricing may harm the long-run competitiveness of the bills/bonds auctions by driving the smaller primary dealers out of the primary market. Especially so, if the primary dealers, which are successful at auctions, have the option to buy securities at the auction price the day after the auction or receive the benefit of being joint lead managers for future syndicated issues. This would motivate the bigger primary dealers to overbid at auctions and to compensate with other benefits as described above.
Spain	Some PDs have complained. The Spanish Treasury is studying the issue.
Sweden	No.
Switzerland	No.
United Kingdom	While there are no immediate concerns, though the UKDMO is aware that any prolonged/ excessive overbidding could compromise future auctions particularly if primary dealer profitability was reduced to the extent that the commercial viability of the model was brought into question. Therefore, we remain vigilant in this regard.
United States	We are not concerned that excessive overbidding at auctions could compromise future funding auctions; however, overbidding phenomenon may signal insufficient supply in the market and we closely monitor the balance of supply and demand to promote the efficiency of market.

Q4 (D) Do you have (and use) flexibility to adjust the issued amount during the auction to reduce the gap between the secondary market level and the cut off price?

Australia	AOFM does not adjust the amount issued during a tender.
Austria	Prior to each multiple securities auction a total issue amount (for all bonds to be auctioned) is announced. After the auction deadline has expired the issuer decides on the basis of the final bids how to allocate the announced total issue amount between the auctioned bonds considering secondary market levels. The total amount is not adjusted during or after the auction and always corresponds to the announced total issue amount prior to the auction. In case of single security auction the total amount is set prior to the auction and is allocated without any modification. The issuer has the right to withdraw planned issues up to 1 hour after the auction deadline.
Belgium	(multi-price method) Exceptional circumstances aside, we have some flexibility to adjust the issued amounts within a pre-announced aggregate range. However, we would not use this flexibility with the specific aim to bring back the average auction price closer to the secondary market price. We will consider the relative aggressiveness of bids together with our strategic goals in terms of the liquidity of individual bond lines and of the maturity of the issued bonds when deciding on cut off prices.
Canada	The Government of Canada does not adjust the amount that is issued at auction. The Government of Canada securities auctions have been and remain fully covered. The Government pre-announces the amount being auctioned in the Call for Tender, which is normally released one week prior to the auction and does not adjust the pre-announced amount during the auction. However, the Government does reserve the right to accept or reject any or all bids, in whole or in part, including, without limitation, the right to accept less than the total amount specified in the Final Call for Tenders.
Chile	We have the flexibility to reduce the amount allocated in each issuance up to 20%. In this regard, the reduction of the amount allocated allows to reduce the final yield, when it is too far from the market, or repeat the auction
Czech Republic	The issued amount may be adjusted depending on the bids distribution. The described gap between prices is not typically the key reason.
Denmark	We aim to be transparent about the amount we want to issue, but we have some degree of flexibility in changing the issued amount taking the demand into account. Normally is it not an issue. We do not use the flexibility to reduce the gap between the primary and secondary market levels.
Finland	No
France	The gap between the bids submitted and the secondary market level is one parameter among many ones that we use in order to choose the amount of each bond we issue within the range announced before the auction.
Germany	No
Hungary	Yes we have, and we do use it, but usually to react to high or low demand and if there is a significant gap between the cut off price and the average price of the auction (tail). Adjusting issued amount only help to reduce the spread of primary and secondary market levels if the demand is low and the auction yield curve is steep according to our experiences.
Iceland	Usually we don't have significantly gap between the secondary market and the cut off price since Primary dealers´ offer prices in the auctions that are in line with the price on the secondary market. However, we can adjust the issued amount if a there appears to be a gap.
Ireland	We typically do not adjust the issued amount during the auction for any reason.
Israel	We do have flexibility to adjust the issued amount during the auction by setting a cut off price. But we never use it.
Italy	Yes. In single (marginal) price auctions both the auction price and the quantity issued is determined discretionally by the Treasury. The amount placed is determined within a predetermined range by excluding bids made at prices that are not suitable with respect to market conditions, on the basis of a ranking in which dealers' bids are listed anonymously. The lowest price among those bid by awarded dealers is the auction (marginal) price which is applied to all awarded dealers.

Japan	We do not adjust the issued amount because of the gap between the secondary market level and the cut-off price.
Korea	No.
Latvia	We have the flexibility to adjust the amount to lower cut-off price. In such a case Treasury may decide to increase the amount sold in single-price auction, if sufficient demand remain. This approach has been used in some auctions.
Mexico	No, the amounts to be issued in each auction are previously defined and announced quarterly in the Federal Government Securities' Auction calendar, consequently, issuance amounts may not change during the auctions. But if the Federal Government considers the results of the auction above market levels it has the option to declare the auction void.
Netherlands	The DSTA always announces a range when it announces auctions. This gives leeway to choose the amount to issue depending on market conditions, development of the auction etc.
New Zealand	Multiprice. Yes, but generally do not follow such a practice, as we prefer market to set price signals.
Norway	We announce the amount two days prior to the auction and we always allot the announced amount as long as there is sufficient volume of bids to cover the auction. Should we not receive sufficient bids, the auction will be cancelled – but this has never happened. We don't have a Post Auction Option Facility.
Poland	There is a possibility to organize supplementary auction (after consultations with investors), on which bonds are sold at a minimum price set at initial sale auction.
Portugal	There is flexibility to issue 1/3 more than what is announced. The IGCP frequently issues more than what is announced in order to reduce the difference between the cut-off price and the secondary market price.
Slovak Republic	Yes. We announce only the indicative intended issued amount. We still can adjust this based on the "attractivity" of the bids. But we try to be close to that announced amount.
Slovenia	The Ministry of Finance has the possibility to adjust the issued amount during the auction taking into account the price (received bids) and funding needs.
Spain	We take advantage of the flexibility provided by the range announced on Monday prior to the auction.
Sweden	Fixed income instruments in Sweden are, by tradition, quoted and traded on yield. The bids in the electronic auction platform are also expressed in yield terms. Yes, we have flexibility to adjust the issued amount downwards. We have the possibility to reduce the offered volume by cutting at a lower yield than the cut-off price (maximum yield/lowest price) for the total volume would imply. Usually, the bond auctions are cleared at mid-market. However, in rare cases, in particular in inflation-linked bonds and T-bills, we have reduced the volume, i.e. issued less than offered.
Switzerland	Federal Treasury announces an issuance calendar in December for the following year. The calendar for T-bonds comprises the auction dates and the planned issuance volume for the year. A day prior to the T-bond auction the Treasury releases the maturity / maturities that will be issued without a targeted issue amount. Hence Federal Treasury has full flexibility to determine the issued amount and allocation price. In most auctions the cut off price is within the bid-ask-spread observed on the secondary market; in some cases Treasury offers a premium with a cut off price slightly below bid-price levels to meet its implicit short-term targets.
Turkey	Yes. At the end of each month the Treasury is releasing Domestic Borrowing Strategy for the coming three months. In these Strategies, the Treasury only announces total amount of borrowing, but not pre- announced security specific size, so that depending on the market conditions and bidding behaviour of the investors, the Treasury has flexibility to adjust issuance amount of bonds during the auctions.
United Kingdom	No.
United States	No.

Q4 (E) Do you have any other concerns regarding the cut-off price?

Australia	No.
Canada	The Government does not have any concerns regarding the cut-off price. The Government of Canada securities auctions have been and remain fully covered, and the pricing has been and remains competitive. Note that participants in the Government of Canada securities auctions are subject to minimum bidding requirements: • Nominal bonds: The minimum level of bidding must be at no more than 10 basis points above the highest accepted yield at the auction. • Inflation indexed bonds: Dealers are required to bid at least 50 per cent of their auction limit at yield that does not exceed 10 basis points above the higher of (i) the auction cut-off and (ii) the yield in the secondary market prior to the auction.
Chile	No.
Czech Republic	No.
Denmark	We do not have forced bidding. A large variation in bids can lead to a gap between secondary price and cut-off price. Cut-off price is usually within the bid-ask spread. If the demand is extraordinary high or low we have the possibility to adjust the issuance.
France	Tail, overbidding, healthy price action before and after the allocation, consistent allocation with regard to the demand.
Germany	No.
Hungary	No.
Iceland	No.
Ireland	No.
Israel	We usually concern the cut off price will be "off market" - in comparison to the secondary market.
Italy	As for the competitive yield auctions used for the issuance of T-bills (BOT), a minimum acceptable (or safeguard) yield is calculated in order to avoid that the weighted average yield is negatively influenced by bids made at yields that are not in line with the market. Similarly, a maximum acceptable (or exclusion) yield is calculated in order to exclude any speculative bids from the auction.
Japan	No, we do not. In any case, it is difficult to provide a concrete assessment on the adequate level of prices, since they are determined as a result of competitive auctions in which each market participant places bids based upon its own market outlook and calculations.
Korea	No.
Mexico	No.
Netherlands	No.
New Zealand	Multiprice. No.
Norway	The auctions generally clear at a premium to the secondary market, but so far we have not experienced that the cut off price has been so "off market" that this has been a concern for the DMO.
Portugal	No.
Slovak Republic	If possible, we try to set the cut-off price at the level, before a significant jump up in the price of the next bid (first derivation).
Spain	We monitor and aspire to contain the size of the auction tails (spread between the cut-off price and the weighted average price).
Sweden	No.
Switzerland	No.
Turkey	No.
United Kingdom	There is a risk, in exceptional circumstances, of the cut-off price being at a level that represents a significant concession to mid-market prices. This may be of particular concern with the single-price format, given that all the stock on offer would be sold at that price (assuming no bids were rejected by the issuer). However, the DMO does reserve the right in such exceptional circumstances not to allot all of the gilts on offer at an auction, where it judges bids to be at an unacceptably deep discount to the prevailing market level.
United States	No.

Section B: Multiple Stock Auctions

Q B1 Do you use multiple-stock auctions (multiple series per auction)? If yes, please specify the bond type (discount, fixed-rate, floating-rate, inflation-indexed, etc.) and maturity, for which this auction method is used

	Yes	No	Bond type and maturity
Australia	X		Treasury Bonds – AOFM standard practice was the issuance of multiple stocks at auction between 1982 and 2000 (with a few exceptions). After Feb 2000 AOFM has only once issued multiple stock at one tender/auction (in July 2005). Treasury Indexed Bonds – Multiple stock auctions were used infrequently during single price auctions (to Jul 2013). The last TIB multiple stock auction was in late 2011 for a 9 year and 19 year maturity. No multiple stock tenders have been held since TIB issuance changed to multiple price auctions in July 2013. Treasury Notes – Multiple stock auctions were commonly used for TN's (discount short term security) between 2000-03 and 2009-14 (NB: no T-Notes were issued from October 2003 – March 2009), the last of which was in January 2015 for 92 and 141 day maturities . No multiple stock auctions of T-Notes have been held since January 2015 though it remains an option.
Austria	X		Fixed- or floating rate; for all maturities
Belgium	X		Fixed Rate Discount/Bills
Canada	X		Discount/Bills
Chile		X	
Czech Republic	X		Medium-term and long-term domestic bonds* *The pre-announced fixed size of individual bonds is not binding and the sold amount may be adjusted according to bid amount with a high degree of flexibility. So the format of the auction can rather be viewed as simultaneous auctions of single bonds
Denmark	X		(Fixed-rate, Inflation-indexed, T-bills)
Finland	X		Fixed rate, 5y-30Y
France	X		Nominal bonds and inflation-indexed bonds (all medium and long term bonds)
Germany		X	
Hungary	X		In case of fixed rate bonds several bonds are offered at the same time but amounts are fixed for each bond (not aggregated)
Iceland	X		• Fixed rate • Inflation linked It is common to offer more than one bond in a single auction, but DMO never sell for a pre-announced fixed size.
Ireland		X	
Israel		X	
Italy	X		All types of bonds with the exception of zero coupon securities (6 and 12-month BOT and 24-month Certificati del Tesoro Zero Coupon (CTZ)). We use multiple-stock auctions particularly for inflation linkers and off-the-run bonds.

Japan	X		We conduct liquidity enhancement auctions for every off-the-run issue. The auctions are implemented in three zones separated by remaining maturity. Bond type: Fixed rate Maturity: 1~39 years remaining (divided into 3 zones: 1~5y, 5~15.5y, 15.5~39y)
Korea		X	
Latvia		X	
Mexico		X	
Netherlands	X		Fixed-rate: long end auctions
New Zealand		X	
Norway		X	
Poland	X		for all maturities of: discount bonds, fixed-rate bonds, floating-rate bonds, inflation-indexed bonds,
Portugal	X		Fixed-rate bonds Bills
Slovak Republic	X		Could be all with explanation in Question 2
Slovenia	X		for all TBills (Discount): 3-month TBills 6-month TBills 12-month TBills 18-month Tbills Bonds (Fixed-Rate) Up to two bonds per auction (as mentioned, the first bond auction after 2007 is planned to be introduced next year)
Spain	X		discount and fixed-rate, all maturities.
Sweden	X		Fixed -Rate Inflation-Linked Discount/Bills
Switzerland	X		T-bonds (Federal Treasury only issues fixed-rate bonds)
Turkey		X	
United Kingdom		X	
United States		X	
Total	**20**	**12**	

Q B2 If the answer to B1. above is "yes", what are the reasons for their use (e.g. to provide flexibility to investors, to minimize operational costs etc.)? Could you please explain the details of the issuance mechanics

Australia	Treasury Bonds - Multiple stock auctions (when utilised) were primarily used to offer investors options when bonds were issued regularly but infrequently (i.e. monthly - every few months). Since 2000 (except for Jul 2005) TB's have not been issued at multiple stock auctions. Treasury Indexed Bonds – Similar to Treasury Bonds multiple stock auctions were held when auctions were less frequent, providing investors with more options. T-Notes - Multiple stock auctions of short term securities (T-Notes) were originally held to provide investors with different maturity options. T-Notes were not used as a funding instrument at all between October 2003 and Mar 2009. The re-introduction of the instrument came in part as a response to the Global financial crisis (GFC). At this point multiple stock auctions were used to successfully reintroduce the security (after over 5 years with no issuance) and to quickly build up cash balances. Issuance mechanics: Multiple stock auctions are held as two (or more) separate auctions on the same day (they are held in the same manner as a regular tender) at the same time. Tenders are held on the AOFM tender system (currently Yieldbroker).
Austria	Reasons • Provide additional flexibility to the issuer • Addressing investors' demand on different points on the curve Issuance mechanics: After the deadline of the competitive auction the issuer decides, on the basis of the submitted bids, how to allocate the announced total issue amount between the bonds auctioned.
Belgium	For our fixed rate OLO auctions, we issue more than one bond at a time (typically between two and four). In doing so we wish to make sure that liquidity in each of the outstanding bonds is in line with market demand for those bonds and that dealers can satisfy the investor demand they observe in the market. We therefore choose what lines to auction after consultation with each of our Primary Dealers. Issuing several bonds per auction, as a smaller country, also contains an element of risk mitigation as often an individual bond line will not attract sufficient size to be able to issue the full auction amount. For our bills TC auctions, we follow a fixed pattern of issuance, with auctions twice per month, once a 3 and 6 month bill and once a 3 and 12 month bill. All monthly maturities are fully fungible so as to end up with a curve consisting of 12 liquid bills. We gauge the market before each 12-month bill auction to capture market feedback but issuance amounts are mostly rather stable.
Canada	The Government of Canada issues its treasury bills in three tranches (3-month, 6-month and 12-month) in a single auction on a bi-weekly basis. Since treasury bills are relatively less actively traded than nominal bonds, offering all three tranches simultaneously accords investors with different investment profiles greater flexibility and allows for better matching of risk exposures in the short end of the Canada curve. Issuing the three tranches in one auction also decreases operational costs, albeit on a marginal scale, since three operations are combined into one.
Chile	Not applicable.
Czech Republic	More varied maturity choice for investors More flexibility for MoF in terms of maturity profile management, duration, coupon structure etc.
Denmark	It provides flexibility for the investors and for us. We announce the two bonds - we are selling at the auction – 3 trading days in advance. If investors tell us they have a large interest in a specific bond, we usually decide to issue that bond. If the market has changed after the announcement, the two bond strategy gives us a larger degree of flexibility in finalising the auction.
Finland	Offer liquidity to multiple points on the curve, and increase auctioned volume without increasing the number of auctions
France	We use this system as it allows to issue a bigger amount at the same time (and so minimizes operational costs) and gives us the flexibility to adjust the quantity of each bond issued depending on the demand expressed by primary dealers through their submissions at the auction. This system gives us also more flexibility to reach the global issuance target announced before the auction with the particular bonds issued/tapped.
Germany	Not applicable.

Hungary	In case of fixed rate bonds we offer 3 bonds at the same time (3Y, 5Y and either 10Y or 15Y). However, the offered amounts are announced separately for each three auction, so the sizes cannot be aggregated. (In this respect these are actually 3 separate auctions that run in parallel.) Nevertheless, if the demand is different in the particular tenors we can decide to increase or reduce the accepted amounts separately. By offering 3 bonds we want to provide flexibility for investors and the actual demand for different tenors can be quite different.
Iceland	Provide flexibility to investors and therefore reduce the risk of auction failure due to low demand. Decrease the number of auctions during the year reduce the operational cost as well.
Ireland	Not applicable.
Italy	Reasons for their use are the need for flexibility when the nature of the bonds and/or market conditions make it difficult the announcement of a specific issuing size for each individual bond to be auctioned. Under these circumstances, two or three bonds may be offered together for an overall aggregate size and the actual allocation to the individual securities is made on the basis of demand.
Japan	We use liquidity enhancement auctions to maintain and improve the JGB market liquidity, and to minimize the authority's financing costs. We conduct liquidity enhancement auctions exclusively for PDs every other month for issues with 1~5 and 15.5~39 remaining years, and every month for issues with 5~15.5 remaining years. We use the yield-spread-competitive, multiple-price method. As of fiscal year 2016 (FY2016), we plan to issue a total of 9.6 trillion yen by these auctions, and will decide the details of the auctions, such as the distribution of issuance amount to each zone, based on discussion with market participants.
Latvia	Not applicable.
Mexico	Nowadays the Federal Government doesn't make use of the multiple stock auction mechanism, but it does carry out several simultaneous single auctions.
Netherlands	Multiple stock auctions give the possibility to offer liquidity in the bonds where liquidity is most needed. In 2016 the DSTA did not do any multiple stock auctions, but has done so in the past.
New Zealand	Not applicable.
Poland	The final offer and the supply of Treasury Securities depends on the market situation and results from the consultations with investors. Types of securities and the range of global nominal amount is announced 2 days before the sale auction. Bids are accepted up to the pre-announced volume. Issuing multiple series per auction (i.e. adapting issuance policy to market circumstances, including demand in different segments of the Treasury Securities (TS)): • provide flexibility to investors, • minimizes the risk of financing/refinancing
Portugal	TBills: In the TBill auctions we used to issue 2 lines per auction (a reopening/tap and a new line) in order to give liquidity to existing Bills and issue a new line. In 2015, we introduced a method of issuance in which we auction 2 lines as well, but depending on whether the month is odd or even we issue a new 12 months bill and reopen the 6 months one or we reopen both the 11 month and 3 months Bills. In this way, we do a Bills auction every month but bills only mature every 2 months, causing them to be larger and consequently more liquid. We did this as we noticed that our Tbills turnover was decreasing. TBonds: We started to auction multiple lines per auction in 2015, as we noticed that it would give more flexibility to investors, it would also give flexibility to the issuer when deciding where to cut-off, and would make it easier to issue off-the-run bonds, as it allows to issue lower amounts than what would be the case if it was solely auctioned.
Slovak Republic	We usually do 2 or 3 bond auctions at the same time. We announce intended amount for each particular bond. But if the bids in one bond are more favourable we accept more of that bond and less of the other bond, so the total amount is more in line with cumulative announced amount. The reasons are mostly: - More flexibility to investors – we are small country, some of our investor have demand for short term bond while others want to buy long bond at the same time. We do the auctions only once per month - Cost optimization – as we are small country with small nominal debt, one investor with one

	substantial bid can significantly affect the auction. And if this bids is at a good price, we tend to accept more of this bond and less of the other one.
Slovenia	The Ministry of Finance offers up to four TBills per auction. The main reasons are: - to provide flexibility to investors and in turn attract a broader range of investors, - easier cash management for the issuer due to the possibility of funding with different maturities, - lowering operational costs. The Government TBill auctions are executed according to the Rules of the Republic of Slovenia. The auctions of government securities are carried out through the Bloomberg Auction System (BAS). Treasury Bill auctions are executed in a single phase by competitive bidding, using a Dutch algorithm. Invitation to the Primary Dealers is sent through Bloomberg Auction System (BAS) at least five business days before the auction date. The general public is notified of the auction by the publication of the offer to the public to purchase the securities on the Ministry of Finance's website. Primary Dealers submit the bids in their own name and for their own account as well as for the account of investors via BAS. Primary Dealers are not obliged to submit bids in their own name and for their own account. Each Primary Dealer can submit an unlimited number of bids. The minimum bid amount is €1,000 for the Treasury Bills. The bids submitted are ranked according to price in descending order. Should the total amount of bids with prices up to the lowest price accepted (the cut-off price) be higher than the size of issue that the Ministry decides to place, the bids with the cut-off price are allotted on pro-rata basis. Bids for the T-Bills are accepted at the uniform price (the lowest bid price accepted). Settlement Delivery Versus Payment (DVP) occurs on T+2 with the Primary Dealers whose bids are accepted at the auction. Each Primary Dealers receives the amount of bills which totals the amount of accepted bids at the auction.
Spain	We announce a target issuance range mostly due to flexibility reasons. The expected issuance amount should be around the middle of the range. The amount issued will be fine-tuned towards the upper or lower end of the range in response to, among other circumstances, the interest rates bid. The objective is to maintain a closer command of the interest rates, marginally increasing issuance when advisable, while reserving the right marginally to reduce it when the prevailing conditions are unattractive. Issuance mechanics: - The specific Letras del Tesoro to be auctioned are fixed at the beginning of the year when the calendar is announced, and are therefore known in advance - Bonos & Obligaciones to be issued are announced on Friday prior to the auction, 2pm Central European Time (CET). - Aggregate size announced for all auctions on Monday prior to the auction, 2pm CET.
Sweden	We most often offer two series of bonds/Inflation-Linked/bills at each auction. Each bond is offered for a pre-announced fixed size. We believe that we get broader interest from end-investors and primary dealers by giving more flexibility. Within our guidelines, we have the last couple of years become more flexible, accommodating market demand when liquidity changes.
Switzerland	To provide T-bonds to different investor classes To meet the targeted issue amount To meet the targeted issuance strategy Details of issuance mechanics: • See answer D) • For each series separate offers may be submitted to all banks in Switzerland and to banks abroad which have a sight deposit account with the Swiss National Bank (SNB) and the necessary infrastructure. These banks submit the offers to the Swiss National Bank within the subscription period (9.30 to 11.00 am) via the electronic trading platform. At the end of the subscription period Federal Treasury make the allotment for each series on the basis of the price structure (shape of demand curve, offer prices compared to secondary market prices) and the targeted issuance volume for all series as a whole.
United Kingdom	Not applicable.
United States	Not applicable.

Q B3 What are the implications, if any, of multiple-stock auctions for end-investor demand and primary dealerships?

Australia	Not applicable.
Austria	As the auction dates are limited, by using multiple-stock auctions more bonds with different tenors can potentially be tapped to meet the demand and increase their liquidity by increasing their outstanding volume. - Consistent increase of liquidity for a larger number of bonds with a limited number of auction dates - Even supply of bonds corresponding to the demand of primary dealers/investors
Belgium	In the way we try to organize them, we believe they allow us to respond fairly directly to investor demand. We believe this reactivity is appreciated by the dealers and the investor community and therefore contributes to the attractiveness and liquidity of our bond market.
Canada	No internal research has been conducted to assess the impact of multiple-tranche treasury bill auctions on end-investor demand and primary dealerships. However, both academics and practitioners concur that investors tend to lower their risk premia on particular securities when their demand for securities is properly met, suggesting that multiple-tranche treasury bill auctions might contribute to lowering the Government of Canada's cost of issuance of securities.
Chile	Not applicable.
Czech Republic	Wider choice of debt characteristics available
Denmark	The multiple bond auctions have the implication that the end-investor have less chance of controlling the cut-off price even if they only have demand in one specific bond. The two bond strategy gives us a larger degree of flexibility in finalising the auction. Further to that more lines of issuance will be on auctions during the year with 2 bonds per auction.
Finland	Increasing liquidity should help PD's market making
France	There is no clear implication of multiple-stock auctions for end-investor demand. For primary dealers, it makes the auctions somewhat harder to manage and monitor, but this higher complexity goes along with a better adjustment of our bond supply with the primary dealer demand (more different bonds are issued at each auction).
Germany	Not applicable.
Hungary	Offering several different tenors at the same time gives more flexibility to the issuance program. Either the investors or the issuer can react to the changing market behaviour and demand accordingly by increasing the amounts on the tenors where the demand is higher and/or decreasing the amount where the demand is lower.
Iceland	There are no implications.
Ireland	Not applicable.
Italy	In case of multiple-stock auctions involving off-the-run bonds, we do not apply the Auction Aggressiveness Index Ratio to primary dealers, given that in this case the secondary market levels are harder to detect and less representative of uniform market valuations.
Japan	Since liquidity enhancement auctions supply off-the-run issues, PDs could utilize their balance sheets without holding unnecessary inventory. Thus, PDs could flexibly meet the diverse needs of end-investors corresponding to each investor's portfolio profile. Moreover, because liquidity enhancement auctions lower the risks of PDs to hold short positions and promote market liquidity, end-investors become motivated to acquire highly liquid bonds. Liquidity enhancement auctions provide an incentive for being a PD. PDs are exclusively allowed to participate in liquidity enhancement auctions and, unlike in auctions for current issues, they are not subject to a minimum purchasing responsibility.

Latvia	Not applicable.
Mexico	There is no experience in the Mexican sovereign debt market regarding multiple-stock auctions.
Netherlands	The DSTA typically only issues a very small amount of its annual issuance in multiple-stock auctions (none in 2016), so the implications of these auctions on investor demand and PDs is difficult to gauge.
New Zealand	Not applicable.
Poland	Series of bonds as well as the amount offered on auctions is resulting from the market conditions and consultations with investors. This provides flexibility to investors.
Portugal	Multiple-stock auctions allow the supply of off-the-run bonds (i.e. bonds that would not be auctioned otherwise because demand is significantly lower than the current benchmarks, and would not be enough to do an auction just with those bonds), but that does not mean there's no demand for these bonds, in fact there is demand, but in lower amounts. By doing multiple-stock auctions we can supply different points on the curve and satisfy multiple pockets of demand, increasing liquidity in the curve and stimulating end-investor demand in other points of the curve other than the current benchmarks.
Slovak Republic	This is a long practice in Slovakia, the PDs are aware and satisfied with this.
Slovenia	In our view multiple-stock auctions for TBills provide for a broader investor base as more investment opportunities (different maturities) are presented to investors. However, given the recent low interest rate environment, the majority of investor demand is concentrated in the longer part of the TBill curve (12 and 18-months). We did not detect any impact on the primary dealership with respect to multiple-stock auctions however one must note, that we do not require from primary dealers to participate (buy a certain percentage of the issue) at the TBill auction.
Spain	Primary Dealers must manage some degree of uncertainty, as they do not know in advance how the announced aggregate range is going to be split between the references to be auctioned.
Sweden	Options to choose between several securities in the primary market should create a more attractive market for investors. Liquidity support by new supply from auctions, facilitates primary dealers' market making.
Switzerland	End-investors get more flexibility / possibilities to meet their investment needs.
United Kingdom	Not applicable.
United States	Not applicable.

ORGANISATION FOR ECONOMIC CO-OPERATION AND DEVELOPMENT

The OECD is a unique forum where governments work together to address the economic, social and environmental challenges of globalisation. The OECD is also at the forefront of efforts to understand and to help governments respond to new developments and concerns, such as corporate governance, the information economy and the challenges of an ageing population. The Organisation provides a setting where governments can compare policy experiences, seek answers to common problems, identify good practice and work to co-ordinate domestic and international policies.

The OECD member countries are: Australia, Austria, Belgium, Canada, Chile, the Czech Republic, Denmark, Estonia, Finland, France, Germany, Greece, Hungary, Iceland, Ireland, Israel, Italy, Japan, Korea, Latvia, Luxembourg, Mexico, the Netherlands, New Zealand, Norway, Poland, Portugal, the Slovak Republic, Slovenia, Spain, Sweden, Switzerland, Turkey, the United Kingdom and the United States. The European Union takes part in the work of the OECD.

OECD Publishing disseminates widely the results of the Organisation's statistics gathering and research on economic, social and environmental issues, as well as the conventions, guidelines and standards agreed by its members.

OECD PUBLISHING, 2, rue André-Pascal, 75775 PARIS CEDEX 16
(20 2017 02 1 P) ISBN 978-92-64-27125-8 – 2017

www.ingramcontent.com/pod-product-compliance
Ingram Content Group UK Ltd.
Pitfield, Milton Keynes, MK11 3LW, UK
UKHW051240300926
15471UKWH00015B/1403

9 789264 271258